The Motherless Child in the Novels of Pauline Hopkins

The MOTHERLESS CHILD *in the Novels of* PAULINE HOPKINS

JILL BERGMAN

LOUISIANA STATE UNIVERSITY PRESS
BATON ROUGE

Published by Louisiana State University Press

Manufactured in the United States of America
First printing

DESIGNER: Barbara Neely Bourgoyne
TYPEFACE: Arno Pro
PRINTER: McNaughton & Gunn, Inc.
BINDER: Acme Bookbinding, Inc.

An earlier version of chapter 4 appeared as "The Motherless Child in Pauline Hopkins's *Of One Blood*," in *Legacy: A Journal of American Women Writers* 25 (2008): 286–98, copyright © 2008 University of Nebraska Press.

Library of Congress Cataloging-in-Publication Data
Bergman, Jill, 1963–
The motherless child in the novels of Pauline Hopkins / Jill Bergman.
p. cm.
Includes bibliographical references and index.
ISBN 978-0-8071-4729-0 (cloth : alk. paper) — ISBN 978-0-8071-4730-6 (pdf) — ISBN 978-0-8071-4731-3 (epub) — ISBN 978-0-8071-4732-0 (mobi)
1. Hopkins, Pauline E. (Pauline Elizabeth) —Criticism and interpretation. 2. American fiction—African American authors—History and criticism. 3. American fiction—Women authors—History and criticism. 4. African American women authors—Intellectual life. 5. Children in literature. 6. Mothers in literature. 7. Parental deprivation in literature. 8. Identity (Philosophical concept) in literature. I. Title.
PS1999.H4226Z57 2013
813'.4—dc23

2012007254

The paper in this book meets the guidelines for permanence and durability of the Committee on Production Guidelines for Book Longevity of the Council on Library Resources. ♾

For Lois Peterson Bergman (1929–1993), who first taught me about mothering, and for Emma, who has continued the lesson. And above all, for Brady, who supports me and bears with me with kindness, patience, and humor.

Sometimes I feel like a motherless child
Sometimes I feel like a motherless child
Sometimes I feel like a motherless child
A long ways from home
A long ways from home

—African American spiritual

The desire of the mother is the origin of everything.

—JACQUES LACAN, *Ethics*

CONTENTS

ILLUSTRATIONS

ACKNOWLEDGMENTS

I HAVE INCURRED a number of debts in writing this book. In its early stages, I had the good fortune of working with—and being encouraged and inspired by—Nina Baym, Robert Dale Parker, and Janet Lyon at the University of Illinois. I was privileged to work with Karen Offen, Marilyn Boxer, and a number of other tremendous scholars in the National Endowment for the Humanities seminar on "Motherhood and the Nation State." The members of the Pauline Hopkins Society have been a great help, drawing on their extensive knowledge of Hopkins's life and work to point me in new and fruitful directions. The University of Montana provided research support, and Sue Samson and the interlibrary loan folks at UM's Mansfield Library gave me invaluable assistance with my research. The Summerfield Baldridge Book Subvention Fund provided support for costs associated with publication. The editors at Louisiana State University Press, John Easterly and Margaret Lovecraft, and the rest of the team, have been wonderful to work with, and their outside readers provided invaluable feedback on the manuscript. I am deeply indebted to my research assistant, Sarah Knobel, without whose fine attention to detail and endless library hours I would still be tracking down references and checking facts. Finally, I owe much to Emma, who mastered the pep talk during this process, and to Brady, who read more versions of the manuscript than anyone should have to. I'm lucky to have you both.

The Motherless Child in the Novels of Pauline Hopkins

INTRODUCTION

The Motherless Child in the Post-Reconstruction United States

> Every mother's son among them seemed to be in search of his mother; every mother in search of her children. In their eyes the work of emancipation was incomplete until the families which had been dispersed by slavery were reunited.
>
> —AGENT FOR THE FREEDMEN'S BUREAU (qtd. in Litwack 230)

> It is a common custom . . . to part children from their mothers at a very early age. . . . For what this separation is done, I do not know.
>
> —FREDERICK DOUGLASS, *Narrative of the Life . . .*, 242

IN HER FINAL NOVEL, *Of One Blood; or, The Hidden Self*, serialized in the *Colored American Magazine* from 1903 to 1904, Pauline Hopkins's protagonist, Reuel Briggs, a mixed-race man passing for white, serves as the doctor for an archaeological expedition in Africa. While there, he discovers that he is heir to the throne of Meroe in Ethiopia, the source of Western civilization, according to the novel. This discovery precipitates his exposure as an African American. In a highly sentimental moment, one of his fellow travelers confronts him with the racial identity he inherited from the black mother he has denied, a confrontation that recalls the trauma of his past: "Reuel stood for a moment, apparently struggling for words to answer the dying man's assertion, then fell on his knees in a passion of sobs agonizing to witness. 'You know then, Jim, that I am Mira's son?'" (593). His emotional acknowledgment of his traumatic past and his maternal heritage functions as the catharsis necessary for healing and facilitates personal and political change for himself and others.

We might say that Hopkins's entire oeuvre leads up to this scene, which offers a distillation of one of the major themes in her work and the focus of this study: the centrality of the mother—both her absence and her recovery—in the formation of a national African American identity. Joining the private and the public, the individual and the communal, the topos of motherlessness describes the psychological and political condition of African Americans in the post-Reconstruction United States and offers an enabling rhetoric for rebuilding that fragmented community. This trope figures widely in the literature and the songs produced by the African American diaspora because it resonates deeply with the group's experience. We can define a literary tradition around motherlessness by observing its manifestation in the novels of Pauline Hopkins. The purpose of this study, therefore, is the identification and analysis of motherlessness as a significant trope in stories of the African diaspora's experience in the United States. While much attention has been given to African American writers' response to master narratives of ideal womanhood, the significance of the mother—and specifically the lack or loss of the mother—as a literary pattern that has psychoanalytic and postcolonial, personal, and political relevance has not yet received its critical due. Addressing this gap in African American literary scholarship, this study introduces the trope of motherlessness, theorizes its multiple levels of resonance, and demonstrates its applicability using the work of Pauline Hopkins as a test case, particularly fruitful for this form of study.

In her four novels, Hopkins treats motherlessness on two interconnected planes. First, adopting the popular model of much nineteenth-century sentimental fiction, she portrays the motherlessness of her characters as a psychological condition. Motherlessness marks her characters with a deep, sometimes unacknowledged melancholy and a sense of lack that, as we shall see, resonates with Freudian theories of subject development. This personal level of motherlessness serves as a fitting motif for Hopkins's novels in that it accurately represents African Americans' lived experience. Under slavery, children were routinely rendered motherless through their mothers' sale or death. Ironically, women became motherless as they were robbed of their rights and abilities to mother their children. After emancipation, the mother-child bond remained vexed as families separated under slavery began the all-but-impossible task of finding one another and as mothers' inability to protect their grown children against outrageous violence became a source of grief. In short, the childless mother became motherless herself as she was denied her right to raise and protect her children, denied her own motherhood.

The personal condition of motherlessness came to represent metonymically the political condition of civic alienation and powerlessness experienced by African Americans, both under slavery and in the escalating racism of the post-emancipation United States. For this diasporic community, violently separated from its "motherland" and enjoying few rights in its new national "home," motherlessness functioned as a metaphor for national alienation. The spiritual from which I draw the title of this study illustrates this double meaning of motherlessness. The singer is presumably an adult who "sometimes feels" like a motherless child rather than actually being a child or being without his or her biological mother. Linking mother and home, the song draws on prominent domestic ideology, but it also resonates in terms of nationalism. The longed-for mother signifies both the biological mother of the individual and the "ancestral origin of a people" (Sundquist 529). This "child's" distant home may be the place where she lives with her family, or it may be Africa, the source of the heritage that identifies her and, in this way, signifies her homeland. Although born in the United States, the "child" cannot consider this land her home because she does not enjoy the rights to which an American citizen is entitled. Signifying at once the private and the public, the individual and the communal, the rhetorically powerful concept of motherlessness communicates the far-reaching concept of national alienation. In short, being a "motherless child" means more than being a child without her or his biological mother. It means being an individual or a group torn from one homeland and unwelcome in another.

This dual image not only signifies a condition of displacement, fragmentation, and loss, but also raises the prospect of redemption by suggesting that such a condition might be reversed by the mother's restored presence. The restoration of the mother figures in several ways in Hopkins's work, as we shall see. On the personal level, the personal or biological mother—an actual character in the novel—may return to the motherless child. On the more abstract political level, the disenfranchised community may experience a reversal in fortunes, finding itself in possession of privilege or power. Its marginalized motherland and the identity connected to it gain new respect and the "child" comes to enjoy the benefits that accompany citizenship, such as civic rights and a sense of belonging. In an extreme manifestation of the mother's restoration, representatives of powerful Mother Africa go to the displaced children to rectify their condition of national alienation. Reclaiming the mother—or the Mother, as this figure takes on collective and national resonance—becomes a means for the African American community to construct a cultural identity by celebrating its heritage and forging a unified frame of reference for national belonging and recognition. Stuart Hall, in "Cultural Identity and Diaspora," identifies such a strategy in the cinema of the Caribbean. "By representing or 'figuring' Africa as the mother of these different civilizations," Hall argues, texts seek to "restore an imaginary fullness or plentitude, to set against the broken rubric of our past" (224–25). In her fiction, Hopkins imagines just such a restoration, and *Of One Blood* registers the culmination of this project, one in which she counters the "broken rubric" of both the African American past under slavery and the post-Reconstruction present with the story of her protagonist's travel to a maternally figured Ethiopia, where he finds a proud racial heritage, citizenship, and national unity all brought into being by the restoration of the National Mother.

My concern in this book is to identify motherlessness as an under-examined trope in African American literature and to analyze the novels of Pauline Hopkins as important representatives of that overlooked literary tradition. I seek to unpack motherlessness as a signifier, examining the multiple and intersecting ways that the composite image of the personal mother and the National Mother becomes a vehicle, sometimes for a hopeful message of healing, national unity, and civic entitlement, and at other times for a despairing lament over the nationally sanctioned racism that seems to render hope futile. I focus on the novels not because they are the only place that Hopkins deploys the trope of motherlessness—indeed, motherlessness appears in the variety of genres Hopkins worked in throughout her career—but rather because they provide a fertile ground for the study of this literary tradition. With this longer form

Hopkins has the opportunity to develop the ethos of melancholy central to motherlessness and to explore the ramifications of this condition for her fully developed characters. This trope can be found in work by many African American writers: Frances Ellen Watkins Harper, Harriet E. Wilson, William Wells Brown, and Julia C. Collins, to name a few. My goal in this study, however, is to sound the depths of motherlessness in the work of one writer as an exemplar of its broader occurrence.

Mothers and Motherlessness: The Legacy of Domesticity

In Hopkins's novels, the presence of the mother and, more, her deeply felt absence recall the domestic ideology so popular in the mid-nineteenth century. Reflecting the values of the new middle class, which emerged with the industrial revolution between 1820 and the Civil War, domesticity touted the home—theoretically isolated from the gritty marketplace—as a haven, a locus of moral instruction and nurturance for children and of restoration and retreat for men. Reigning over the home, the idealized mother provided unsurpassable love and strong moral guidance for her family. Her gentle instruction took the form of influence; she did not force but rather swayed her children and husband along the right path. These "mothers of civilization," as Mary P. Ryan terms them, provided "internal restraints" on a potentially anarchic society bred by the increasingly competitive individualism now expected of the American male (147).[1] Through the mother's presence and influence, the comforting notion of "hearth and home" gained meaning.

The modern reader may balk at the false consciousness that enticed middle-class women to subscribe so wholeheartedly to this ideology. As Elizabeth Ammons observes, the idealization of mothers in the home began at precisely the moment when economic changes in the nation may have offered new possibilities of independence for women.[2] Nevertheless, subscribe they did, and enthusiastically. It was the notion of women's influence that made this ideology palatable. If mothers molded their sons into moral citizens and statesmen, if they influenced their husbands to make moral decisions in the workplace and the White House, then surely they wielded power. Nina Baym sums up this guiding philosophy: "Woman, if she can preside over the home space, will then be not out of the world but at the very center of it" (49).[3] Many of the architects of domestic ideology focused on this ideal. Catherine E. Beecher, for one, held that positive change in society could be brought about by bringing maternal ethics—based on the believed moral superiority of women—to bear not only on the private home but on all aspects of American life. More ambitiously, she advocated a central role for women in the nation's global leadership: "to American women . . . is committed the exalted privilege of extending over the world those blessed influences, which are to renovate degraded man" (37).[4] Understanding the home as a microcosm of society, adherents of domestic ideology imagined a world in which women used their influence to promote a loving community ethic as a remedy to society's ills. They believed that "female, and specifically maternal, love offer[ed] the foundation upon which to build a new social order" (Ammons, "Stowe's Dream" 181). In short, domestic ideology gave women an avenue through which they could participate in the all-important project of American nationalism.

The nineteenth-century domestic novel emerged as a vehicle for domestic ideology. Its goal: "to recruit the emotional energies of masses of women for a civilizing mission" (Ryan 147). Domestic novels realized the vision of domesticity in the service of the nation by portraying young women learning to become the virtuous, even saintly, mother ideal. These heroines—sometimes under the tutelage of their own mothers, but more often guided by a surrogate—learned to contribute to the project of building and strengthening a nation organized around the principles of motherly love. Believing that "God's values were domestic, even if the concept of God himself remained masculine," writers of the domestic genre "propose[d] a maternal, loving ethic in opposition to prevailing patriarchal values" (Baym 44, 15). Jane Tompkins, in her analysis of *Uncle Tom's Cabin,* describes this cultural project: "The popular domestic novel of the nineteenth century represents a monumental effort to reorganize culture from the woman's point of view. . . . *Uncle Tom's Cabin* . . . is the *summa theologica* of nineteenth-century America's religion of domesticity, a brilliant redaction of the culture's favorite story about itself—the story of salvation through motherly love" (124–25). Much of the sentimental domestic fiction of the nineteenth century shared this goal.[5]

Paradoxically, these novels often highlighted the redemptive power of the mother with her absence, or with her failure to fulfill the ideal of motherly love.[6] In *Uncle Tom's Cabin,* to take one example, recall little Eva's anti-mother, satirically named Marie, whose self-absorption renders Eva effectively motherless. As Mammy and Tom provide surrogate mothering, Eva overcomes this obstacle and emerges as a maternal figure herself, nurturing the unloved, motherless Topsy. Eva's love redeems Topsy, who goes on to serve society and the world as a missionary, embodying domestic ideology's tenet that the private reaches the public. Harriet Beecher Stowe's strategy was far from idiosyncratic; Susan Warner's Ellen, Maria Susanna Cummins's Gerty, E. D. E. N. Southworth's Capitola, Elizabeth Stuart Phelps's Avis, even Edith Wharton's Lily suffer the effects of motherlessness, overcoming or being overcome by this disadvantage in varying degrees.[7]

Through much of the nineteenth century, American domestic ideology and its wildly popular literary vehicle were primarily the terrain of the white middle class, but in the wake of emancipation, as African Americans took on the task of defining their place in the United States, they found political possibilities in the sentimental domestic novel as well. Many black women turned to domesticity as one of their strategies, adapting middle-class domestic and motherhood ideals for their own purposes, and treating "maternal values as the ethical alternative and logical corrective to racial injustice in America" (Ammons, "Stowe's Dream" 176–77).[8] Similar, perhaps, to European American women after the American Revolution who sought ways to adopt the new republic's egalitarian rhetoric and to participate in the new national project,[9] African Americans in the wake of emancipation sought the means by which to claim the citizenship granted them by the Fourteenth Amendment.

A number of scholars have examined the ways in which late nineteenth-century African American women writers took up domestic ideology in their work, noting especially their appropriation of domesticity's model of idealized womanhood. Excluded from popular definitions of "woman," classified as breeders rather than mothers under slavery, and stereotyped as lascivious jezebels, African American women often found themselves —both during and after slavery—excluded from dominant notions of

"Woman," an exclusion famously articulated by Sojourner Truth's question, raised at a women's rights convention in 1851: "Ar'n't I a woman?"[10] Such scholars as Claudia Tate, Elizabeth Ammons, Hazel V. Carby, and Deborah McDowell have explored the ways in which African American women writers sought to dismantle prevalent stereotypes of black women by portraying heroines who embody the traits of True Womanhood.[11] Tate, for example, attributes the popularity of domestic ideology among African American women to the growing belief in the importance of the "bourgeois decorum" modeled in the domestic novel as a means of racial uplift (*Domestic Allegories* 4). Ammons notes that, seeking to dismantle prevalent stereotypes about African American women, writers portrayed female characters as beautiful, motherly, and highly moral in order "to demonstrate the vicious untruth of the 'wanton' theory underlying rape-lynch mythology" (Ammons, *Conflicting Stories* 30). Carby, in her aptly named study, *Reconstructing Womanhood,* identifies the "dominant domestic ideologies and literary conventions of womanhood which excluded [black women] from the definition 'woman'" and examines the ways "black women intellectuals reconstructed [these ideologies] to produce an alternative discourse of black womanhood" (6). McDowell describes the goal of African American women writers in this way: "Conscious of the fact that a reconstruction of black female sexuality was required, these writers assumed a revisionist mission in their work, one based on a belief that they could substitute reality for stereotype. That substitution would assist a larger and related mission: to elevate the image of the entire black race. In so doing, they naively believed, they could eliminate caste injustices" (38). This argument certainly applies to the work of Pauline Hopkins, and each of the above-mentioned scholars has read her work in this light to some extent. Characters such as Sappho and Grace from *Contending Forces: A Romance Illustrative of Negro Life North and South* or Dianthe from *Of One Blood* embody many of the traits typically associated with domesticity's idealized womanhood. And if Hopkins does not engage in a wholesale adoption of True Womanhood, she nonetheless situates her work in the context of the ideology even as she subtly critiques aspects of it.[12]

The scholarly focus on African American writers' appropriation of the ideal of womanhood has illuminated this body of literature most usefully. I would argue, however, that womanhood is not the only aspect of domestic ideology that African American writers found appealing. If claiming ideal womanhood was a fruitful avenue for race activism made available by domestic ideology, the notion of motherlessness, drawing on the model of family and thus opening the door to community cohesion, resonated more deeply for the post-Reconstruction race community and offered greater possibilities for political work.[13] We find the groundwork for this strategy in black nationalism and its response to exclusion from the nation: activists in this movement looked to form a nation of their own, based not on geographic boundaries but on common heritage and race unity. According to historian Wilson Jeremiah Moses, "Black nationalism has sometimes, but not always, been concerned with the quest for a nation in the geographical sense. But often it has been 'nationalism' only in the sense that it seeks to unite the entire black racial family, assuming that the entire race has a collective destiny and message for humanity comparable to that of a nation" (17).[14] If, as Moses indicates, black nationalism conceived of the budding nation in terms of "family," domesticity and its emphasis on motherhood served as an enabling ideology and the domestic novel as a promising vehicle for creating a "post-diasporic national fantasy" (Berlant 558). It would be an easy step from domesticity's quest for the lost mother to the African American community's search for a National Mother, the African heritage that unites them. Indeed, the domestic novel's focus on mothers and motherlessness may have been the most attractive characteristic of that genre for African American authors. If African American women had a vexed relationship with domesticity's notion of ideal womanhood, as scholars have correctly noted, their relationship to the ideology of motherhood was equally troubled by a long history of thwarted motherhood under the American institution of slavery.

Mothers and Motherlessness: The Legacy of Slavery

The conditions experienced by mothers and children under slavery have become quite familiar, thanks to a number of illuminating studies on the subject.[15] In the "peculiar institution," motherhood was primarily an economic role; slave owners valued young female slaves as "breeders" and encouraged slave women to think of both their reproductive capacity and their children in financial terms. As Hazel V. Carby explains, a slave woman's "reproductive destiny was bound to capital accumulation; black women gave birth to property and, directly, to capital itself in the form of slaves" (24–25). Children led to "capital accumulation" not only for slave owners but, in some cases, for the mothers. Herbert G. Gutman cites evidence from plantation business ledgers that female slaves were rewarded with such items as a small pig or a new dress, or privileges such as Saturdays off, for giving birth and for sustaining the lives of their children for a given number of years (75–77).[16]

I do not mean to suggest that motherhood for white women existed apart from economics. Far from it. Feminist theorists such as Mary Wollstonecraft, Sarah M. Grimké, and Charlotte Perkins Gilman described marriage as a form of prostitution for white women—a relationship in which a woman's economic support depended upon the performance of her sexual and reproductive duties.[17] Harriet Jacobs insightfully identified the economic vulnerability of white plantation mistresses and black female slaves as the source of tension between Linda Brent and her master's wife.[18] Nevertheless, the experience of motherhood was worlds apart for these two sets of women, and domestic ideology provided one of the stark contrasts between slave motherhood and white, middle-class motherhood. While domesticity as it applied to middle- and upper-class whites in the antebellum period held motherhood as an exalted, almost sacred, state that downplayed the economics of the role while it glorified women and called for their respect and protection, motherhood for slave women was reduced explicitly to the material. Plantation owners classified them as breeders and justified rape as a means of increasing the "stock" of laborers. Moreover, while motherhood for middle-class white women brought—at least theoretically—a modicum of power to these agents of domesticity, motherhood for slave women functioned to reinforce "the reproduction of the relations of production" by reproducing "the values and behavior patterns necessary to maintain the system of hierarchy" (Spillers 79). In other words, reproduction further diminished power by helping to guarantee ongoing enslavement.

If parturition was troubled for enslaved women, so was the rearing of children. Slave mothers had little or no control over their relations with their children. Always threatened with the possibility of having their children sold away from them, slave mothers became a parody of idealized motherhood. As Hortense Spillers explains, in slavery, motherhood loses its sacredness as a "female blood-rite/right" (75). Encouraged to bear children, slave women were often prohibited from mothering them, a prohibition that fostered another form of motherlessness: that of being barred from one's role as and right to mother. Children, of course, suffered from motherlessness in slavery by being separated from their mothers by sale or perpetually threatened with such a separation, and so became actually or effectively orphaned.[19] In this way, most African American slaves could claim the experience of motherlessness.

The end of slavery did not mark the end of motherlessness, but rather expanded its reach. After emancipation, families that had been separated began the arduous task of trying to reunite. One man walked more than six hundred miles in search of his wife and children.[20] According to an agent for the Freedmen's Bureau, "every mother's son among them [the freed slaves] seemed to be in search of his mother; every mother in search of her children. In their eyes the work of emancipation was incomplete until the families which had been dispersed by slavery were reunited" (qtd. in Litwack 230). Significantly, although all types of family members—siblings, aunts, uncles, cousins, fathers—searched for their loved ones, this agent metonymically characterizes the large community's search as the search of mother for child, child for mother. In spite of their efforts, however, most families who had been divided under slavery never reunited. As late as the turn of the twentieth century, items in black newspapers advertising a family's search for its missing members demonstrated the ongoing effects of slavery's disruption of family life, the extended separation of children from mothers.

Motherlessness as Literary Trope

Given this history, we are not surprised to find motherlessness to be a recurring theme in African Americans' cultural productions. Indeed, as one explores this body of literature, one finds motherlessness to be central to enough texts as to merit recognition as a literary tradition. It is the goal of this study to read Hopkins's novels as exemplary of such a tradition. Motherlessness found a voice in multiple venues, both during and after slavery. Olaudah Equiano's account of his experience of abduction and slavery, published in 1789, described his separation from his family, including his mother. He sets up the pain of his separation from her by describing their closeness: "As I was the youngest of the sons, I became, of course, the greatest favorite with my mother, and was always with her; and she used to take particular pains to form my mind" (46–47). When he and his sister are taken from their home, he invests all his emotional connection to his family in the ongoing proximity to his sister, his one remaining family member. The two siblings comfort each other over the loss of their family, "bathing each other with [their] tears" (48). Losing his sister, the last connection to family, is agonizing: "she was torn from me . . . while I was left in a state of distraction not to be described. I cried and grieved continually" (48).

In his 1845 *Narrative of the Life of Frederick Douglass,* Frederick Douglass articulates more specifically the child's experience of motherlessness:

> My mother and I were separated when I was but an infant—before I knew her as my mother. It is a common custom . . . to part children from their mothers at a very early age. . . . For what this separation is done, I do not know, unless it be to hinder the development of the child's affection toward its mother, and to blunt and destroy the natural affection of the mother for the child. That is the inevitable result. (242)

The separation from his mother deprives Douglass of the typical feelings of a child for his mother so that her death makes little impression on him. Douglass's depiction of his experience of motherlessness and the systematic undermining of the bond between mother and child provided a highly charged sentimental image that proved very useful to abolitionists. Motherlessness signified particular hardship in the domestic novel, and abolitionists exploited this familiar model for their white audiences, who revered the role of the mother and believed the mother-child bond to be sacred. Accounts of the horrors of slavery were often couched in terms of the atrocities practiced against mothers and children. Casting the experience of slavery in these terms, therefore, became a rhetorically savvy means of appealing to the emotions of a nineteenth-century audience steeped in domestic ideology.

The emphasis on motherlessness was not strictly strategic, however, as indicated by another vehicle for this image: the slave spirituals, or "sorrow songs," as W. E. B. Du Bois termed them (2). These songs of the American slave community did not seek to communicate with a white audience as the slave narratives did. Rather, they functioned—as the blues later would—as a means of mourning, rehearsing, and sharing painful experiences, and of seeking comfort.[21] For this reason, they perhaps offer less mediated access to the deployment of the mother image. One song expresses the pain and loss of motherlessness with the wistful phrase, "Mother, rock me in the cradle all day." Another song laments, "Sometimes I feel like a motherless child / A long ways from home" (Sundquist 508, 581). These songs decry a lack that came to represent the alienation and powerlessness experienced under slavery. Moreover, and as Eric Sundquist explains, the songs express both personal and national longing in that they recall "the ancestral origin of a people as well as the familial origin of an individual" (529). The instances of motherlessness in the spirituals, then, suggest that this image was significant for the African American community as it spoke to and for itself to create the story of a common past, not as it attempted to translate its experience for a white audience.

Further evidence that motherlessness resonated meaningfully for the African American population resides simply in the fact that one repeatedly encounters it in works by African American authors. Harriet E. Wilson's *Our Nig; or Sketches from the Life of a Free Black* (1859) establishes motherlessness as a central condition for the novel's titular character with the final sentences of the first chapter: "Frado waited for the close of day, which was to bring back her mother. Alas! it never came. It was the last time she ever saw or heard of her mother" (23). Julia C. Collins's novel, *The Curse of Caste; or The Slave Bride,* serialized in 1853 and reprinted in 2006 by Oxford, tells a classic "tragic mulatta" story of a heroine who has no knowledge of her mother, "not even her name" (5).

Frances Ellen Watkins Harper's *Iola Leroy* (1892) will serve as a model of this tradition which, I argue, Hopkins works within and exemplifies. A close, brief look at *Iola Leroy* will give some indication of how the trope works in the literature. The novel establishes its interest in motherlessness early on with the introduction of Robert Johnson, a slave. Other than his name, the author provides only one detail to give readers insight into this character: he "had been separated from his mother in his childhood" (7). The novel's central character also appears as a motherless child for a time. Iola is the daughter of a slave-owning white man, Eugene Leroy, and his wife, Marie. Marie had been a slave and she remembers "being torn from her mother while clinging to her dress" (69). As Eugene's wife, Marie enjoys the privileges of the mistress of the plantation, but her husband neglects to make her freedom official, so after his death, her African heritage is exposed and she is remanded into slavery, along with her children. Iola knows nothing of her racial identity until she becomes a slave. The revelation of her race brings the full extent of her motherlessness into relief. Not only has she been separated from her mother with her sale, but she has discovered her national orphan status, removed from the American citizenship she took for granted. The novel then follows Iola through her separation from, search for, and eventual recovery of her personal mother and the racial heritage that links her to her National Motherland.

Iola's motherlessness manifests itself in traits we shall see in Hopkins's heroines. She experiences melancholy based on a sense of lack, "feeling the sad missing of something from her life" (54). A classic tragic mulatta figure, Iola could pass for white, but she determines to follow her mother and embrace the racial identity inherited from her. When a white doctor falls in love with her and offers to marry her, he attempts to assuage her concerns by offering to share his mother: "What is to hinder you from sharing my Northern home, from having my mother to be your mother?" (116). The answer is clear to Iola. Her mother is the source of her identity, and the absence of her mother is the cause of her deepest pain: "Oh, you do not know how hungry my heart is for my mother!" (117). Loyalty to her mother is tantamount to loyalty to her race. Her sister, on her deathbed, fervently charges Iola to "stand by mama!" (118). Her future husband, too, conflates loyalty to mother with loyalty to Motherland. He rejects the fortune offered to him by his paternal grandmother—a wealthy white woman. As he later explains to Iola, "My mother . . . faithful and true, belongs to that race. Where else should I be?" (263).

Iola and Dr. Latimer's commitment to mother and Motherland prompts them to return to the South, where they believe the race community most needs them. Iola works with a church, teaching Sunday school and offering programs for mothers and children. Her husband, thanks to his kindness and skill, becomes the "good doctor," known not only for his medical acumen but also for his patriotism and good citizenship. Iola's reunion with her mother has put her into the proper relationship with her National Mother, motherless no more.

The widespread use of this trope suggests that motherlessness, growing out of the lived experience of many African Americans, signified effectively as African Americans sought to tell a story that not only recovered a common past but also attempted to produce a unified identity that would equip them for the present. We turn now to an analysis of the multiple levels of relevance for the trope of motherlessness, and the reasons behind that relevance for African American literature.

Africa: The Mother Imago

The systematic destruction of families and the routine separation of children from their mothers under slavery resulted in a profound sense of insecurity and alienation for African Americans. The personal devastation of kinship ties paralleled the national decimation of citizenship ties as slave catchers abducted individuals from their homelands and divested them of their indigenous names and their national home.[22] Once on American shores, the experience of American slavery compounded this displacement. In addition to the separation of children and mothers, whether real or threatened, the paternalism of the slave system infantilized all slaves regardless of age, registered in part by the common usage of "boy" in racist discourse or by the practice among slavery's defenders of casting Africans in the role of children needing guidance and supervision. Significantly—and fundamentally to this study—these experiences of loss and alienation fostered an image of the personal mother and of Africa as the Motherland as an imago, a wistfully idealized locus of comfort and belonging.

We can understand the individual's and the community's relationship to the mother more fully through the lens of psychoanalytic theory, the critical methodology that informs this study. In her 1998 *Psychoanalysis and Black Novels: Desire and the Protocols of Race,* Claudia Tate addresses what she assumed would be the "misgivings that many African Americans have about the relevance of psychoanalysis to black literature" and she cites those misgivings as an explanation for the "general absence of psychoanalytic models in black intellectual discourse" (5). The narrow focus by psychoanalysis on gender construction and its tacit presumption of whiteness has led to the assumption that the discipline has little to say about racial difference or hierarchies. As a result, scholars of African American culture have in the past hesitated to apply psychoanalytic models to African American literature.[23] In recent years, however, scholars have answered these objections, supporting Tate's assertion that "psychoanalysis can tell us much about the complicated social workings of race in the United States and the representations of these workings in the literature of African Americans" (Tate 5). Hortense Spillers, to name one example, posits the suitability of psychoanalysis for understanding African American experiences under slavery: "these 'threads cable-strong' of an incestuous, interracial genealogy uncover slavery in the United States as one of the richest displays of the psychoanalytic dimensions of culture before the science of European psychoanalysis takes hold" (77). Following the lead of these scholars and others, I find that psychoanalytic models offer important insights into the deeply seated concept of motherlessness for the individual and into its reverberations for the community.

Sigmund Freud's oedipal model of individual development did much to establish the notion of the absent mother in American culture. The well-known family romance that forms the basis of the oedipal complex centered on the suppression—real or symbolic—of the mother as crucial to the proper development of the subject and, by extension, of civilization. Significantly, Freud's oedipal model describes not only the development of the individual and the role of motherlessness in that process, but it also insists upon the importance of motherlessness to the health and development of the community or nation. Terry Eagleton describes this Freudian notion: "It is clear that the child in [the pre-oedipal] state is not even prospectively a citizen who could be relied upon to do a hard day's work" (154). In order to be properly initiated into subjecthood, Freud claimed, the individual must reject her or his initial infantile attachment to and desire for the mother, turning instead to identification with the father. Rather than the mother's absence functioning as an obstacle to overcome or a sign of chaos that must be put right, as in the domestic novel, this model figured the mother's absence (or at least her diminishment) as the goal. The rejection of the mother and the identification with the father figures as a key step in the development of the ego, that balance between id and superego that allows the subject to function in society.[24]

Building on Freud's theories, Jacques Lacan argues that during the pre-oedipal stage, the state of the original symbiotic relationship with the mother, the child develops a concept of a unified self and a sense of plenitude deriving from it (although, Lacan insists, this is a false or imaginary sense of unity). The father's intrusion into this relationship in the form of the Law of the Father, forbidding the close, potentially incestuous relationship between child and mother, ushers the child into the social world and the Symbolic Order that assigns social roles and dictates proper behavior in society, including the repression of the original desire for the mother. Separation from the mother and the accompanying loss of the believed sense of fullness or plenitude experienced in that relationship elevate the mother as, in Lacan's words, "the prehistoric Other that it is impossible to forget—the Other whose primacy of position Freud affirms in the form of . . . something strange to me, although it is at the heart of me" (71). In short, "the desire of the mother," says Lacan, "is the origin of everything" (283).

Treating the African American community as a collective subject in Freud's oedipal model clarifies the impossible position occupied by that group. We can recast the drama of the Freudian "family romance" with the African American community as the subject, African heritage and the idealized nation of Africa as the Mother, and the dominant white culture of the United States as the Father. Under slavery, children followed the condition of the mother, inheriting African heritage, or "black blood," from their mothers; in this way the mother came to represent the source of African lineage and African American culture. As Lauren Berlant explains, "the slave mother was the 'country' into which the slave child was born, a realm unto herself whose foundational rules constituted a parody of the birthright properties of national citizenship" (559). Parody indeed. This "mother" deviated drastically from the domestically empowered antebellum ideal; African heritage from the mother resulted in marginalization and disempowerment, and Africa itself—far removed from the lived experience of most African Americans, both slave and free—existed primarily as a distant imagined ideal of a mother figure.

The father's "no," which prohibits the intimate connection between child and mother, figures in the racism of the late nineteenth-century United States that devalues African heritage and deems only European ancestry as an acceptable marker of Americanness. The collective African American subject recognizes its circumscribed place in American society by virtue of its connection to the Mother, who stands in a marginalized position in relation to the Father. The subject therefore comes to understand that it must reject this powerless Mother in order to be successfully articulated as a rights-bearing citizen. Here I build on Hortense Spillers's widely cited essay, "Mama's Baby, Papa's Maybe," in which she examines the status of the mother in the African American community and the roots of that status. Taking as her text the edict that the child follows the condition of the mother—*partus equitur ventrem*—Spillers probes this notion: "But what is the 'condition' of the mother? Is it the 'condition' of enslavement the writer means, or does he mean the 'mark' and the 'knowledge' of the *mother* upon the child that here translates into the culturally forbidden and impure?" (79, emphasis in original). In the turn-of-the-century United States, the time that Hopkins was writing, the condition inherited by African Americans was the latter. The degradation of the Mother as "culturally forbidden and impure" leads the "child" to look to and identify with the Father. According to Freud's formulation, when the child sees that the phallus or source of power is not available from the mother—that she is effectively castrated—that child turns to the father as the source of the power-wielding instrument.

Although this study centers on the post-Reconstruction era, the period in which Hopkins wrote her novels, the condition of motherlessness as I theorize it here developed over many years, emerging variously in each stage of history. Two crucial moments constitute the key events in Freud's theory: the loss of the mother and the intrusion of the father. We can locate the initial break from the Mother in the mass abduction from Africa, beginning in the early seventeenth century, which was the slave trade. Spillers describes this experience—specifically the infamous Middle Passage—as a site of the systematic and intentional breakdown of the African subject's kinship groups and identity. The experience of the Middle Passage figures as the crucial moment of separation from the Mother and intrusion of the Father. Prior to this time the subject enjoyed a close bond with its Mother, in so far as Africa figures as the Mother. Classified as property and separated from family and home, the African subject, displaced to a new and strange country, becomes motherless. Equiano's account of his experience of abduction portrays motherlessness during this stage.

Following the 1808 ban on the foreign slave trade, the second stage was the time of the well-established "peculiar institution," a period with approximately four million enslaved African Americans in the southern United States and a thriving domestic slave trade. For people of these later generations who had never lived in Africa, the moment of separation from the Mother might occur in the initial recognition of the nation's disparagement of the subjects' African heritage and the understanding that they would need to repudiate the Mother, whose heritage provided the justification for their enslavement or marginalization. Harriet Jacobs's narrative of life in slavery perfectly describes such a moment. Fortunate enough to be kindly treated as a child, she lives in ignorance of her status as a slave and enjoys a pre-oedipal connection to her mother for six years: "When I was six years old, my mother died; and then, for the first time, I learned, by the talk around me, that I was a slave" (10). Fittingly for my argument, Jacobs's sense of her national motherlessness—defined by her circumscribed role as a slave—coincides with the advent of her personal motherlessness—through the death of her biological mother. We find a similar phenomenon in the pre-emancipation section of Hopkins's first novel, *Contending Forces: A Romance Illustrative of Negro Life North and South.* Grace Montfort's children discover their relation to the Law of the Father when their mother's suspected blackness renders them no longer citizens but slaves. Her subsequent suicide leaves them, like Jacobs, doubly motherless.

The legacy of these two periods followed the community throughout slavery and after emancipation. Stories of abduction, of separation from kin and homelands, of the domestic slave trade and the auction block passed from generation to generation, and the loss engendered by that experience continued to be felt. The experience of motherlessness in the

African American community, therefore, stretched over these stages of slavery in America and beyond, for as long as its identity with Africa—its Mother imago—excluded it from access to privileged American citizenship and identification with the National Father of the United States.

Emancipation therefore figures as another major historical moment in the oedipal drama when the Father imposes himself into the African American community's ongoing relation with the Mother of African heritage. It is at this point that the possibility of identifying with the Father becomes available, at least theoretically. With the extension of rights and citizenship to all persons through the Fourteenth Amendment, emancipated slaves believed they had the opportunity to identify with the Father and had access to the power and privilege of American citizenship. It did not take long, however, for the black "child"—the developing subject or citizen—to discover that the Fourteenth Amendment promise of citizenship and equal protection was, in practical terms, virtually meaningless. That is to say, identification with the Father was still not an option for the black child.[25] The virulent racism of the defeated South, along with its ongoing resistance to federal control of states' rights, eventually brought the failure of national Reconstruction efforts. In the ongoing oedipal drama, the collective African American subject came to recognize the powerlessness of the Mother and the need to cling to the Father of white society for rights and citizenship.

To return to the Freudian model, then, the oedipal transition rarely goes smoothly for either the individual or the community subject, and that is certainly true for the African American "child." In Freud's original formulation, the child who emerges from the oedipal complex remains divided between the conscious life of the ego and the unconscious or repressed desire for the plenitude it believes it experienced in its preoedipal relationship with its mother.[26] The collective African American subject experiences its own schism in that, paradoxically, its achievement of separation from the Mother is prohibited even as it is required. If the letter of *partus equitur ventrem* no longer held sway, its spirit abided well into the twentieth century with the "one drop rule," which classified as black any person with a single drop of "black blood" (Davis 4–6). Forced to retain their identification with the Mother, persons of African heritage lacked the rights and status that would allow them fully to enter the dominant order. As Hortense Spillers observes, "under the press of a patronymic, patrifocal, patrilineal, and patriarchal order" in the United States, the slave, the emancipated slave, and the post-Reconstruction African American individual who, by law, follows the condition of the Mother becomes "the man/woman on the boundary, whose human and familial status, by the very nature of the case, had yet to be defined" (396).

We come, then, to a paradox: under the regimes of slavery and post-emancipation racism, African Americans experienced a form of mistreatment and exclusion on account of their maternal heritage, marginalization that rendered them both materially and symbolically motherless. The terms of the civic disempowerment taking place officially under slavery and less formally but no less legally sanctioned in the post-Reconstruction era, however, barred them from identifying with the civilly recognized and empowered Father. In other words, they were prompted to reject their Mother even as they were prohibited from identifying with their Father.

This loss that accompanies the motherlessness imposed by the Father manifested itself in the condition Freud described as melancholia. In his 1917 essay, "Mourning and Melancholia," Freud examines the effects of grief in response to "the loss of a loved person, or to the loss of some abstraction which has taken the place of one" (243). Freud distinguishes mourning from melancholia in that mourning is a temporary condition: in mourning, the individual believes that the lost object can be relinquished or replaced and, therefore, that she will get over her grief, as she eventually does. In melancholia, however, the sufferer experiences a long-term, pathological condition of loss (246). An additional contrast and a significant one for my argument: unlike the mourner, who experiences a specific and known loss, the melancholic may experience the sense of loss while being unable to identify the object of loss. Freud explains:

> In yet other cases one feels justified in maintaining the belief that a loss . . . has occurred, but one cannot see clearly what it is that has been lost, and it is all the more reasonable to suppose that the patient cannot consciously perceive what he has lost either. . . . This would suggest that melancholia is in some way related to an object-loss which is withdrawn from consciousness in contradistinction to mourning, in which there is nothing about the loss that is unconscious. (245)

This kind of unidentifiable loss effectively describes the motherlessness of the post-Reconstruction African American community. With the refrain, "sometimes I feel like a motherless child," the singer refers to a nebulous sense of lack that affects his experience, but which he cannot connect to a specific absence. The singer experiences this lack powerfully, feels lost, alone, unprotected, just as a child would experience the loss of his or her mother.

A number of scholars have theorized the condition of melancholia as it pertains to the experience of racism. In racial melancholia, the subject has lost—or has never possessed—the rights of citizenship so freely available to members of the dominant race. Racial melancholia, therefore, is the state of displacement or abjection that results from the experience of being a person of color in dominantly white America. According to Anne Anlin Cheng, author of *The Melancholy of Race: Psychoanalysis, Assimilation, and Hidden Grief,* racial melancholics have internalized the discrimination—both formal (institutionalized) and informal—designed to prevent their full assumption of American citizenship (17); they have come to accept their status as the Other against which dominant white society defines itself. Postcolonial scholars David L. Eng and Shinhee Han focus on the way melancholia illuminates the processes of assimilation in this country (344). They argue that because the "ideals of whiteness . . . remain unattainable" for persons or groups visibly marked as racially Other, the processes of assimilation are left "suspended, conflicted, and unresolved" (345). To put it in the terms of my argument, because identification with the white Father of dominant American society is both required of and prohibited for African Americans, they remain in a state of limbo marked by melancholia. Eng and Han extend their argument beyond the individual to the race community: "For . . . groups of color, suspended assimilation into mainstream culture may involve more than severe personal consequences; ultimately, it also constitutes the foundation for a type of national melancholia, a national haunting" (347).

Motherlessness and the Colonial Subject

The paradoxical position of the African American oedipal subject replicates the position of the colonial subject, as scholars working in the field of postcolonial studies have described it.[27] Vijay Mishra and Bob Hodge, for example, put it this way: "There is always, in the colonial regime, a tantalizing offer of subjectivity and its withdrawal which, for the colonized, momentarily confirms their entry into the world of the colonizer only to be rejected by it. The colonized never know when the colonizers consider them for what they are, humans in full possession of a self, or merely objects" (278). The status of object for the colonized as a conquered people is tantamount to the civil disempowerment of post-Reconstruction African Americans based upon their maternal heritage. Just as Freud's oedipal model places the pre-oedipal mother in a devalued, abject position (Sprengnether 2), so the colonial project devalues pre-colonial history, distorting, disfiguring, and destroying the past of the oppressed (Fanon, *Wretched* 210).

Given this parallel, it is not surprising to find similarities in the strategies of postcolonial and feminist psychoanalytic theorists, both students of theories of power and oppression. Psychoanalytic scholars have rejected Freud's marginalization of the mother, identifying the pre-oedipal mother not as the obstacle to the subject's proper development, but as a source of power and possibility. Madelon Sprengnether and others have discovered in Freud's work indications that even Freud finds the mother more powerful than he lets on: "The pre-oedipal mother, in Freud's unsystematic treatments of her, emerges as a figure of subversion, a threat to masculine identity as well as to patriarchal culture. Never a major figure in Freud's theory, which revolves around the drama of the father-son relationship, she has a ghostlike function, creating a presence out of absence" (5).[28] Julia Kristeva identifies the disruptive power of the remnants of the pre-oedipal phase in "semiotic" language play, attributing to such play the possibility of undermining the Symbolic Order, associated with the Law of the Father (62–67).

Similar to feminist efforts to revalue the mother in Freud's theory, postcolonial scholars advocate efforts to revalue the colonial subject's Motherland. Frantz Fanon's description of the colonized subjects' recovery of the past bears a striking resemblance to feminist treatments of the pursuit of the pre-oedipal mother: "native intellectuals, since they could not stand wonder-struck before the history of today's barbarity, decided to go back farther and to delve deeper down; and, let us make no mistake, it was with the greatest delight that they discovered that there was nothing to be ashamed of in the past, but rather dignity, glory and solemnity" (*Wretched* 210). Stuart Hall echoes Fanon, touting the importance of rediscovering "hidden histories" as part of the process of recovering the postcolonial subject's cultural identity. He sees in the work of Jamaican photographer Armet Francis, for example, efforts to represent Africa as the Mother, and to use that representation to restore the pre-oedipal plentitude lost with the denial or repression of that Mother. Yet, he insists upon the mythical nature of a unified heritage or shared history as a defining element of cultural identity. Indeed, "as well as the many points of similarity, there are also critical points of deep and significant *difference* which constitute. . .—since history has intervened—'what we have become'" (Hall 224–25, emphasis in original). Africa, as a source of origin, as a Mother, becomes figurative, a unifying metaphor for, in Benedict Anderson's words, "an imagined community." And yet, Hall explains, its imaginative quality makes it no less real:

> Cultural identity is not a fixed essence at all, lying unchanged outside history and culture. . . . It is not a fixed origin to which we can make some final and absolute Return. Of course, it is not a mere phantasm either. It is *something*—not a mere trick of the imagination. It has its histories—and histories have their real, material and symbolic effects. The past continues to speak to us. But it no longer addresses us as a simple, factual "past," since our relation to it, like the child's relation to the mother, is always-already "after the break." It is always constructed through memory, fantasy, narrative and myth. (226, emphasis in original)

This work of memory, fantasy, narrative, and myth—this "re-telling" of the past (224)—is the work that goes on among numerous post-Reconstruction authors who address the paradox of the African American community's relationship with the Mother by recuperating and reclaiming that Mother as a representative of a glorious past and a source of belonging and national entitlement.[29]

Hopkins had a keen awareness of the condition of African Americans in the United States, and particularly of their devaluing as a people. She describes the effect of slanted history: "To the Negro is denied the stimulus of referring to the deeds of distinguished ancestors, to their valor and patriotism. He is distinguished only as the former slave of the country. Truth gives him the history of a patriot, a brave soldier, the defender of the country from foreign invaders, a 'God-fearing producer of the nation's wealth."[30] Like the artists described by Hall, Hopkins dedicates herself to retelling the African American story. Her novels represent the plight of the African American community in terms of motherlessness and the longing for the plenitude available in a pre-oedipal relationship with the Mother. She fills her work with mothers, both lost and found, real and symbolic. As we shall see in the chapters that follow, drawing on the domestic novel form, Hopkins invests the familiar trope of the absent mother with cultural and political significance, allowing her to imagine the restoration for her community of the plenitude that the dominant culture of the United States withholds. In answer to the alienation and marginalization imposed by white society in the post-Reconstruction United States, Hopkins uses the figure of the mother—so powerful during the heyday of the cult of the Mother—as an image of Africa, the pre-oedipal Mother and the source of the proud history that Hopkins believed accompanied African heritage.

Pauline Hopkins as a Race Activist

Pauline Hopkins's life fitted her for the work she undertook. Her early life coincided with twenty very turbulent years in African American history. Born to free parents in 1859, she grew up in Boston during a period of optimism brought about by the North's Civil War victory, emancipation, and the passage of the Fourteenth Amendment granting citizenship to former slaves. She came of age with the shattering of optimism brought about by the failure of Reconstruction in 1877. But Hopkins did not sit quietly on the sidelines of this drama: she created her own—literally. It was during these years that she took to the stage, launching her career as not only a playwright and performer, but also as a strong spokesperson for her race.

Although readers today know Hopkins primarily as an author and editor, her experience as a playwright and performer has received increased attention in recent years.[31] In 1875, at just sixteen years of age, Hopkins made her musical debut in the Progressive Musical Union, an African American choral group. Two years later, she played the lead role in the musical, *Pauline, or the Belle of Saratoga.* With this premiere, Hopkins joined her extended family's long tradition of "using the arts to promote racial uplift and raise political awareness" (Lois Brown, *Hopkins* 72), a practice that would inform the rest of her performing and writing career. Indeed, her family was part of her musical enterprise in the form of the Hopkins Colored Troubadours, a professional arts group. Hopkins was also actively writing at this time, and in 1877 she applied for the copyright for two plays: *Aristocracy—A Musical Drama in 3 Acts* and *Winona.* With her well-received third play *Peculiar Sam; or, The Underground Railroad, a Musical Drama in Four Acts,* Hopkins earned recognition in the African American theater culture of her day. Brown points out that *Peculiar Sam* (later titled *The Slaves' Escape*) distinguished Hopkins as "the first African American dramatist to emerge in the post–Civil War era and the first American playwright to write and star in her own play on American slavery" (139). Hopkins left her musical career for the perhaps more lucrative and certainly more dependable work of a stenographer. But her passion for music continued, and as we shall see in chapter 4, Hopkins maintained her faith in the power of music to move people.

Hopkins's place in history equipped her with a keen understanding of the political and racial situation that characterized the late nineteenth and early twentieth centuries; this understanding prompted her to make her voice heard. In 1900, she published her first novel, *Contending Forces,* and joined the staff of the *Colored American Magazine* as contributor and eventually editor. Through her work at the magazine and her contacts with others in Boston's wide and politically active African American community, Hopkins participated in the ongoing race uplift efforts. Numerous turn-of-the-century African American women used the rhetoric of motherhood and the image of the mother as a means of claiming access to the important public work of "race progress."[32] In her 1892 essay, "Enlightened Motherhood," Frances Ellen Watkins Harper drew on the familiar rhetoric of domesticity as taking place in the home but extending well beyond it: "the home is an institution older than the church and antedates school, and that is the place where children should be trained for useful citizenship on earth" (285–86).[33] Anna Julia Cooper, in her 1886 address, "Womanhood: A Vital Element in the Regeneration and Progress of a Race," extolled the importance of mothering: "Woman, Mother,—your responsibility is one that might make angels tremble and fear to take hold! . . . The training of children is a task on which an infinity of weal or woe depends." Later, she describes more precisely this responsibility: "A stream cannot rise higher than its source. The atmosphere of homes is no rarer and purer and sweeter than are the mothers in those homes. A race is but a total of families. The nation is the aggregate of its homes" (59, 63).[34] Carrie W. Clifford, a member of the Ohio Federation of Colored Women's Clubs, argued that women should be granted the vote on the basis of their ability to care for their children. Indeed, given their insight into the needs of children, she said, "the wonder grows that her voice is not the *first* heard in planning for the ideal State in which her child, as future citizen, is to play his part" (185, emphasis in original). The National Association of Colored Women's prioritizing of "Mother, Home, Child" as its primary focus further evinces the popularity of the belief that the concrete notion of mothering and the quotidian practice of childrearing held implications for the development of the race community that extended well beyond the individual family (Boris 218).[35] These activists and others called upon the image of the mother and the work of mothering as a political strategy to articulate the "quintessential Americanness of black women" (Berg 21), and in this way, to justify their increased participation in the public sphere, specifically in the arena of nation-building and racial uplift.[36]

A similar strategy was deployed by white activists. Even as enthusiasm for the promise of domestic ideology waned among the white middle class, the rhetoric of motherhood as crucial to the project of nation building continued to be heard from a variety of sources. White women wishing for power on the national scene and in the arena of policy-making claimed motherhood as a divinely ordained role that uniquely qualified them to attend to the national concerns of children and made them crucial players in the project of nation building. A well-known proponent of this type of reasoning, Charlotte Perkins Gilman, drew her evidence from evolution theory, arguing that women are the primary agents of human progress and that, thanks to their natural tendency toward giving and nurturing life (as opposed to the violent and destructive impulses natural to males), women belong in positions of national leadership.[37] While black spokespersons' arguments resembled those of their white contemporaries, finding in motherhood an avenue through which to justify their work in national and local concerns, their references to the motherlessness of the African American community and to a broadly conceived, symbolic National Mother as a rallying point for that community sets their rhetoric apart. Anna Julia Cooper described the African American race as a child needing maternal guidance: "young and full of the elasticity and hopefulness of youth" and yet "particularly sensitive to impressions" (144–45).[38] Although Cooper here makes the familiar call for model mothers, she also constructs a collective, familial identity for the race community, raising the possibility or necessity of a collective Mother, the Mother writ large, to nurture this young and hopeful community. Likewise, and as we have seen, the nineteenth-century black nationalist movement figured the African diaspora as a family, calling for unity among all from the Motherland, based on "the feeling on the part of black individuals that they are responsible for the welfare of other black individuals, or of black people as a collective entity, simply because of a shared racial heritage and destiny" (Moses 20). In other words, according to the tenets of black nationalism, people of African heritage saw themselves as members of an extended and oppressed family who needed to return to their Mother.

Throughout this study, I refer to this Mother, the Mother writ large, the collective ideal representing the potential unity and community of the African diaspora, as the National Mother. With this term, I seek to capture the idealized notion of African heritage as a source of national belonging. The forced denial of the Mother is rejected by claiming the Mother. The African heritage—"black blood"—attributed to that Mother and denigrated by dominant American society is upheld as positive and sought after. "National" points to not just the cultural and racial heritage, but to an idealized notion that full citizenship would accompany the claiming of that maternal heritage, bringing an end to the civic alienation suffered under the influence of the National Father. (Similarly, I refer to the nation of the United States, marked by racist institutions and a refusal to recognize its African children as rights-bearing citizens, as the National Father, in keeping with the oedipal model by which I have defined motherlessness for the post-Reconstruction African American community.)

The term "National Mother" also seeks to distinguish from both the motherhood ideal celebrated in nineteenth-century domesticity that focused primarily on individual mothers and from the individual mother characters that populate Hopkins's novels. Certainly, we see in her work various motherless characters returning to or reclaiming an individual mother. The story of Reuel, with which this chapter opened, serves to illustrate this distinction. As we shall see in more detail in chapter 4, Reuel recalls his personal mother, her words, her nurturing acts such as tucking him into bed at night. In the emotional climax, he reclaims that personal mother, openly declaring, "I am Mira's son." But by reclaiming his personal mother, Mira, he also reclaims his National Mother, the African heritage he inherited from Mira. He reclaims his connection to the Africans who have hailed him as their future king. In short, he has recovered both the personal mother, Mira, and the National Mother, Africa and African heritage.

The sometimes subtle distinction between the personal mother and the National Mother as I describe it can be seen in Frederick Douglass's account of his life, where he demonstrated the dual function of the mother for family *and* community cohesion in his narrative. He explains that the loss of his mother led to the breaking down of kinship ties with his siblings, regardless of the fact that they all lived together in the same house: "the early separation of us from our mother had well nigh blotted the fact of our relationship from our memories" (260). Spillers comments on his statement: "The *physical* proximity of the siblings survives the mother's death. They grasp their connection in the physical sense, but Douglass appears to mean a *psychological* bonding whose success mandates the *mother's* presence" (76, emphasis in original). The racial uplift program as Hopkins and her contemporaries imagined it grew out of just such an assumption. If, as Spillers asserts, "the destructive loss of the natural mother, whose biological/genetic relationship to the child remains unique and unambiguous, opens the enslaved young to social ambiguity and chaos" (76), then the motherless child of the race community, subject to the violence and chaos of the post-Reconstruction United States—the National Father—is prey to the same "social ambiguity." Hopkins casts the dilemma of the African American community in terms of motherlessness, and focuses on recovering a connection with a National Mother.

In the chapters that follow I map and analyze Hopkins's use of the metaphor of motherlessness and the National Mother as a means of articulating and exploring her vision for racial uplift and the development of a national identity for African Americans. I look not only at the optimism but also at the doubt reflected in her work, the times in which motherlessness seems insurmountable in the face of the National Father's dominance. Overall, however, Hopkins remains steadfast in her commitment to a national vision, brought about through maternal redemption.

Chapter 1, "'The blessed relief of tears': Maternal Redemption in *Contending Forces,*" reads Hopkins's first novel, published in 1900, as her first extended treatment of motherlessness. Through the mixed-race characters of John Langley and Sappho Clark, respectively villain and victim, Hopkins illustrates the intertwining of individual and community motherlessness. The mulatto/a figure, so popular with turn-of-the-century novelists, pointedly embodies the oedipal struggle between identifying with the white father or the black mother, and thus resonates multiply in *Contending Forces,* as the novel's title suggests. Motherlessness emerges in the novel as a state akin to the psychoanalytic condition of melancholia, and the cathartic power of tears as a response invests the novel's relation to the sentimental domestic novel with deeper psychoanalytic significance. John Langley's rejection of his mother in favor of courting the approval of white society leads him to betray Boston's African American community in order to make individual professional gains. In contrast, Sappho's mourning over the loss of her child and her own lost motherhood brings about healing as she confronts the memory of the violent assaults that led to her current state and resolves to reclaim her son and her identity as mother. Her personal melancholy and healing are invested with national significance as her catharsis leads to restored unity for the rest of her community. With its focus on sentimentalism and the recovery of the past, the novel participates in the same communal cathartic work that Ralph Ellison would attribute to the blues: "an impulse to keep the painful detail and episodes of a brutal existence alive in one's aching consciousness" (78). Thus the catharsis implicit in the novel weaves together the political and psychoanalytic threads of *Motherless Child*'s argument. With Sappho's story, Hopkins dramatizes maternal redemption—the notion forwarded in the domestic ideology of salvation through motherly love—as a means of healing motherlessness, reintegrating individuals into their community, and inching that community toward the assumption of full citizenship in the United States.

The following two chapters examine novels in which Hopkins shifts her focus from Mother Africa to the National Father of the United States, pointedly placing blame for the African American community's motherlessness on the Father of dominant white society. Chapter 2, "Motherlessness in the Nation's Capital: The National Father in *Hagar's Daughter*," locates the father figure in the political machine of Washington, D.C. The novel highlights its national interests not only with the setting but also with the underlying story of the biblical Hagar, whose child was denied a place in his father's nascent nation of Israel and so was forced to identify with his Ethiopian mother. The National Father comes under criticism for his failure to invite African Americans into full national belonging in the United States, thus barring them from oedipal identification with him. At the same time, it criticizes that Father as unworthy of identification due to immorality in the form of sexual exploitation of African American women. Bringing together Freud's treatment of the oedipal crisis as necessary to civilization and Gail Bederman's work on masculinity and civilization, this chapter probes Hopkins's complex championing of maternal heritage as a source of national identity and civilization superior to that available from the National Father. In *Hagar's Daughter*, the abundance of dramatic moments, hidden identities, and narrow escapes—as befitting a serialized novel—do not distract the reader from the novel's important message: the nation's government seat, as a site of racist corruption and immorality, establishes the moral failure of the National Father.

Hopkins's third novel, *Winona*, takes readers to another site of national significance: the western frontier. Set in "Bleeding Kansas"—that territory engaged in a violent contest over whether it would join the Union as a free or a slave state—*Winona* tells the story of, once again, a mixed-race woman divided between identification with her African American mother and her Anglo-American father. During their escape from slavery in Missouri, Winona and her adopted brother, Judah, team up with John Brown and his men in their fight against the vicious Missouri rangers. Chapter 3, "'Somethin's gwine happen': National Warning in *Winona,*" again offers a critique of the National Father, this time focusing on brutal violence. Revising Frederick Jackson Turner's argument of ten years earlier, that the true American character develops out of encounters between the civilized European and the "savage" Indian, *Winona* attributes true savagery to the proslavery southerners while the African American characters and those sympathetic to their cause emerge as the only hope for the nation's civilization.

While all ostensibly ends well in the novel, with Winona inheriting her father's fortune and poised to marry the man she loves, the novel also sounds a note of warning. Judah's emergence as a prophet figure sets this text in the tradition of the American jeremiad as he foresees a tragic end for the nation if such racist violence continues. Motherlessness remains pointedly present as Winona's father effectively erases her mother from her history. Nevertheless, Hopkins ends the novel with the voice of another prophet, an old woman who speaks as a representative of African American folk wisdom. Granted the last word in the novel, this sage optimistically predicts the restoration of the Mother with a change in circumstances for her people: "somethin's gwine happen."

Something does indeed happen in Hopkins's final novel, *Of One Blood; or, The Hidden Self:* her protagonist's search for his personal mother and National Mother culminates in his assumption of the throne in Ethiopia. Maternal figures abound in this story: most notably, the protagonist's mother seems to merge with Africa itself, a ghostly presence wooing her children back to her. With this novel, Hopkins harkens back to her early career as a playwright and musical performer, imagining music as the channel for reconnection with African heritage. Chapter 4, "Finding Mother Africa: *Of One Blood* and Hopkins's National Vision," sets the novel alongside W. E. B. Du Bois's *The Souls of Black Folk* (published the same year as the final installment of *Of One Blood*), which celebrates the national import of the music created by the African American community. For both Hopkins and Du Bois, music serves as a vehicle for recovering a repressed (pre-oedipal) past, which Hopkins perceives as crucial to the project of recovering the National Mother. *Of One Blood* registers the culmination of this project as she counters the "broken rubric" of both the African American past under slavery and the post-Reconstruction present with a story of proud racial heritage, namely the Ethiopianist position that Ethiopia is the true source of Western civilization. The novel does not end with unqualified optimism; on its last page, her protagonist ponders the ongoing threat of the National Father, even reaching to the shores of Africa. Nevertheless, the reunion of the protagonist with his Mother reverberates with promise and hope for the national progress of Americans of African descent.

As we shall see, in all of Hopkins's novels missing mothers haunt the characters, and the condition of motherlessness marks not only individuals but entire communities. As in the domestic novel genre, motherlessness figures as a debilitating condition that must be overcome. The post-Reconstruction African American community faces an overwhelming, nationally enforced degree of motherlessness for which there are no simple solutions. Ultimately, Hopkins's oeuvre does not imagine an easily achieved maternal redemption; in fact, three of her four novels end with serious misgivings about their characters' futures. Nevertheless, Hopkins explores the possibilities afforded by the pre-oedipal mother, her memory, and the power of that memory. As they rediscover the past, bringing that history to bear on the present, Hopkins's novels offer a cathartic experience for readers, an opportunity to sympathize with the characters' motherlessness and to recognize their own. The novels provide a model for discovering a "glorious past" and for revaluing and celebrating the National Mother of African heritage.

CHAPTER ONE

"THE BLESSED RELIEF OF TEARS"

Maternal Redemption in *Contending Forces*

> Then came the blessed relief of tears—like a flood—they relieved her overcharged brain and saved her reason. . . . At length she rose from that seat resolved that come what would she would claim the child and do her duty as his mother in love and training. She would devote her life to him.
>
> —*Contending Forces*

IN HER PREFACE to *Contending Forces: A Romance Illustrative of Negro Life North and South,* Hopkins describes her first novel as a "somewhat abrupt and daring venture"—a surprising claim, given her history in the public arena as an actress, singer, and playwright. Although she began writing fiction almost immediately after her stage career, working on and even registering a copyright for the partially complete *Hagar's Daughter* in 1891 (Lois Brown 163), financial necessity caused her to take up stenography, a career she pursued until 1899. During this time, although she joined Boston's community of race activists, she was not in the public eye as she had been, and may have felt, therefore, that her first novel, published in 1900, would seem like a sudden shift. Nevertheless, if this was a daring venture, it was not ill-conceived. She had given a good deal of thought to the endeavor and the purpose behind it. The novel's preface outlines her vision for her new vocation. Hopkins announces that her purpose for the novel goes well beyond simple entertainment, having far-reaching political goals.[1] Her primary goal for her foray into "the field of romantic literature" is to "raise the stigma of degradation from my race" (13), to restore and heal the race community. Fiction, she believed, could be the means for uniting and uplifting the African American community in the face of rampant violence and discrimination: "Fiction is of great value to any people as a preserver of manners and customs—religious, political and social. It is a record of growth and development from generation to generation" (13–14).

Significantly, Hopkins characterizes the important work of recovering and retelling stories as the particular purview of women: "The colored race has historians, lecturers, ministers, poets, judges and lawyers,—men of brilliant intellects who have arrested the favorable attention of this busy, energetic nation. But, after all, it is the simple, homely tale, unassumingly told, which cements the bond of brotherhood among all classes and all complexions" (13). Here Hopkins deploys the well-established dialectic between masculine and feminine, head and heart, public and private. She sets the typically public, nationally oriented work of historians, judges, lawyers, and epic poets—which she identifies as the work of "men"—against the unassuming "homely tale," presumably the work of women. She appears, with this diminutive classification of storytelling, to accept the traditional valuing of public work over private. As the lines quoted above attest, however, she challenges that ranking, crediting storytelling with the important national work of preserving the manners and customs of a people and of recording the nation's growth, work identified by Nira Yuval-Davis and Floya Anthias in *Woman, Nation, State* as one of the ways women take part in nationalism as "active transmitters and producers of the national culture."[2] So doing, Hopkins attributes national significance to the sometimes feminized and undervalued work of storytelling, the work she now takes on.[3]

With her reference to the particular contribution of women, Hopkins may also have had in mind the sentimental, domestic literary form, a form made popular by white, middle-class women writers of the nineteenth century and used by black and white women alike through the turn of the century. As we shall see, with its focus on motherhood, its ethos of sympathy, and its promise of maternal redemption as a means of addressing both personal and national ills, the domestic novel comported perfectly with Hopkins's purpose and, as such, provided a fitting vehicle for depicting the African American community as a motherless child. Through the mixed-race characters of John Langley and Sappho Clark in *Contending Forces,* Hopkins illustrates the intertwining of individual and community motherlessness and explores the possibility of maternal redemption, achieved by reclaiming and reaffirming an alliance with the Mother who was the source of racial identity and who had been denied by the oedipal directive of subject development under white oppression.

Motherlessness and Melancholia: The Oedipal Dilemma in Contending Forces

Having outlined her goals in the preface, preparing her readers for what lies ahead, Hopkins launches into her project of recuperating the race community's history by telling a story that spans the past and the present. The novel tells the history of the Montfort family, beginning in the early nineteenth century with their arrival in the United States from Bermuda. Charles and Grace Montfort, along with sons Charles and Jesse, come to the United States in order to avoid the British law that would require them to emancipate their slaves. Although they support this law in principle, Charles believes he will lose too much money if he follows the emancipation schedule outlined by British law. He comes to North Carolina, then, with the plan of freeing his slaves within the next few years. His new neighbors disapprove of his plan, fearing that it will lead to unrest among their own slaves, so they hatch a scheme to undermine the Montforts' position in society by circulating a rumor that Grace Montfort has a "black streak in her" (41). This suspicion, along with the community's fear of Montfort's liberal leanings, gives Anson Pollock ample justification for killing Charles and claiming Grace and her sons as his property. Unable to accept her fate, Grace drowns herself, leaving her sons and her personal maid, Lucy, to a life with Pollock. He sells the young Charles to an Englishman, who takes the boy to England with him. The Englishman attempts to free Jesse, but before succeeding, Jesse escapes to the North, where he marries and has a family. The brothers never reunite.

The novel then jumps forward to the late nineteenth century to tell the story of Jesse Montfort's descendents. His daughter, Elizabeth "Ma"

Smith, is widowed with two grown children, Will and Dora. Will—a character loosely modeled after W. E. B. Du Bois—works as a bellhop at a Boston hotel, but is saving for college where, we understand, his keen intellect will stand him in good stead. Dora helps her mother with the boarding house they opened after the death of Dora's father. When Sappho Clark, a beautiful woman with a mysterious past, takes one of their rooms, Dora immediately receives her as a friend and Will soon falls in love with her. Unfortunately, Dora's fiancé, John Langley, a man motivated by greed, also develops an attraction for Sappho. Unwilling to give up Dora and the property she will bring to their marriage, he takes a circuitous route to Sappho. He discovers her secret—that she has a son as the result of rape—and attempts to use this information to blackmail her into becoming his mistress. Unwilling to be with Langley, but also convinced that Will would reject her if he knew her history, Sappho secretly leaves the boarding house. She reclaims the son who has been living with her aunt and takes him to New Orleans, her original home. All works out, of course, as we expect of the domestic novel. Dora breaks her engagement with John Langley when she learns of his cruelty to Sappho and marries, instead, her longtime friend, Arthur Lewis—a character modeled after Booker T. Washington. Eventually, Will finds Sappho, convinces her of his continued devotion, and marries her. Most dramatic—and typical of the remarkable coincidences often found in this genre—an Englishman who meets Will at a dinner discovers that the Smiths are the descendents of Jesse Montfort, whom he came to the United States to find. The grandson of Charles Montfort Jr., he explains that his family has been in litigation with the U.S. government, suing for damages over the treatment of the Montfort family, a suit that eventually results in an award of $150,000 for Mrs. Smith.

Motherlessness forms a backdrop against which the novel's action takes place. In the early Montfort family, both children enjoy a pre-oedipal closeness to their mother—the plenitude described by Jacques Lacan in the oedipal drama. They "followed their mother closely" and "resembled her in the beauty of their features" (40). Jesse, the "young darling of his mother's heart" (31), bears a "still greater resemblance" to his mother than does his brother (40). Although the children have their mother, the text foreshadows their paradoxical motherlessness, stating that they "followed their mother," a phrase ominous in its similarity to *partus equitur ventrem*. The children's bodies carry the physical mark or features of their mother, although the only feature the text makes explicit is "beauty." In fact, the reader never knows if Grace is of African descent, if she has "black blood" that she has passed on to her children. The information of her racial heritage grows entirely from rumors circulated by neighbors jealous of the Montforts' wealth and resentful of their more liberal opinions about slavery. They attempt to find and read signs on her body that mark her with African heritage. Bill Samson, one of the outspoken and disgruntled neighbors, asserts confidently, "Thar's too much cream color in the face and too little blud seen under the skin for a genooine white 'ooman" (41). Later, Samson and another man confirm this reading by inscribing another set of marks: the "raw gash" of the whip. Allison Berg explains that such marks serve the construction of race and take on concrete meaning:

> Taking turns in a whipping that also serves to brand Grace as a slave, Pollock's overseers lay claim to Grace by marking her with visible lines of blood. Her allegedly black blood externalized and literalized—the racial privilege suggested by her "tender white back" overwritten by marks testifying to her racial difference—Grace becomes wholly identified with the "contaminated" bloodline that both motivates and justifies their actions. (35)

By leaving Grace's racial heritage uncertain, the novel points to an understanding of race as a construction, a fiction. And yet, this fiction has very real consequences.[4] Grace's African heritage becomes fact at this moment, and her sons by law follow not only her actions and appearance but her newly determined racial and political condition as well.

This scene not only gives Charles and Jesse an African mother; it also takes her away. The entrance of the Father—the representative of white society, taking the form of a white man wielding a phallic whip—disrupts the children's pre-oedipal plenitude. Lucy, their mother's maid, takes the boys away from their mother to prevent them from witnessing the violence, so the whip separates them literally as well as symbolically from their mother (70). The Father is also represented by the law—the Lacanian Law of the Father. Hopkins portrays a number of casual conversations—

seemingly unconnected to the novel's main plot—between the residents of the Montforts' North Carolina town, but a common thread emerges in the repeated references to the town's application of the law as a means of upholding racial distinctions and enforcing the hierarchy of power. For example, one man appears before a judge and is sentenced to whipping for his plans to marry a slave (36–37). Another spends time in jail because he accidently shot someone's dog when he meant to hit a free black man. The shooter explains that the law would have excused the killing of the black man, but the dog was a valuable asset "thet had tred hundreds o' runaways" (38). In these cases, the law appears as an instrument used to secure the place of whites over blacks. Harryette Mullen, in her discussion of women's slave narratives, identifies legal discourses as "the tools of the master" and asserts that these tools "are used like an iron bit to mute the resistant slave woman's mother tongue" (83). *Contending Forces* bears out Mullen's claim: the law plays an important role in controlling Grace Montfort, the newly created slave woman, and in maintaining the racial hierarchy that Charles Montfort threatens. According to one law-abiding citizen, "we jes don't spec' to hav' no foolin' 'bout this yer question of who's on top as regards a gentleman's owning his niggers, an' whomsoeveder goes ter foolin' with that are pertickler pint o' discusshun is gwine ter be made a eggsample of, even if it's a white man" (36). By this standard, the law justifies Montfort's murder, making an example of him for planning to free his own slaves while others will remain enslaved. As one of his killers explains, "It's the law of the United States that ef eny man is caught creatin' dissatisfacshun among the slaves he deserves death, and death he gits" (62).

The loss of their mother, effected by the Law of the Father, figures as the central hardship for this part of the novel. In his study of sentimental novels, David J. Denby identifies the central obstacle, or "misfortune," that serves as the foundation for the sentimental novel as "that which disrupts a previous state of happiness, and which must then be overcome as a condition of the re-establishment of an ulterior happiness which will represent the closure of the text" (72). For Charles and Jesse, the "misfortune" central to the sentimental plot is the advent of their motherlessness. Indeed, "after the loss of their mother, the two lads clung very closely to each other" in an attempt to find comfort and, perhaps, to find their mother metonymically through another family member (71). Anson Pollock, the agent of this misfortune, agrees to sell Charles, the older son, to an Englishman because he fears that Charles is "too old to forget" his mother and the brutality that led to her death. Remembering and identifying with his African American mother would prevent his identifying with the dominant white society that represents the Father in this oedipal drama and ultimately undermine his loyalty to Pollock (73). Pollock is right. When faced with the prospect of leaving his brother for England, Charles exclaims in an apparent non sequitur that in fact indicates his broader psychic state of motherlessness: "I hate to leave Jesse. O mama, mama, my beautiful mama!" (74).

Contrary to Pollock's theory, however, the younger Jesse is no more capable than Charles of forgetting his mother. Pollock tries to beat the memory out of him, flogging him for rebelling against his new position (74). Eventually, Jesse learns to feign forgetting; his childhood and his close connection to his mother "appeared to slip from him," and he behaves as Pollock requires. Nevertheless, the memory of his mother continues to haunt him, much as the "Other" that Lacan says is "impossible to forget" (Lacan 71), or the "previous state of happiness" that, according to Denby, comes before the loss—a "previous state" that recalls the preoedipal condition: "Sometimes at night, when rolled in his blanket on the hard floor, he would weep over the painful past. Then he would feel the touch of a tiny hand upon his eyelids. It was his mother's hand; he knew it to be so. Then he would lose himself in sweet dreams and awaken in the morning refreshed and comforted" (76–77). In a dream state, a state Sigmund Freud posited as an access point to repressed or hidden desires, Jesse finds his mother and believes her to be with him. Jesse's memory of his mother's delicacy, indicated by her "tiny hand," links her to the womanhood ideology of the period generally reserved for white women and so further establishes her racial indeterminacy. Nevertheless, if Jesse remembers her as delicate, tiny, and white, he also willingly embraces the racial legacy he inherits from her. After his escape from Pollock, he decides to "cast his lot with the colored people of the community" (78) and in this way seeks to identify with the Mother rather than the Father. When he meets the family he will eventually marry into, he reinforces this identification by extending motherly attention to one of the children, offering to "rock the cradle" of the fretful child (79). Such an identification signals his continued search for the mother, a search he never fully realizes. In spite of the formation of his own family, he continues to suffer from motherlessness. Just as Charles's impending separation from Jesse causes him to long for his "mama," so Jesse experiences a "fit of despondency" when the letters from his brother—a representative of his family and his mother—no longer come. Eventually, his daughter would report, he "died of a broken heart" (375). Jesse experiences the enduring and irreplaceable absence leading to a "long term, pathological condition of loss" (Freud, "Mourning" 216) which, as we saw in the introduction, Freud classifies as melancholia and comports with the condition of motherlessness.[5] Jesse's state indicates the deep-seated lack felt by the child missing the pre-oedipal connection to her mother. No, Jesse does not forget his mother. Indeed, he seems to die thinking about her.

The novel emphasizes Jesse's motherlessness with a broader condition of motherlessness in the form of racial melancholia. While still in Bermuda, Montfort observes a group of slaves dancing "to the strange monotonous music of drums without tune, relics of the tom-tom in the wild African life which haunted them in dreamland" (26). Although they may never have heard African drums firsthand, the slaves experience a subconscious "dreamland" memory of the pre-oedipal state of closeness to Mother Africa. The memory of the Mother continues to reverberate for the slaves in North Carolina. Working in the cotton field, they sing to "bring solace to their sad hearts" regardless of the fact that some of them "may not have known why they were sad" (60). This unidentifiable but always present sadness echoes the unknown longing for the pre-oedipal mother—the "previous state of happiness"—and the melancholia growing from an unknown loss.

After the story of Jesse, the novel jumps forward to tell the story of Jesse's daughter and her family. Much has changed in the fifty or so years that have passed. Most significant, of course, is the abolition of slavery. Also different for this part of the novel is the setting. From the slaveholding South the story moves to post-emancipation Boston, which the novel praises as "New England's freest city" (115). Being the "freest" does not, however, make it ideal. The novel critiques the city's racist employment practices, and the narrator's sarcastic description of this discrimination as unexpected from "the descendants of the liberty-loving Puritans" (83) indicates a complex assessment of Hopkins's hometown.[6] Nevertheless, in Hopkins's fictional Boston, we find a strong community of race activists. The American Colored League and an active church group, most visibly populated by women, provide cohesion to the city's race community. And yet, if the novel's setting has changed, an ethos of motherlessness still lurks, even in this apparently happy and well-adjusted society. As with the slaves in Montfort's fields, motherlessness for this 1896 race community often takes the form of an unnamed or unrecognized lack. Dora, for example, suffers from a "long-felt [but unspecified] want" (98), to which her relationship with Sappho Clark ministers, at least to some extent.

The novel further signals the community's motherlessness with its complex treatment of conjure and supernaturalism. Alongside the primary plot line of the Montforts and their descendents, the novel includes several humorous characters and plots providing comic relief against the emotionally and politically charged content of the novel's primary plot.[7] Stories such as the competition between Mary Jane Robinson and Ophelia Davis or the courtship and marriage between Ms. Davis and Rev. Tommy James reside in the comic register of the novel and contrast with the more serious stories of the principal characters. Readers first encounter supernaturalism through the character of "Doctor" Peters, an uneducated man with a gift for "hoodooin'" (132). The novel portrays Peters sympathetically: the narrator explains that, in spite of his lack of education, he is well read and has a vast interest in science. Nevertheless, minstrelsy dialect marks his speech, identifying him as a character not to be taken too seriously. Before we meet him, Dora invokes him lightly, quoting his "homey" wisdom: "Matches,—love matches,—my child, turn out so badly that a girl hesitates to 'git jined to eny man fer better or worserer,' as Dr. Peters says" (121). In his own narrative of his history of "hoodooin,'" Peters offers a mixture of humor and sincerity. He conflates it with Christianity, explaining that he discovered his powers of magnetism at the same time that he had "'sperinced ruligeon" (132). Yet his application of this apparently spiritual gift to such causes as scaring off watermelon thieves, beating out his rival for love of his future wife, and making money invites readers to discount this portion of the novel as purely comic relief and puts the character in an abject position. Adopting the dominant culture's rejection of supernaturalism, the novel seems to judge Peters's antics as marginal and worthy of contempt, and to invite its readers to do the same.

Later, at the church fundraising fair, it appears that such supernatural powers will again be relegated to the comic thread of the story. Madam Frances, a "spiritualistic soothsayer and marvelous mind-reader," has a booth where she will tell fortunes (197); conjure and supernaturalism here figure as carnival trickery. This classification becomes complicated, however, and the church fair quickly becomes a place where the novel's comic and serious registers meet and mingle. For example, the almost caricatured figures of Ophelia Davis and her cohort appear alongside the developing courtship of the novel's main characters, Will and Sappho, and the perfidy of John Langley. Madam Frances occupies a complex role, serving as entertainment for the fair but simultaneously holding the more serious position of Sappho's aunt and surrogate mother for the motherless Alphonse. Comporting with this complexity, the novel vacillates in its treatment of Madam Frances's abilities. At first, the narrator describes her presence playfully, employing a mock-serious tone to describe the fair participants' enthusiasm over her services, services they imagine to be focused entirely on love and courtship:

> The young people were in a flutter over this particular feature, the men no less so than the women. Who could tell *what* might happen through her agency? Long delayed questions might be asked; unknown feelings might be revealed to anxious hearts. One might buy a lucky charm and present it to his inamorata, and by contact with it her coldness should vanish. Henry might receive a letter whose sweet perfume should banish the thoughts of Susan and turn his wandering heart to its first allegiance. (198)

The fair participants—their frivolousness marked by their youth and their "flutter"—hope to deploy Madam Frances's ability in the pursuit of crushes and young romance. Labeling their belief in Madam Frances's abilities "superstition" and likening her fortune telling to a parlor game, the narrator dismisses this activity as a "simple pastime of innocence" (198).

As the description continues, however—and it does so for far longer than we might expect for comic relief—the narrator links "superstition" specifically to "the Negro's heritage" as something brought "from their native Africa" and compared to similar powers in Egypt, a connection Hopkins would pursue further in each of her novels. Religion professor Yvonne P. Chireau discusses Conjure and Hoodoo as part of the African American spiritual experience. She traces the sources of black American supernaturalism to traditions found in African societies and continued among African slaves in the United States, even as these enslaved persons began to adopt the religious beliefs of the new country. She explains, "Elements of the older African worldview . . . intersected with a network of Anglo-American supernatural traditions. The simultaneous emergence of African-based supernaturalism (later identified as Conjure and Hoodoo) and black Americans' embrace of Christianity resulted in the reinforcement of magic and religion as convergent phenomena" (7). *Contending Forces* reflects this history as it turns from the comic portrayal of Doctor Peters to offer an almost reverent explanation for the source of Madam Frances's supernaturalism, asserting that the "occult arts" were "once the glory of the freshly imported African," but were lost when they were brought to this "foreign shore" (199, 198). The novel links the gifts of Madam Frances and Doctor Peters to their Mother Africa, marking the comic quality now attributed to them as further sign of distance from that Mother, and the culturally common rejection of the practices of these "occult arts" as the Father's prohibition of the African Mother.[8] In this light, the narrator's statement, that fair participants enjoy "the simple pastimes of innocence" (198), becomes a reference to their memory of childlike innocence in pre-oedipal *past times.*

Against the backdrop of motherlessness writ large in the community, two of the novel's main characters offer fuller portrayals of motherlessness through the popular nineteenth-century trope of the mulatto/a. A representation of fragmented identity, the mulatto/a had captured the imaginations of writers long before Hopkins took it up and continued to do so well into the twentieth century. The mixed-race figure resonated so deeply with writers in part because it crystallized the identity conflict ignited by the race community's oedipal conflict. While we recognize the spurious nature of biological categorizations based on blood or race, the nineteenth-century legal and national discourses invested a great deal of faith in the notion of the mulatto/a as a "juridical term that constrains citizenship by ante- and postbellum law and force" (Foreman 506). Thus, the notion of the mulatto/a as a figure divided between two biological identities (however constructed those identities may be) comes to represent the more significant phenomenon of being torn between two civic identities, the building blocks of the oedipal drama. The conflict faced by mulatto/a figures often came down to choosing which of their heritages to embrace and identify with. Would they repress their African heritage—deny their black Mother—in order to identify with their white Father and claim all the rights and privileges associated with whiteness? Would they, as P. Gabrielle Foreman expresses it, "slip phenotypically white bodies over the border into a Fatherland of 'whiteness' that promised (material) racial rewards, recognition, and inheritance" and, we should add, national belonging (Foreman 507)?

John Langley, the antagonist in the Boston portion of the novel, descends (coincidentally) from Anson Pollock, the white man behind the Montfort murders, and Lucy, Grace Montfort's black maid. Langley does not attempt to pass for white, but—in accordance with the oedipal directive—he actively rejects the Mother in an effort to identify with the Father and gain the power and privilege he hopes will follow from that identification. He believes that "association with success would in the end bring the desired quality to any one" (220), and indeed, the pursuit of success for "one" accurately describes Langley's endeavors. In this community-oriented novel, Langley stands out as a character selfishly driven by individual ambition. His "devotion" to Dora, his fiancée, derives from her family's financial stability and the boarding house that she would undoubtedly bring to the marriage (220). Because he is a lawyer, his association with the law establishes his alignment with the Law of the Father, as we saw in the earlier part of the novel. He has his office in the business district of Boston, "among the most reliable lawyers in the profession" (220).[9] His hiring of white office staff in his law practice as a means of courting the business of white clients leads members of the American Colored League to believe him to be "as prejudiced toward black people as any Anglo-Saxon" (226), a charge further signaling his identification with the Father.

The novel does not, however, cast blame entirely on Langley for his choices. It points—at least in part—to literal motherlessness in his upbringing as the cause of Langley's lax moral character and weak relationship with his rightful community—the figurative motherlessness he experiences. Born into slavery, he was sold at six months of age to a man "who farmed Negro babies for the market" (380). After emancipation, he found himself a "half-starved beggar in the city streets, a deserted child claiming kindred with none" (335). He decided to leave the South and go to the North, which had been portrayed to him as something of a "fairyland"—a place of beauty and safety that would appeal to the sense of loss we have seen in the motherless child. Typical of the subject separated from the pre-oedipal mother, he has a memory of "a woman, presumably his mother," somewhere in "the dim past" (221). So, in a sentimentally coded scene, a young John Langley starts his journey "at an age when the loving mother trembles to have her darling exposed to the perils of the busy streets without a strong hand to guide him through its dangers" (335). The absence of his mother is irreparable: years later, when he finds her, he detests her low status and, beyond sending her money, has little to do with her.

Langley exhibits the split psyche that these conflicting impulses incite, a splitting that David L. Eng and Shinhee Han attribute to the person of color attempting—and failing—to achieve assimilation, "one who exhibits a faithful allegiance to the universal norms of abstract equality and collective national membership at the same time as he displays an uncomfortable understanding of his utter disenfranchisement from these democratic ideals" (349). We see this split in a crucial scene in which Herbert Clapp, a white politician, offers Langley the position of city solicitor in exchange for attempting to pacify the American Colored League as they discuss their response to racial violence in the South. Although he seems determined from the start of the conversation to accept Clapp's offer, Langley engages in a strangely conflicted debate, arguing passionately on behalf of the race community to which he belongs and against the decision he will ultimately make. Clapp tries to persuade Langley to support what might be described as an accommodationist response to the recent violence: "It is the duty of every one of us to wait for justice, and not to countenance excitement and bloodshed. . . . [I]f the colored people are only patient for a while longer, this thing will be settled amicably" (235). He attempts to enlist Langley's assistance in suppressing the community's anger by appealing to his loyalty as a citizen. "If you love your country as you should," he urges, "you will be willing to sacrifice a little for the good of the whole" (233). But Langley recognizes that "the whole" excludes him as a black man, and that he enjoys only limited citizenship as long as he maintains the black identity inherited from his mother. He points to this inequity in his response to Clapp: "Yes, you give us a bootblack stand in the corridor of the State House, and think we are placated" (231). Nevertheless, in spite of this insight, he accepts Clapp's offer of advancement in public office, choosing to believe the promise that if he identifies with the Father by ambitiously seeking the approval of white society and success according to its terms, and rejecting or weakening his ties to his African heritage and community, he will eventually achieve full citizenship, with a seat at the table of government rather than a bootblack stand in the corridor.

Sappho and the Tragic Mulatta Tradition

Also a mulatta figure, Sappho invokes the popular tradition of the tragic mulatta, a character used by white abolitionist writers to bemoan the "'one drop' of 'black blood' that distanced [them] from the traditional sentimental heroines" (Bost 675). The "tragic" view of these figures extended beyond white writers, however. Bost cites William Wells Brown's *Clotel; or, The President's Daughter,* a novel Hopkins undoubtedly knew, as an example of the tragic mulatta story.[10] According to this trope, "mixed blood . . . acts as a reminder of an original rape and of the imbalance of power that led to coerced sexual relations between white men and black women." Later writers, however, including Hopkins, revised that figure, finding a way for mulatto/a characters to be "empowered by their 'betweenness.'" Working within and against the sentimental novel tradition, these writers subvert the "tragic" model, making their characters not victims but advocates for their race community (Bost 675–76). The stories of Grace and Sappho illustrate that revision, and demonstrate the crucial role maternal redemption plays in it.

Grace Montfort's story serves as a precursor to Sappho's and lays important groundwork for the reader's understanding of Sappho. For example, Sappho's rape echoes the rape of Grace Montfort. Although

Hopkins does not make Grace's rape explicit,[11] highly sexualized images appear in the scene, suggesting rape as well as physical beating:

> She uttered a wild cry of agony as the rough hand of Hank Davis was laid upon her to tear her garments from her shrinking shoulders. . . . The air whistled as the snaky leather thong curled and writhed in its rapid, vengeful descent. A shriek from the victim—a spurt of blood that spattered the torturer—a long, raw gash across a tender, white back. . . . Another shriek, a stifled sob, a long-drawn quivering sigh—then the deep stillness of unconsciousness. Again and again was the outrage repeated. Fainting fit followed fainting fit. The blood stood in a pool about her feet. (68–69)

Grace's nakedness, the phallic whip, and the blood at her feet all indicate that she has been raped. Grace's treatment embodies the tragedy of the tragic mulatta. Unable to accept the consequences of her purported black blood (slavery, rape), she follows the example of Brown's character, Clotel, and drowns herself. Grace's response indicates her internalization of white society's definition of her as impure, as not a "genooine 'ooman" by the terms of True Womanhood (41).

The paired stories of Sappho and Grace serve to illustrate Hopkins's claim that little has changed for African Americans since emancipation. Like Grace, Sappho too becomes a victim of rape. When Sappho was fourteen, living with her family in New Orleans, her uncle, the white half-brother of her former slave father, abducts her and keeps her as a sexual slave in "a house of the vilest character" for three weeks (260). Here Sappho's story revises another aspect of the oedipal model, a revision we will see repeatedly in Hopkins's novels. In Freud's figuring of the family romance, the father intervenes between mother and child on the basis of the incest taboo. His intrusion seeks to interrupt the potentially incestuous relationship between mother and child. In Sappho's story, however, the threat and ultimate perpetration of incest comes from Sappho's uncle who, as a member of a white, former slave-owning family, serves as a representative of the white Father. Following the precedent in which the white Father disparages the African Mother, the uncle attempts to cast blame for his actions on Sappho and her maternal heritage, claiming that Sappho "is no better than her mother or her grandmother" in that, as a black woman, she knows nothing of virtue.[12] But the novel's placement of blame is clear. With this revision, the novel challenges the Father's insistence on the child's rejection of the Mother, highlighting the historical fact of rape as a mainstay of the "peculiar institution" and the Father's culpability in that crime.

With so many similarities between these two stories, the differences between them—specifically, the difference between Grace's and Sappho's responses to rape—stand out. Initially, Sappho's response to her experience resembles Grace's. At the birth of her child and the advent of her identity as a mother in a New Orleans convent for black women, she asks the sisters to report that she died in childbirth and changes her name. Putting an end to her identity, she figuratively enacts the suicide that Grace literally performs. As a rape victim, Sappho has her motherhood paradoxically taken from her even as it is forced upon her: "Her feeling of degradation," the novel explains, "had made her ashamed of the joys of motherhood, of pride of possession in her child" (345). As Kate McCullough asserts, "rape strips the African American woman of her right to 'motherhood,' to a voluntary and nonalienated relationship to her offspring, placing her in the same cultural space as her enslaved foremothers" (39). The trauma of Sappho's rape separates her from her son just as Grace's suicide takes her from her children. Leaving Alphonse in the care of her aunt, Sappho experiences only a detached, dispassionate relationship with him. When she talks about him, her language indicates no feeling and little connection aside from a vague sense of responsibility: "That money will do what you wish for the boy, Aunt Sally. . . . There is no need for him to know" (278–79). She avoids calling Alphonse by name and offers no opinion on his upbringing. She rejects her son as the embodiment of her past and the paradoxical embodiment of her motherlessness. By abdicating the responsibility of raising Alphonse, she effectively denies her own status of mother, effecting another level of motherlessness for herself. In other words, at the same time that Sappho figures as a "motherless child," she also has become a "childless mother."

Although the novel does not reveal Sappho's background until more than halfway into the story, Sappho evinces her motherless condition from her first appearance, exhibiting the melancholia of motherlessness in several ways. She is drawn to the domestic warmth of Ma Smith's boarding house, and she experiences an immediate emotional attraction to Mrs. Willis, a woman she meets at the sewing circle held there: "For a moment the flood-gates of *suppressed feeling* flew open in the girl's heart, and she longed to lean her head on that motherly breast and unburden her sorrows there" (155, emphasis added). A complex figure, Mrs. Willis boasts a proud past as both a domestically driven wife and mother and an ambitious advocate for racial uplift.[13] Now a widow with grown children, she has turned her energies to women's club work and entrepreneurship. Although Sappho does not know the true object of her longing—as she explains to Will, she suffers from "shadows," unclear even to her (310)—she quickly perceives Mrs. Willis's maternal qualities and is tempted to unburden the secret of her dark past. Her defenses are too deeply entrenched, however, and she suppresses the vulnerability she is not ready to give in to: "she drew back as from an abyss suddenly beheld stretching before her," and is left with the same unfilled lack that she felt before (155). Sappho's son, Alphonse, left to be raised by Sappho's aunt, barely develops as a character, functioning primarily as an illustration of the community's motherlessness. He is "melancholy," with the "shadows of life heavy upon" him, shadows that he perhaps shares with his mother. Embodying the sadness of the motherless child, he exhibits "no desire for the frolic and fun which belongs to the golden days of childhood" (201).

Another expression of motherlessness takes the form of a longing for home. While describing the racism she has encountered in her work as a stenographer, Sappho exhorts Dora to "thank God every day for such a refuge as you have in your home" (128). Since "home" and "mother" are linked in domestic ideology, the mother being the crucial figure in the home, Sappho's longing for home implicitly expresses a longing for mother. On another occasion, as Sappho contemplates her growing attraction for Will, she fears the effect her past will have on his feelings for her. She exclaims, "Oh, the happiness of home and love! must I be shut from them forever?" (182). Sappho's statement draws on the metonymic relationships between the home, the personal mother, and the imago of the Mother of racial heritage, Mother Africa, and her promise of acceptance and belonging.

Hope in Sorrow: Maternal Redemption

In this context of palpable pain and loss, the novel explores possibilities for healing. Motherlessness can be remedied through the restoration of the mother. Moreover, if that restoration is brought about by the melancholia of motherlessness, then melancholia becomes productive. Lacan explored this productivity in the form of catharsis, which he understood as the healing or "release of emotional tension achieved through recalling a repressed traumatic experience" (244). Here we do well to distinguish racial melancholia from the "propensity towards lamenting and complaining" described and rejected by Richard Wright.[14] Far from a site of debilitation or pathology, melancholia—the African American community's emotional response to motherlessness—emerges as a source of catharsis, of personal and political power in *Contending Forces.* The negotiation of the oedipal directive under the conditions of a racist society, the condition of motherlessness, becomes a space of possibility, of productivity, of rebuilding. It becomes an opportunity to transform the disenfranchised individual or community from one "subjected to grief to . . . a subject speaking grievance" (Cheng 7); that is, it becomes a way to secure political agency. Eng and Han, too, see possibilities for power in melancholia. In contrast to Freud's disparagement of "the melancholic's inability to 'get over' loss," they celebrate "the melancholic's absolute refusal to relinquish the other . . . at any costs" (364). And José Esteban Muñoz, in *Disidentifications: Queers of Color and the Performance of Politics,* sees possibilities for communal activism and healing particularly relevant to motherlessness as a condition of the post-Reconstruction African American community: "Communal mourning, by its very nature, is an immensely complicated text to read, for we do not mourn just one lost object or other, but we mourn as a 'whole.'" This mourning, he asserts, is not "a self-absorbed mood that inhibits activism. Rather, it is a mechanism that helps us (re)construct identity and take our dead with us to the various battles we must wage in their names—and in our names" (qtd. in Eng and Han 365, 363).[15]

The African American community under slavery understood the promise of melancholia as a vehicle for building community cohesion and harnessed that possibility in the sorrow songs. As is well known, the content of the songs signified on multiple levels, masking political messages of resistance and escape within lyrics of traditional Christian doctrine. But more than that, the songs lamented the collective experience of slavery. As discussed in the introduction, a number of these songs grieve for the singer's condition as "child" or a "motherless child" and imagine or conjure the presence and power of the Mother, calling upon her to "rock me in the cradle" and longing to get to the "home" she represents. The sorrow songs rehearsed the hardship and pain of the community's experiences under slavery. Like Ralph Ellison, who emphasized the emotional power of music and art over intellectual or philosophical power, Hopkins joins this tradition, drawing on the domestic novel form with its commitment to the power of sentiment. She refers to this goal in the novel's preface, calling for literature that will "faithfully portray the inmost thoughts and feelings of the Negro" (14), that will—in other words—represent and dwell on the sentimental aspects of the African American experience.

The telling of Sappho's story exemplifies the novel's commitment to the effort to "keep the painful details and episodes of a brutal existence alive" (Ellison 78) as a means of achieving community cohesion and transcendence. Rather than dramatizing the events of Sappho's past in direct narrative, the novel tells her past through the indirect narration of Luke Sawyer at the meeting of the American Colored League, which has convened to plan the members' response to recent lynchings in the South. The effect of this choice is powerful. Rather than presenting this horrific history in the virtual isolation of an intimate conversation between narrator and reader, the novel brings the reader into the community, convened on the basis of a shared experience of marginalization and suffering, and relates the event in this setting. Sappho's story, then, becomes part of the larger narrative of the systematic and violent marginalization of the motherless race of African Americans, and the telling of the story functions to unify the community around its shared pain and to induce the community's catharsis. Her story is told spontaneously, as an intervention in a meeting designed to "look at the question [of lynching] dispassionately" (241–42), a meeting in which the first speaker charged his audience of "rational people" to be "calm and logical" (245–46). After two "logical" speakers, Luke Sawyer addresses the crowd, not from a standpoint of calculated reason but from his personal experience. Reminding readers of the contrasting discursive formations described in the novel's preface, he eschews the rhetoric of lecturers, ministers, and lawyers. Instead, he tells a story. As a boy he saw his family murdered by white men who objected to the competition presented by his father's business. Years later, having been taken in by Sappho's father, he was the one who carried Sappho from the brothel where she had been repeatedly raped. His story elicits a strong response from his listeners, who experience the emotional release Lacan attributed to catharsis: "The house was filled with the cries and groans of the audience. Sobs shook the women while the men drank in the words of the speaker with darkening brows and hands which involuntarily clinched themselves in sympathy with his words" (258). Responding as a collective body, the community shares Sappho and Luke's pain because—on some level—it is their own repressed pain. Later, the narrator, too, becomes part of the community, offering a response to Sappho's plight. In a rare slip into a prophetic voice, the narrator bemoans Sappho's motherlessness, expressing the emotion that Sappho cannot: "Such incidents are not uncommon in any community where slavery has cast its baleful shadow. . . .We may right a wrong, but we cannot restore our victim to his primeval state of happiness. Something is lost that can never be regained" (332). A departure from the third-person voice narrating the rest of the novel, this intrusive narrator steps in to direct the emotional response of her readers. The narrator speaks knowingly—as if from firsthand experience—of the loss that cannot be regained.[16] With its foregrounding of healing through catharsis, *Contending Forces* looks forward to the blues novel, a genre that would build on Ellison's notion of "fingering" loss as a means of transcending pain, of recovering and building community, in short, as a means achieving the "blues philosophy of endurance and hope" (Tracy 132).[17] But with its particular focus on motherlessness as the source of pain, the blues novel more compellingly looks back to the domestic, sentimental novel and the maternal redemption modeled in that form.

Maternal redemption restores a character to her or his proper relation to society through a catharsis prompted by the restoration or replacement of the lost mother. As Jane Tompkins so persuasively argues, *Uncle*

Tom's Cabin modeled this trope exquisitely, making it the consummate example of "salvation through motherly love" (125) and a valuable starting point from which to understand the trope. Maternal redemption appears repeatedly in *Uncle Tom's Cabin*. In each scene, the love and pity of a maternal figure, the recovery of a lost mother figure, or the embracing of one's own mothering ability has the power to restore hard-hearted characters to virtue or to heal emotionally damaged characters. Cassie, hardened by years of sexual abuse and separation from her own children, experiences redemption through Tom's maternal style of love and sacrifice, and through the opportunity to recover and extend her own motherly love to the motherless Emeline. The generous and unquestioning love found in the maternal haven of the Quaker settlement softens the anger of runaway slave George Harris. The emotionally charged argument of Mrs. Byrd, inspired by the death of her own child and the sight of Eliza, who stands to lose her son, moves Senator Byrd to tears and persuades him to renounce his legalistic and unfeeling stance on fugitive slaves. And in a quintessential moment of maternal redemption, the precocious Eva provides the motherly love needed to redeem the seemingly intractable Topsy:

> "Oh Topsy, poor child, *I* love you!" said Eva, with a sudden burst of feeling . . . ; "I love you, because you haven't had any father, or mother, or friends;—because you've been a poor, abused child! I love you, and I want you to be good. . . . I wish you would try to be good, for my sake;—it's only a little while I shall be with you."
>
> The round, keen eyes of the black child were overcast with tears;—large, bright drops rolled heavily down, one by one, and fell on the little white hand. Yes, in that moment, a ray of real belief, a ray of heavenly love, had penetrated the darkness of her heathen soul! She laid her head down between her knees, and wept and sobbed,—while the beautiful child, bending over her, looked like the picture of some bright angel stooping to reclaim a sinner. . . .
>
> St. Clare, at this instant, dropped the curtain. "It puts me in mind of mother," he said to Miss Ophelia. (306–307, emphasis in original)

Maternal redemption requires an emotional response by the would-be redeemed, and Topsy's tears function as both the means and evidence of her redemption. St. Clare's comparison of Eva to his mother emphasizes the maternal character of Eva's action. As an agent of maternal love and redemption, Eva brings about redemption not only for Topsy but for Aunt Ophelia as well who, moved by Eva's example, determines to love Topsy herself after Eva's death. Topsy's improved behavior and her eventual work as a missionary to Africa, then, are attributed to the motherly love shown her by Eva and Ophelia.

These familiar tropes of motherlessness and maternal redemption anticipate the literary means Hopkins uses for exploring, respectively, the problem and solution for the post-Reconstruction African American community. Denby describes this work of the sentimental novel: "read and wept over, [the novel] is to be the site of a community of like minds drawn together by their common reaction to a common scene" (Denby 80). In *Contending Forces,* Hopkins attempts to harness the melancholia of her audience, the African American community rendered motherlessness by the dominant society's disparagement of its African heritage, and put it to work to bring about activism and healing. The sentimental, domestic novel form effectively describes this condition and therefore works well as a means of addressing the motherlessness of the race community and imagining the Mother's restoration, the pinnacle of Hopkins's racial uplift agenda. Maternal redemption speaks directly to the misfortune—the "lack"—that Hopkins's work portrays. In this way, *Contending Forces,* subtitled "A Romance Illustrative of Negro Life North and South," goes beyond a simple story of romance for two couples culminating in marriage. It becomes a romance in the quest tradition as this African American community searches for and attempts to recover its lost Mother.

Maternal Redemption in Contending Forces

We return, then, to Sappho's story to see the workings of maternal redemption and her successful quest for the lost mother. Sappho's story serves as a corrective to Grace's experience. Grace embodies the tragic mulatta trope by her identification with the National Father who judges rape to be the appropriate treatment of a black woman. Like Frantz Fanon's black schoolboy educated with lessons of the "white man who carries truth to savages,"[18] Grace has been raised to think of herself as a white woman. The discovery (or rumor) of her black blood—what Carla L. Peterson would call a "threatening racial indeterminacy" (46)—and the rape that her racial identity justifies bars her from the ideal of womanhood as she has come to understand it and foreshadows the life she can now expect to live. Therefore, defeated by the values of the dominant white society, she chooses death over identifying with her African heritage and living with the price of that identification. Sappho, on the other hand, rejects the values that destroy Grace, choosing instead maternal redemption. Langley inadvertently prompts her empowerment as he attempts to force upon her the same identification with the National Father's values that destroyed Grace. He challenges Sappho's authentic or "genooine" womanhood by accepting her uncle's earlier judgment—that she knows nothing of virtue and is worthy only of being a sexual companion—and offers her the prospect of being his concubine rather than wife, returning her to the sexual slavery she experienced years earlier. His threat of exposing her past and her son does not have the desired effect, however; Sappho rejects his effort to classify her according to the standards of dominant white society.

Although Sappho resists Langley's threats, his insult along with the end of her relationship with Will (which she assumes the revelation of her past will precipitate) plunge her into a state of outrage and a desire for revenge which, the narrator tells us, threaten to do her irreparable damage (341). However, she avoids this danger through an emotional catharsis—described in a chapter entitled "Motherly Love"—worthy of the classic sentimental novel: "Then came the blessed relief of tears—like a flood—they relieved the overcharged brain and saved her reason" (342). Rather than continuing to keep her secret, she resolves to reclaim her son and, in so doing, to find and reclaim her own motherhood. She feels sorrow and guilt over her rejection of motherhood and over the fact that she has "felt nothing for the poor waif but repugnance." She determines to "claim the child and do her duty as his mother in love and training. She would devote her life to him" (342). The first night she spends with her son in her arms, her redemption is made complete as "something holy passed from the sweet contact of the soft, warm body into the cold chilliness of her broken heart" (346). Experiencing maternal redemption, Sappho rejects patriarchal and white standards that seek to define her as outside the parameters of middle-class womanhood or motherhood. She reclaims the motherhood that has been taken from her and thereby experiences the maternal redemption that allows her eventually to reunite with Will, marry, and take her proper place in the community and the nation.

Ultimately, John Langley strives for maternal redemption as well, but perhaps too late. He has rejected his mother and has betrayed the community she represents in favor of his drive to succeed through identification with the National Father. Even the means of his death mark this pursuit: he joins a group of "daring adventurers who were allured from home by the dazzling promise of immense fortunes to be dug out of the earth in the new Eldorado—the Klondike gold-fields" (398). Here, the drive for fortune is set against "home" and mother, according to the code of the domestic novel. His quest points to a lack that must be filled, but he misreads this lack as material, and as such engages in a misdirected quest. Although his recent experience with Sappho and the Smith family inspires him to "do good among his fellows as a sort of atonement for his early mistakes," he postpones that goal until after he has amassed a large fortune (399). When Madam Frances foretells his death on the ice fields, he dismisses her warning, further signaling his rejection of his African heritage through this art that was "once the glory of the freshly imported African" (199).

Langley's exploits comport with the imperialistic drive of the United States for international property and control, efforts that were rife at the time Hopkins wrote *Contending Forces.* She signals this interest with the opening of the novel, set in the British colony of Bermuda. As several scholars have observed, a number of African American authors at the turn of the century vigorously opposed U.S. imperial efforts, which they recognized as similar to and dependent upon racist practices within the United States.[19] According to Frederick Wegener, "even a brief survey of [African Americans'] work at the turn of the century would find very few American writers of African descent . . . who did not . . . include some critique of imperialism in their challenge to apartheid in the United States, or failed to see in the advent of empire the worldwide dissemination of racially oppressive conditions at home" (484).[20]

If Langley's embrace of imperialism indicates his desire to identify with the National Father, the gendered politics at work in the nation's ventures further support his rejection of the Mother. Anne McClintock has identified the patriarchal agenda of imperialism, arguing that those efforts culminated "in the regeneration of the authority of the white father" as the "head of the global Family of Man" (234). In short, imperialism was a project of "paterfamilial restoration" (240). McClintock notes that popular stories depicting undertakings similar to Langley's chose their subject matter because of the gendered possibilities afforded by them. In her analysis of popular adventure novels by British writer (and Hopkins contemporary) Henry Rider Haggard, for example, McClintock attributes Haggard's interest in the genre to his "fear of female generative authority" or motherhood (236).

Haggard's fiction offers a fantasy of female containment and restores the Father as imperial authority.[21] *Contending Forces* rewrites this form, replacing Haggard's paterfamilial restoration with maternal redemption. Although Langley's death, alone on an ice field, may seem a fitting end for him, given his selfishness, greed, and betrayal of his community, ultimately the novel offers some compassion for this character. At the moment of his death, he indicates regret at rejecting his mother. His final prayer nearly conflates god and mother as he calls, "O God! Receive my soul. Dear, dear mother" (401). When we learn that he descends from Pollock, the agent of the hardships suffered by the Montfort family, Langley's life becomes further evidence of the "strangely tangled threads in the lives of many colored families" and of the long legacy of the damage done by slavery (373). So, while Langley has certainly been a traitor, the novel ultimately understands him as another victim of motherlessness.

Maternal Redemption as Racial Uplift

The maternal redemption experienced by Sappho and sought by Langley projects the broader possibility of maternal redemption for the community and the nation. Having established the individual and community motherlessness resulting from the oedipal separation from the mother, the novel offers an antidote in the form of a maternally organized community, and that community in turn points to the possibilities to be realized in the form of national maternal redemption. As in the domestic novel, in which the home often functions as a microcosm of the nation,

Contending Forces establishes motherhood and maternal redemption as the engine behind racial uplift, the hope of the African American community and its place in the nation. Hopkins highlights the centrality of national issues by setting the bulk of the novel in 1896, a significant year in African American history. The years prior to 1896 had been something of a roller coaster in American race policy. The *Dred Scott* case of 1857 had declared all blacks—slave or free—to be ineligible for American citizenship; shortly after the Civil War and following on the promise of emancipation, the Fourteenth Amendment reversed the *Dred Scott* decision, granting African Americans due process and equal treatment under law. Little more than a decade later, after Reconstruction efforts met with resistance in the southern states and were eventually abandoned by the U.S. government, the promise of emancipation disintegrated into what Rayford Logan has famously termed the "nadir" of race relations in the United States. In this context, the *Plessy v Ferguson* case of 1896 institutionalized widespread discrimination, granting the constitutionality of racial segregation through the hollow justification of "separate but equal" rhetoric. Against this backdrop of racist national law (and emphasizing the Law of the Father), *Contending Forces* portrays true nationalism as the maternally organized community, governed instead by Mother Law.

The Smiths' boarding house figures as a haven of motherly love and care, a fact suggested by proprietor's nickname: "Ma." Ma Smith's actions replicate the phenomenon of the "othermother" described by Patricia Hill Collins: a common role for women, during slavery and after, who stepped in to care for children whose mothers were unavailable or absent, whether due to work duties, sale, or death. The othermother became a foundation for political activism among African American women after emancipation, growing into the extended role of "community othermothers," women who thought of all the children of the community as members of their own families, and therefore as their responsibility (129–32).[22] Ma Smith acts as a community othermother for the "children" who live in her home. More than simply providing room and board, she nurses her tenants when they are ill and provides "music evenings or reception nights" as both entertainment and moral guidance. A true disciple of domestic ideology and the spiritual power of home and hearth, "she argued, logically enough, that those who were inclined to stray from right paths would be influenced either in favor of upright conduct or else shamed into an acceptance of the right" through her motherly guidance (102). A microcosm of the maternally organized society imagined by the architects of domesticity, the Smith home and its primarily female tenants bustle with productive activity, organizing a fundraiser for an upcoming church event and holding regular meetings of the sewing circle. With all its activity, this home exemplifies the possibilities for maternal redemption at the community level, leading toward the vision imagined by Harriet Beecher Stowe of "a world reorganized from a feminine perspective, and built upon a belief in salvation through motherly love" (Tompkins 21–22).

The sewing circle, in particular, depicts a symbiotic relationship between domesticity and racial uplift.[23] Exhibiting the virtues of home and domesticity, the sewing circle consists of a group of women gathered in Ma Smith's home to sew items for the local church fundraiser. The gathering involves more than just sewing, however. The introduction of "events of interest to the Negro race which had transpired during the week throughout the country" (143) gives participants the opportunity to discuss and debate race progress. The session depicted in the novel features a guest speaker who attempts to inspire the women in their duty to racial uplift, a duty that has a distinctly maternal quality: "[L]et us cultivate, while we go about our daily tasks, no matter how inferior they may seem to us, beauty of the soul and mind, which being transmitted to our children by the law of heredity, shall improve the race by eliminating *immorality* from our midst and raising *morality* and virtue to their true place" (153, emphasis in original). The speaker transforms *partus equitur ventrem*—"the child follows the condition of the mother"—from limiting to empowering. Rather than inheriting a condition of enslavement, says Mrs. Willis, the children of these race women can inherit such elevated qualities as "beauty of the soul and mind" that will tend toward the improvement and elevation of the race. The sewing circle with its shared goal of uplifting the race and building community contrasts dramatically with the individualism that characterizes Langley's pursuits. In Ma Smith's boarding house and the sewing circle, the novel portrays the "black woman's role in changing history through her solidarity with other women, who help her to forge a new vision that runs counter to the one white culture promulgates" (Campbell 39). In short, the sewing circle becomes a vehicle for the maternal redemption of the community.

The Middle Passage and Return to the Mother(land)

After the passing of several years and the resolution of all conflicts, *Contending Forces* ends with a journey for the principal characters: Ma Smith; Arthur Lewis, Dora, and their daughter, "Little Sappho"; Will and Sappho—now married; and Alphonse, motherless no more. In a final tableau, they stand on the deck of a ship bound for Europe, where they will meet the descendents of Charles Montfort. This will become a familiar scene: in each of Hopkins's novels, one or more of her characters travels across the Atlantic, a journey that pointedly revisits the route of the slave ships.

Paul Gilroy finds positive significance in the image of the ship and the transatlantic voyage in *The Black Atlantic.* He notes that a number of well-known race advocates, including figures familiar to Hopkins such as W. E. B. Du Bois, Ida B. Wells, and Anna Julia Cooper, were politically transformed by their experience of transatlantic travel. He explains: individuals "who begin as African-Americans or Caribbean people . . . are then changed into something else which evades those specific labels and with them all fixed notions of nationality and national identity" (19). By spending time outside of the United States, these travelers gained a new perception of racial difference and racism. Ida B. Wells, as we shall see in chapter 3, became empowered by the respect she garnered in England as compared to the threats leveled at her in her "home" country. The transatlantic travel undertaken by the Smith family in *Contending Forces*—and to some degree in all Hopkins's novels—carries with it therefore the promise that they will get a new perspective on the National Father's rejection of their National Mother and will, in Gilroy's words, "transcend both the structures of the nation state and the constraints of ethnicity and national particularity" (19).[24]

On another level of signification, the journey across the Atlantic pointedly revisits the route of the slave ships and thus draws the reader's attention to the Middle Passage. In keeping with the postcolonial project, described by Stuart Hall and Frantz Fanon, of recovering the past of the colonized subject, the transatlantic journey contextualizes the events of the novel in the history of the slave trade. As Hopkins had charged in the novel's preface, the African American community has the important mission of telling stories that record its growth and that "lie dormant in our history" (14). *Contending Forces* concerns itself with telling the stories of the past, such as the history of the Montforts. The most dramatic example of recovering the past occurs in Sappho's story. She has suppressed the history of her abuse at the hands of her uncle and, when we first meet her, it "lies dormant"—temporarily asleep but capable of being activated. The recovery or activation of that story through Luke's retelling of it and Langley's attempt to use it against her pushes Sappho to recover her son and to claim maternal redemption. With the reminder of the slave trade, Hopkins similarly activates an important memory of African Americans' removal from the National Mother, a history that has been routinely elided in order to maintain the national myths. As Eng and Han assert, "discourses of American exceptionalism and democratic myths of liberty, individualism, and inclusion force a misremembering. . . , an enforced psychic amnesia that can return only as a type of repetitive national haunting" (347). Carl Pedersen sees the possibility, not of haunting only, but of empowerment: "If . . . slave owners and slave traders had willingly severed their bonds with the past, they seemed determined to expunge forcibly the African past among their captives, sensing, perhaps unconsciously, that memory could be a means of resistance and liberation" (43).[25]

The family's trip across the Atlantic and its related image of the Middle Passage, then, serves as a reminder of the national history of the African American community's abduction from its Motherland, and of that community's resultant psychic condition of motherlessness. Hortense Spillers comments on the psychological impact of the infamous Middle Passage, calling it a time of "unmaking" for the African subject: "Those African persons in 'Middle Passage' were literally suspended in the 'oceanic,' if we think of the latter in its Freudian orientation as an analogy for undifferentiated identity: removed from the indigenous land and culture, and not-yet 'American' either . . . we could say that they were culturally 'unmade'" (72). Spillers refers to the unmaking of the subject based on Freud's formulation of development, which requires the recognition of a separation between the self and everything around him or her. "Normally," says Freud of the mature subject, "there is nothing of which we are more certain than the feeling of our self, of our own ego. This ego appears to us as something autonomous and unitary, marked off distinctly from everything else" (*Civilization* 12). Freud attributes the ego's lines of demarcation to the healthy subject, explaining that uncertain or incorrectly drawn boundary lines are typically associated with pathology (13). Following this model, Spillers argues that the dehumanizing Middle Passage erased lines of demarcation and therefore undermined the development of healthy subjects: "removed from the indigenous land and culture, and not-yet 'American' either, these captive persons . . . were in movement across the Atlantic, but they were also *nowhere* at all" (72, emphasis in original). Middle Passage took African subjects backward in their development, Spillers asserts, plunging them into the darkness of an unarticulated ego or self. In this way, she understands Freud's notion of the oceanic as negative or crippling, reading the Middle Passage as a backward journey through the process of development, a dismantling of the psyche, an unmaking of the subject.

Freud's theory of the oceanic, however, also allows for a positive reading, raising provocative possibilities for the motherless child. If the subject goes backward in her development, where does she find herself? Freud explains that the term "oceanic" designates an unusual situation in the subject: that of continued connection between the ego and the external world comparable to that of "an infant at the breast [who] does not as yet distinguish his ego from the external world" (13). In the context of motherlessness, which this study argues to be the prevailing ethos of the African American population in the post-Reconstruction United States, an ethos exemplified in the novels of Hopkins, returning to or reclaiming the condition of the "infant at the breast" holds out the possibility of recovering the pre-oedipal mother, as feminist psychoanalytic scholars have called for. Freud complicates the understanding of the oceanic condition, describing it as rare but ideal:

> Originally the ego includes everything, later it separates off an external world from itself. Our present ego-feeling is, therefore, only a shrunken residue of a much more inclusive—indeed, an all-embracing—feeling which corresponded to a more intimate bond between the ego and the world about it. If we may assume that there are many people in whose

> mental life this primary ego-feeling has persisted to a greater or less degree, it would exist in them side by side with the narrower and more sharply demarcated ego-feeling of maturity, like a kind of counterpart to it. In that case, the ideational contents appropriate to it would be precisely those of limitlessness and of a bond with the universe . . . the "oceanic" feeling. (*Civilization* 15)

Given Freud's idealization of the oceanic as limitlessness, we can also say that a return to the Middle Passage not only prompts a negative memory but also facilitates healing from that trauma. It not only signifies the physical journey away from the mother, but also the psychic reunion with the pre-oedipal mother. As the extended Smith family makes its way across the Atlantic Ocean on board the British Cunard ocean liner, they "unmake" not themselves, but the journey that rendered their ancestors motherless so many years before.

In her first novel, Hopkins takes on the work she believes to be crucial to racial uplift: the work of the novelist or storyteller to retell the African American community's history and, via the sentimental genre, to facilitate the emotional catharsis that such a history requires for healing and redemption for the motherless child. She boldly addresses the realities facing the African American community—in particular, racially motivated violence in the form of lynching and rape—and offers as an antidote a community-based vision of family and restoration with maternal redemption as the basis for survival and healing. As a model for racial uplift, the novel's subplots resonate with maternally oriented possibilities for action. The race community—organized according to a principle of motherly love, in keeping with the domestic ideal the novel emulates—stands in stark contrast to the "lack of brotherly affiliation" and the individually motivated greed "which deadens men's hearts to the sufferings of their brothers" and which Luke Sawyer identifies as "the contending forces that are dooming this race to despair!" (256). In this context, Ma Smith's boarding house, the sewing circle, and the fair all emerge as sites of race activism and maternal redemption. More, as links to the National Mother of African heritage, they provide the alternative to the National

Father of dominant white society which, with a legal system that overlooks violence against African Americans, proves to be an inadequate parent, unworthy of the identification from which it bars its African American "children." Focused on the power and merit of the Mother of African heritage, *Contending Forces* tells a story of maternal redemption for the individual and the community.

CHAPTER TWO

MOTHERLESSNESS IN THE NATION'S CAPITAL

The National Father in *Hagar's Daughter*

Then it was borne in upon him: the sin is the nation's.

—*Hagar's Daughter*

AFTER THE OPTIMISTIC conclusion of *Contending Forces, Hagar's Daughter* comes as something of a surprise. Here, amid the novel's spectacular content—including murder, abduction, disguises, a haunted mansion, a daring escape, and a dramatic courtroom climax—Pauline Hopkins offers a scathing critique of a nation that excludes the Mother of African heritage and the children who identify with her. Building on the equation of the American nation with the father of the oedipal narrative already established in *Contending Forces, Hagar's Daughter* critiques that father as unworthy of his children's identification. Although it extends a modicum of hope for maternal redemption, *Hagar's Daughter* focuses primarily on the enforced motherlessness of the African American race community and sounds a warning for the National Father who rejects his children. Underlying the romp and frolic of this serialized novel that kept Hopkins's readers coming back for more, we find unsettling outcomes for her characters and ominous warnings for the nation's future.

Following the publication of *Contending Forces,* Hopkins serialized three novels in the *Colored American Magazine,* a publication for which she served as contributor and editor from 1900 to 1904.[1] The first of these, *Hagar's Daughter,* ran from March 1901 to March 1902. Hopkins published it under her mother's maiden name, Sarah A. Allen, possibly in an attempt to reduce the number of contributions with her own byline, as several have speculated,[2] but possibly also as a tribute to her mother, with whom she shared a close bond. They had performed together in the Hopkins Colored Troubadours in Hopkins's early years, and she lived with her mother throughout her adult life as a single woman. After her stepfather's death, Hopkins cared for and supported her mother—one of "her closest friends"—until her death (Lois Brown, *Hopkins* 500). With the choice of Washington, D.C., for the novel's setting, she points to such other important "race women" as Anna Julia Cooper, Fannie Barrier Williams, Mary Church Terrell, and Mary Ann Shadd Cary, all of whom claimed D.C. as their home at one time or another. Her choice of Washington also makes an important intertextual reference to the setting of William Wells Brown's novel *Clotel; or, The President's Daughter,* a work she draws on extensively in *Hagar's Daughter.*[3] Brown was an important figure in Hopkins's life, having encouraged her in her future path by awarding her a writing prize when she was fifteen (as mentioned in the previous chapter). But if the setting of *Hagar's Daughter* makes a number of important personal tributes to people she knew and admired, it also serves the significant public purpose of setting the stage for the novel's examination and critique of the National Father.

As she had in *Contending Forces,* Hopkins uses a two-part structure in *Hagar's Daughter.* Set in Baltimore in the early 1860s, the novel's first section relates the story of the kind-hearted plantation owner, Ellis Enson, and his marriage to Hagar Sargeant, daughter of the neighboring plantation's owner. With the birth of their daughter, Ellis's younger brother, St. Clair, loses his place as the heir to the Enson fortune. St. Clair—as cruel and corrupt as his brother is kind—mentions his plight to the notorious slave-trader Walker as they share a drink at the convention of the Confederate States in South Carolina. Conveniently, Walker knows from previous dealings that Hagar was born a slave, left with Mr. Clark Sargeant at the age of five, and raised as his daughter. Armed with this information, St. Clair and Walker travel to Baltimore and confront Ellis with the news that his wife is a slave and, since the child follows the condition of the mother, so is his daughter. Walker produces the bill of sale, and Hagar's own faint memory confirms his claim. After the initial shock subsides, Enson buys his wife and daughter, determining to move his family to Europe, but before they can leave, he is shot and left for dead, apparently at the hands of his unscrupulous brother, who then takes Hagar and the baby to Washington to be sold. Hagar makes a desperate attempt to flee and, failing that, jumps with her child into the Potomac River.[4]

The second part of the novel takes place twenty years later in the high society of Washington, D.C. The plot follows the ongoing intrigues of St. Clair Enson and Walker—now thinly disguised in the new identities of General Benson and his friend, Major Henry Clay Madison—as they scheme to repair their fortunes. Zenas Bowen, a wealthy entrepreneur and new senator from California, has arrived in Washington for the legislative season with his daughter, Jewel, and his wife (Jewel's stepmother), Estelle. Jewel's engagement to Cuthbert Sumner, General Benson's private secretary, promises to bring together not only the young people but their substantial family fortunes. Benson and Madison have designs of their own for those family fortunes, however; they plan for Madison's beautiful daughter, Aurelia, to seduce Cuthbert and marry him herself, thus leaving Jewel Bowen vulnerable to General Benson's overtures. Aurelia succeeds at splitting up the couple, but when Jewel resists the general's advances and reunites with Cuthbert, Benson contrives to frame Cuthbert for the murder of his stenographer and to abduct Jewel, keeping her prisoner in the now abandoned Enson Hall until the end of Cuthbert's trial. There ensues a dramatic story of intrigue, disguises, fantastic escapes, and revealed identities. In the end, thanks to the bravery and pluck of Ellis and Hagar's former slave, Aunt Henny, and her granddaughter, Venus, Jewel escapes; Aunt Henny provides important testimony in the trial that acquits Cuthbert; Ellis Enson is discovered to still be alive; Estelle Bowen is revealed as his wife, Hagar; and Jewel is discovered to be Hagar and Ellis's daughter. Zenas Bowen having recently died, Hagar and Ellis reunite, and Jewel attempts to come to terms with her newly discovered black identity and Cuthbert's confirmed racism. When Cuthbert's love for Jewel overcomes his bigotry, he seeks her out at Enson Hall, only to discover that she has died of Roman fever while traveling abroad.

Paradise Lost

Hopkins sets the opening of her novel squarely in the tradition of the southern pastoral, portraying the Enson plantation in idealized terms:[5]

> The morning sun poured its golden light upon the picturesque old house standing in its own grounds in one of the suburban towns adjacent to Baltimore—the Baltimore of 1858 or 1860.
>
> The old house seemed to command one to render homage to its beauty and stateliness. It was a sturdy brick building flanked with offices and having outbuildings touching the very edge of the deep, mysterious woods where the trees waved their beckoning arms in every soft breeze that came to revel in their rich foliage. This was Enson Hall. (30)

If the trees and breezes are content in this setting, waving "arms" or reveling in branches, the slaves enjoy their situation as well. Here, Aunt Henny and her daughter, Marthy, happily and lovingly care for their newly married master and mistress, Ellis and Hagar, isolated from the cruelties of family separation or physical brutality that often characterized the experience of slavery: "It was a happy household; . . . the sting of slavery, with its demoralizing brutality, was unknown on [the Sargeant and Enson] plantations, so recently joined" (44). In this Edenic setting, Hagar enjoys the role of "Eve's perfect daughter" (46). Even after her marriage and the birth of her child, she wears "spotless white," a testament to her "pure nature" as she—Madonna-like—cradles her baby in her arms (44). Ellis's gentleness marks him as almost feminine. He shows no interest in politics or the impending war, and his brother considers him "mild and peaceful" to the point of being "womanish" (49, 23). Indeed, when Hagar hears Ellis approaching in the garden, prior to their courtship, she mistakes him for her mother (36–37). Thus, Hopkins opens the novel in an ideal setting: a feminized Eden populated with mothers or mother-like figures.

Of course, Hopkins's "portrayal of the South as a plantation idyll" (Greene 6) must be read as tongue-in-cheek, simultaneously mocking the proslavery novel tradition and hinting at an inevitable fall.[6] The expectation is heightened by the placement of this hyperbolic portrayal of the happy plantation immediately after a chapter depicting St. Clair and Walker's conniving. Their conversation occurs at the convention "which ushered in the birth of the glorious Confederate States of America" (8). Hopkins describes the scene with lines from *Paradise Lost:* "a solemn council forthwith to be held / At Pandaemonium, the high capital / Of Satan and his peers" (8).[7] So doing, she criticizes the southern states' attempt at secession, comparing it to Satan's attempt to overthrow God and heaven. More, the reference lays the groundwork for the comparison between St. Clair and Satan. This characterization will be enforced throughout the novel as St. Clair transforms, when thwarted, from an "elegant society man" to a hissing creature with the "countenance of a devil" (205).

The novel offers several portents of the fall to come. The death of Hagar's mother provides the first warning of the end of the pastoral, maternal life at Enson Hall and previews Hagar's imminent motherlessness (39). The appearance of Isaac, St. Clair's slave sent ahead to the Enson plantation, provides a second warning of impending disaster. At his arrival, Aunt Henny calls him the "lim' ob de debbil," a moniker that accurately characterizes his longtime relationship with St. Clair, who has "the diabolical beauty of Satan himself" and whom Isaac judges to be "a borned debbil" (42, 21, 24). The arrival of this devil, then, in the company of Walker, presages Hagar's "fall" from the position of elevated white plantation mistress to degraded black slave and introduces corruption at the plantation.[8] Edenic images multiply as the discovery of Ellis, apparently murdered by his brother, recalls the biblical fratricide of Abel by Cain. St. Clair Enson then takes Hagar from her pastoral home to the slave market in the capital city where, Walker claims, as a "handsome polished wench" she will be a coveted sexual commodity for "any gentleman" (55).

Hagar experiences a conflicted relationship with the Mother of African heritage, to say the least. Like the story of Grace in *Contending Forces,* Hagar's story resembles the plot of the tragic mulatta so popular among turn-of-the-century authors: a woman raised with the privileges and, often, the prejudices of an upper-class white woman discovers that she has African heritage—"black blood"—most often inherited from her mother. She "follows the condition of the mother" and is, therefore, black. Owing to her internalized racial biases, the discovery of her black heritage devastates her, accompanied as it inevitably will be by any number of abuses: enslavement, poverty, social ostracism, and physical vulnerability, to name a few. The plot typically follows this trajectory in one of two directions: either the discovery of her new identity overpowers her and she takes her own life, or she chooses to embrace the identity inherited from her mother and becomes a valuable and active member of the race community. The tragic mulatta narrative constitutes an ironic story of motherlessness: while the discovery of her identity ostensibly repairs the heroine's initial separation from the mother's African heritage and thus from the National Mother, the heroine has so internalized the Father's rejection of the Mother that she continues in a state of motherlessness even after the recovery of the Mother. The outcome of her story depends upon whether she achieves maternal redemption by accepting her heritage and seeking identification with the Mother or she continues to pursue identification with the Father and thus remains motherless.

Hagar's story begins in the same way as the typical tragic mulatta story. We learn that the woman who has raised her, the woman she thinks of as her mother, is in fact not her biological mother. Born into slavery, she became part of the Sargeant family as a young child, and they raised her as their own. The "terror of her childish heart caused by the rough slave-trader" appears to have wiped out memories of an earlier time and of her slave mother (57). Nevertheless, true to Jacques Lacan's notion of an "Other that it is impossible to forget" (71), memories of her mother and an awareness of her motherlessness haunt her. Just prior to Ellis's approach in the garden, an approach she mistakes for her mother, Hagar "is filled with a delicious excitement, caused by she knew not what" (33). She may not recognize the cause of her excitement, but the fact that she first thinks of her mother when she hears Ellis's approach suggests that thoughts of her mother lurk not far beneath the surface of her consciousness. With the ongoing awareness of her loss, melancholia functions as haunting, keeping her loss ever present (Eng and Han 347).

In spite of this subconscious haunting, her upbringing with the Sargeant family has directed her identification away from the National Mother of Africa to the National Father of the United States. She exhibits a deep interest in and loyalty to the National Father in her fascination with the colonial English roots of American identity, the source of the nation's Anglo-Saxon heritage. As a young woman in the Sargeant family, she was responsible for washing the "heirlooms of colonial china and silver." Hagar takes seriously her responsibility for these artifacts, which she believes link her to a proud family and national heritage. And yet her extreme dedication suggests that she suspects the veracity of her family ties. She makes a misdirected, subconscious attempt to enforce her pedigree: "Not for the world would she have dropped one of these treasures. . . . Not the royal jewels of Victoria were ever more carefully guarded than these family heirlooms" (33). Hagar also frequents Chesapeake Bay, the site of one of the original colonial settlements in Jamestown, Virginia, where "she would dream of life before the Revolution, and in these dreams participate in the joys of the colonial dames" (33).

Hagar's attraction to the colonial period registers more than a desire to solidify her family's place in American history; it indicates her wish to claim the racial heritage attributed to the "Anglo-Saxon Race," a heritage long associated with superiority.[9] According to historian Rogers M. Smith, British American colonists seeking to exclude Native Americans and Africans from the classification of "British subject" used the myths of Anglo-Saxon superiority for support. Notions of American exceptionalism, exemplified by John Winthrop's "citty upon a hill," grew out of confidence in the Anglo-Saxons' unique ability to carry out God's plan.[10] Beliefs in Anglo-Saxon superiority persisted into the nineteenth century, when evolutionary and social evolutionary theories contributed to such ideas: Herbert Spencer, for example, asserted that the Anglo-Saxons' heritage from ancient Teutonic tribes uniquely fitted them for political freedom (Smith 295). He further asserted that while the "interbreeding" among persons of European heritage would improve the "race," "white pairings with blacks . . . and other more 'distant' races would produce only stunted, backward offspring" (quoted in Smith 205).

Hagar's desire to participate in the early years of the nation's development, therefore, points to her repressed knowledge that she does not belong to the class of Anglo-Saxons and her need to assuage that sense of exclusion. Her "dream" of life before the Revolution indicates her subconscious awareness that the nation does not welcome her, that it bars her from identification with the Father and authentic American identity. Hagar's dreams of the colonial period and her longing to participate in this heritage may indicate Hopkins's own sense of exclusion from the nation, and in particular her assertion of her status as a "daughter of the Revolution" in a 1905 speech at Boston's centennial celebration of William Lloyd Garrison. In this speech, she stakes a claim to the American heritage Hagar longs for: "I remembered that at Bunker Hill my ancestors on my maternal side poured out their blood. I am a daughter of the Revolution, you do not acknowledge black daughters of the Revolution but we are going to take that right" (Hopkins, "Address" 355). Reflecting Hopkins's sense of entitlement and her apparent anxiety over the denial of that entitlement, Hagar seeks reassurance that her membership in the Sargeant family—a family with colonial china as family heirlooms—secures for her a share in Anglo-Saxon national identity.

Given Hagar's deep investment in identification with the National Father, the reader is not surprised that, when Walker spoils her dream, thwarting her attempt to identify with the Father and forcing the connection with her African heritage, Hagar recoils from the news. Trying to make sense of her new identity, she searches the face of her slave, Marthy,

> minutely examining the black skin, crinkled hair, flat nose and protruding lips. So might her grandmother have looked. . . . Her mother a slave! She wondered that the very thought did not strike her dead. With shrinking horror she contemplated the black abyss into which the day's events had hurled her, leaving her there to grovel and suffer the tortures of the damned. Her name gone, her pride of birth shattered at one blow! Was she, indeed, a descendant of naked black savages of the horrible African jungles? Could it be that the blood of generations of these unfortunate ones flowed through her veins? (56–57)

Having wholeheartedly adopted the values of the National Father, Hagar experiences horror at the thought that she does not descend from the nation's slave owners, as she believed, but from the slaves. The thought of her African heritage, however, does not "strike her dead." Rather, she responds to her situation with strength, invoking the history of the biblical Hagar as her model.

The Old Testament story of Hagar aligns in important ways with the oedipal model as it figures in Hopkins's work. Hopkins prepared her readers for her serialized novel by including an essay on "Hagar and Ishmael" by Charles Winslow Hall in the *Colored American Magazine* issue preceding the first installment of *Hagar's Daughter.* This essay would remind readers of the details of the biblical story while also emphasizing its relevance to Hopkins's community. In this story, God has promised Abraham that he will father a "great nation," but when his wife, Sarah, does not conceive, she worries that God's promise will not be realized. So she sends her Egyptian servant, Hagar, to Abraham as a surrogate for her. When Hagar conceives, Sarah becomes jealous, and Hagar flees to escape Sarah's rage. An angel comes to Hagar with a promise for the future of Ishmael, her child. He will "multiply . . . exceedingly," but he will not participate, it seems, in the great nation that Abraham's legitimate second-born son, Isaac, will enjoy. Rather, Ishmael will experience adversity: "his hand will be against every man, and every man's hand against him."[11] Although Hagar returns to Abraham and Sarah at the angel's direction, Abraham casts her out after the birth of his legitimate son, Isaac, barring Ishmael from his rightful place in the nation.

This story resonates with Hopkins's novel in two obvious ways: a struggle exists over the child's identification with the mother or the father, and this struggle has national implications. As we have come to expect, the struggle replicates the oedipal narrative in that the child who identifies with its mother and the African heritage she represents is excluded from identification with the white father and the rights and privileges accompanying that identification. Like the biblical figures, Hopkins's Hagar and her child lose their place in the nation because their African heritage defines them as outsiders. Hagar recognizes "the horrible fatality" of her name as she recalls lines from an unknown poem that she had heard "somewhere" and that "came back to her vividly now":

> Farewell! I go, but Egypt's mighty gods
> Will go with me, and my avengers be.
> And in whatever distant land your god,
> Your cruel god of Israel, is known,
> There, too, the wrongs that you have done this day
> To Hagar and your first-born, Ishmael,
> Shall waken and uncoil themselves, and hiss
> Like adders at the name of Abraham.[12]
>
> (58)

Hagar's ability to locate these lines somewhere inside herself offers further evidence of her access to and haunting by the pre-oedipal mother, a haunting described by Lacan in the language of Sigmund Freud's uncanny: "something strange to me, although it is at the heart of me" (71). As she repeats the lines from the poem to herself, she forms a connection with her own suppressed National Mother, a connection that enables her to participate in the biblical Hagar's nationalism and her power. In his rendition of this story for the *Colored American Magazine*—the fourth in a series of "Fascinating Bible Stories"—author Charles Winslow Hall emphasizes the Egyptian Hagar's status as an African mother and Ishmael's legacy as "the son of a Caucasian father and African mother" (304). Hall had emphasized the biblical Hagar's fortitude as she supports Ishmael in the wilderness; similarly, Hopkins portrays a strong Hagar as she confronts her racial identity and returns, with her child, to slavery.[13] Speaking the lines of the poem, Hagar adopts the voice of a prophet, foretelling the fate that awaits Abraham as recompense for his wrongs against her. Far from wishing for her child to identify with its father, the biblical Hagar endorses Abraham's insistence that his child, in effect, follows the condition of the mother. That motherly inheritance becomes a source of power for Hopkins's Hagar. When she speaks to St. Clair, she follows the example of the poem, making her own prophecy: "in spite of the wealth and position you have played for and won, you have seen the last on this earth of peace or happiness" (71). Hagar speaks with power and bravery as she predicts the eventual fall of her tormenter.

Bravery aside, Hagar and her child face a bleak fate, and Hagar knows that they possess few options. Walker speculates that "a handsome polished wench" like Hagar would bring a high price from "any gentleman" (55) at the slave market in Washington, D.C., his anticipated buyer indicating that she will be sold as a sexual commodity.[14] His guess at a separate price for "the pickaninny" suggests they will be sold separately. By jumping into the Potomac River, Hagar solidifies her place in the tragic mulatta tradition: like *Contending Forces*' Grace, she attempts to end her life in an act of desperation and defeat. As we learn, however, Hagar is not defeated. She survives and makes her way to California, where, like Sappho, she adopts a new identity and a new life.

The Unmanly National Father

In contrast to the maternal Hagar, who exhibits strength and courage, Hopkins sets up the masculine national capital—and by extension, the National Father—as immoral and cowardly. With this portrayal, she critiques the nation that rejects the African American community in the oedipal narrative as unworthy of the "child's" identification. Hopkins prefigures this contrast with the difference between the feminized, maternal character of the prelapsarian Enson Hall and Washington, D.C.—the setting for most of the novel—which quickly emerges as something of an old boys' club. The capital is an immoral place controlled by men, similar in character to Satan's council at Pandaemonium evoked by the Confederated States convention earlier in the novel. Of course, Hopkins's portrayal of the capital did not grow entirely from her imagination. The District of Columbia, when created in 1800, shared the slave laws of the state of Maryland.[15] D.C. hardly qualified as a moral leader for the nation: many lawmakers owned slaves, and slavery continued to exist in the capital until 1862. The time period for the novel's later section—1882—recalls the federal government's failure of paternalism, as it had recently abandoned its efforts to reconstruct and democratize the South. Moreover, the novel's brief reference to the 1874 failure of the Freedman's Bank raises the specter of government corruption (117).[16] Against this historical backdrop, the novel portrays the capital as rife with corruption in the form of sexual license and harassment. This characterization first appeared in Walker and St. Clair's attempt to sell Hagar as a concubine (55), but we quickly learn that the sexualization and commodification of women continue twenty years later in "the beautiful capital of our great Republic" (75) as we hear two men at a social gathering frankly assessing the value of several women according to their appearance. The men dismiss the older women out of hand—"we don't waste ammunition on elderly females who have had their day"—and pay attention only to the young and attractive. One of the men succinctly sums up the capital's values: "be beautiful and rich and you will be happy here" (114). Although the women are not slaves to be sold at auction, the fact that one of them is Hagar, now in the guise of Estelle Bowen, provides an uncanny sense of déjà vu, recalling the city's historical participation in the domestic slave trade and casting the men's banter in a sinister light.

The lion's share of transgressions belongs to St. Clair Enson, now refashioned as General Benson. St. Clair had been one of the South's most trusted delegates in its bid for secession (20), and now, twenty years later, his political ambition persists. He dreams of being the "father" of the country and as such he serves as the novel's representative for the nation and the National Father in the oedipal drama (77). (And, lest we've lost track of the biblical Hagar thread in the novel, this National Father's servant, or "limb" as Aunt Henny called him, bears the name Isaac, a reminder of "father" Abraham's legitimate son. Hopkins's Isaac is more accurately an Ishmael, a former slave and very probably the son of a black mother. We know he is the son-in-law of a black mother: he is married to Aunt Henny's daughter. But, like Langley in *Contending Forces,* he seeks the privileges that accompany American citizenship by identifying with the National Father and occupying the position of Isaac, Abraham's legitimate son.) St. Clair/General Benson has engaged in a number of immoral behaviors, ranging from using tax dollars to support his extravagant lifestyle (148) to playing an unspecified role in Abraham Lincoln's assassination (77). He lives at the Willard Hotel (93), an historic site built in the mid-nineteenth century which, Nathaniel Hawthorne once said, "more justly could be called the center of Washington than either the Capitol or the White House or the State Department."[17] Over the years, the Willard housed Presidents Taylor, Fillmore, Pierce, Buchanan, Lincoln, Grant, Taft, Wilson, Coolidge, and Harding. In particular, Ulysses S. Grant's association with the hotel—he reportedly "escaped" to the lobby of the Willard regularly to get away from the stress of the White House—brings with it his reputation for scandal and his legendary tendency to receive "lobbyists" in the hotel lobby, suggesting the type of dealings General Benson engages in with Walker. The novel's mention of this historic hotel, then, associates Benson with its colorful and questionable history.[18]

Benson's general corruption underscores his sexual immorality, which will form the basis of Hopkins's scathing critique of the National Father in *Hagar's Daughter.*[19] Just as the first section of the novel opened with

St. Clair and Walker discussing Hagar as the spoiler of St. Clair's future fortune, the second part of the novel begins with these same two men—now General Benson and Major Madison—this time discussing a woman who spoiled Benson's hopes for a good time at a party. At this social gathering, we learn, the hostess's temperance convictions have kept away "all the women fit for pleasant company," "fit" in this context connoting the possession of questionable moral standards (77). Benson avers that he would "cut and run for it" if he had a wife like that, complaining that "the seat of government is no place for a missionary" (77). Although a relatively benign comment, Benson's opinion that Washington is no place for morality alerts readers to the kind of government and nation he envisions. This section of the novel goes on to focus primarily on Benson's unscrupulous and self-serving dealings with women. We learn of the "many women to whom he had vowed eternal fidelity at one moment, only to abandon heartlessly ['cut and run'] the next at the rise of a new star in the firmament of beauty" (93). He has abandoned a number of lovers, including Major Madison's daughter, Aurelia, and his stenographer, Elise Bradford, with whom he has fathered a child. As Benson serves as the novel's representative of the National Father, his immoral sexual behavior is linked to that Father, showing him to be unworthy of his children's identification.

Gail Bederman's work on masculinity in the nineteenth century sheds some light on the characterization of General Benson, inviting us to place his behavior within the context of the Victorian notion of "manliness" that associated true masculinity with sexual restraint. According to this ideology, sexual desire existed as a natural force in men, but a force to be managed through carefully developed self-control. Middle-class parents encouraged their sons to develop this power of will, considering it to be crucial to their sons' character and to their assumption of the authority that should eventually be theirs: "By gaining the manly strength to control himself, a man gained the authority, as well as the duty, to protect and direct those less manly than himself—whether his wife, his children, his employees, or his racial 'inferiors'" (Bederman 48). Significantly, this ideal of masculinity—in conjunction with the myth of the black rapist—appeared in justifications of southern lynching. By constructing African American men as uncontrollable sexual animals and therefore unmanly, self-restrained white men appeared as truly manly and, in this way, superior. According to this logic, white men were the bearers of civilization, and "black men embodied whatever was most unmanly and uncivilized, including a complete absence of sexual self-control" (Bederman 49).[20] Serving the function of the colonial Other, the fiction of the sexually voracious African American man comforted white men with the image of what they were not, and threatened them with what they could become if they followed the wrong path. Indeed, "without manly self-restraint," the story went, "civilized men would be no better than these vicious savages" (Bederman 49). Thus, African Americans came to signify everything unmanly and barbaric while the ideal of "the white man" signified self-control and civilization. "In colloquial usage," says Bederman, "the terms 'civilization' and 'the white man' were almost interchangeable" (49–50). Hopkins turns this web of signifiers on its head, undermining claims to authority and superiority by linking sexual exploitation and license not to African American men, but to the nation's capital and the National Father.

General Benson has directed his unmanly sexual proclivity at Aurelia Madison, the daughter of his co-conspirator, Walker/Madison. Initially, Aurelia appears as anything but a victim, functioning as an antagonist for most of the story. She conspires with the villains—her father and her ex-lover—agreeing to revive her past relationship with Cuthbert Sumner in order to get his fortune and thereby make Jewel Bowen available for General Benson's attentions. For this, Benson will reward her with the sum of one million dollars. Reader alliances shift, however, as we learn that Aurelia has been a victim of Benson's sexual exploitation. The novel provides a clue to Aurelia's complex status early on by staging her first appearance in the story at the theater, where Jewel and Cuthbert have gone to see "Modjeska . . . interpret the heart-breaking story of 'Camille'" (90). Hopkins would have become familiar with the Polish actress, Helena Modjeska (1844–1909), who played Camille to rave reviews in New York in 1878, just as Hopkins was preparing for her own performing career, which would begin in 1879 with the debut of her musical, *Peculiar Sam; or, The Underground Railroad* (Wallinger 35). *Camille* was a stage version of a novel by Alexandre Dumas fils, entitled *La Dame aux Camelias.* Based on Dumas's relationship with Marie Duplessis, it tells the story of the love affair between a courtesan and a young man who cannot afford to keep her in the lifestyle she prefers. Unwilling to sacrifice the wealthy life she can lead as a courtesan, she rejects her lover. She eventually learns to choose love over riches, but the lesson comes too late, and she dies of consumption. Hopkins sets up a number of similarities between Camille and Aurelia. Aurelia appears as a something of a courtesan herself, a dazzling beauty "with a mature air of a woman of the world" (90). She has formed sexual relationships with several men of means, including General Benson, who appears to be wealthy, and Cuthbert Sumner, who is in fact wealthy. Those relationships now over, Aurelia is left alone. Although her history resembles the "heartbreaking story of 'Camille,'" the racial component of her story distinguishes it. In one of *Hagar's Daughter*'s many dramatic revelations, we discover that Aurelia is a "quadroon," the daughter of her father's slave, a motherless child who never knew and therefore does not remember her mother (107, 245). This secret makes her a "willing tool" and an easy victim for General Benson (159). Elise Bradford, another of Benson's victims, describes the plight of Aurelia and women like her:

> Aurelia in a measure deserves our pity. The loveliness of Negro women of mixed blood is very often marvelous, and their condition deplorable. . . . Socially, they are not recognized by the whites; they are often without money enough to but [*sic*] the barest necessities of life; honorably, they cannot procure sufficient means to gratify their luxurious tastes; debauched whitemen [*sic*] are ever ready to take advantage of their destitution, and after living a short life of shame, they sink into early graves. (159)

Through Elise, Hopkins casts Aurelia as a Camille who uses sex to make money, but Aurelia's vulnerability frees her from judgment. Aurelia joins the ranks of Hopkins's characters who have been victims of "debauched" white men: Grace Montfort, Sappho Clark, Hagar Sergeant Enson.[21] The primary debauched white man in *Hagar's Daughter,* Benson plays a significant role in Aurelia's exploitation. Knowing her racial heritage and her desire to conceal it, he wields over her the power of master over slave. And although Aurelia does not die, once her mother's identity is revealed, the world of white high society where she sought acceptance rejects her, and she vanishes (272).

Benson's sexual exploitation of Jewel Bowen differs from his treatment of Aurelia primarily because he believes Jewel to be white. She represents a commodity to him, however, in that she will inherit her father's very substantial fortune. His sexual harassment works primarily behind the scenes, arranging the destruction of her relationship with Cuthbert Sumner. Once he has cleared the field, he attempts to ingratiate himself into her affections. As they dance one evening at a ball, he uses sexually loaded banter as he flirts:

> "Are you pleased with Washington?"
> "Oh, yes; but I miss the freedom of the ranch, the wild flight at dawn over the prairie in the saddle, and many other things."
> He looked at her with glowing eyes: "There we have congenial tastes. I am never so happy as when in the saddle." (119)

This rather surprising bit of sexual innuendo, delivered with a leer, exposes Benson's character both to the reader and to Jewel, who recoils at his licentiousness. Benson's sexual freedom quickly turns to violence; when Jewel refuses his numerous advances, he responds with harsh words, then threats, and eventually abduction and a fraudulent scheme designed to put her and her wealth into his hands.

Benson's treatment of Elise Bradford is the most fully realized and the most violent example of sexual exploitation in the novel, serving to demonstrate most persuasively his deep depravity and the inadequacy of the National Father. Elise's situation as she describes it to Cuthbert resembles that of the "negro women of mixed blood" whom she pities. Indeed, as Carla Peterson has observed, the novel leaves her racial identity uncertain (46). It provides a number of hints, however, that prompt the reader to wonder about her racial identity. Born in Kentucky, she was motherless—an orphan raised by her "othermother" aunt. When she arrives in Washington, General Benson hires her to work as a stenographer, the same profession held by Sappho (of *Contending Forces*) and Hopkins herself, indicating that this profession was available to African American women. Her fear of poverty and her desire for "official wealth, power, and opportunity" point to her wish to identify with the National Father and make a place for herself in white society, just as Dumas's Camille sought a place in high society. This desire makes Elise vulnerable to Benson's advances, which leave her a single mother. As she tells her story to Cuthbert, she expresses the shame often experienced by victims of sexual abuse: "How can I tell you? Oh! the shame of it all will kill me" (156). The shame does not kill her, however; Benson does.

Hopkins completes her characterization of General Benson's violence and sexual excess with testimony from white characters, characters who have access to citizenship and therefore rightfully identify with the National Father. Such "political self-impeachments by whites"—in effect, the "negation of white citizenship"—amount to a pronouncement "by whites about the unworthiness of white people to lead America in official and everyday life" (Berlant 562). Ellis Enson and Elise Bradford—both white or apparently white characters—offer political self-impeachments, casting doubt on the merit of the National Father. Elise, having experienced the same sexual exploitation as the novel's black characters and having witnessed the corruption of the nation's capital, makes an unsurprising critique of the racial prejudice of the nation: "It is killing the black man's hope . . . in every avenue; it is centered against his advancement. . . . As life, real life, has unfolded to my view, I have come to think that there is nothing in this prejudice but a relic of barbarism" (159–60). Elise deploys the language of civilization, so central to the doctrine of manliness, challenging the Anglo-American claims of superiority and privileged citizenship based on civilization by denouncing their behavior as barbaric (Bederman 23).[22] Ellis Enson, too, has had time to reflect on the shortcomings of the nation, having been separated from his wife for twenty years by the nationally sanctioned racist institution of slavery. He denounces the hypocrisy of "Puritan new England philanthropy" that extends to black Americans "every privilege but the vital one of deciding the question of the commonest personal liberty which is the fundamental principle of the holy family tie" (271).

These denunciations by Elise and Ellis are borne out by General Benson, whose treatment of Aurelia, Elise, and Jewel indicts him as the devilish character he was shown to be earlier in the novel. Moreover, as a representative of the National Father, his traits characterize the nation. Berlant's study of sexual harassment and exploitation as a national issue provides a useful model for understanding Hopkins's strategy in her characterization of Benson. Berlant asks, "What would it mean to write a genealogy of sexual harassment in which not an individual but a nation was considered the agent of unjust sexual power? Such an account of these complaints would provide an incisive critique of the modes of erotic and political dominance that have marked gender, race, and citizenship in America" (553). Hopkins writes just such a genealogy in her novel, starting with Hagar's enslavement and proposed sale as a sexual commodity and continuing through Elise's murder and Jewel's abduction. Although slavery's function as a site of nationally sanctioned sexual abuse is well known, Hopkins demonstrates—as she asserted in her preface to *Contending Forces*—that little has changed since emancipation, and the abuse of power facilitated by the master-slave relationship continues into the post-emancipation United States. In this way, as Berlant has argued, "America becomes explicitly . . . accountable for the sexual exploitation it authorizes in the guise of the white male citizen's domestic and erotic privilege" (554). With her damning portrayal of the nation's capital—a metonymy for the nation itself—as a site of masculine corruption, Hopkins denounces the National Father as unworthy of the identification of his children, just as the biblical Hagar had denounced Abraham.

The Mother in the Land of the Father

It is to this site of immorality and—according to Bederman's formulation—unmanliness, the site of her attempted sale as a sexual commodity, that Hagar returns. She has undergone a significant transformation in the twenty years that have lapsed, taking a new name—Estelle—as a marker of that change. She pursues her oedipal directive by denying her identification with the Mother and clinging instead to the socially acceptable Father. Although she is already a motherless child according to the terms of the oedipal directive, her motherlessness is compounded by the loss of her child through the traumas of slavery, in this case by choosing to end her child's life rather than see her live as a slave.[23] Like Sappho, she has given up her mothering identity by sacrificing her child and essentially burying its mother, Hagar. The impact of this loss does not leave her, however, and years later when General Benson threatens her stepdaughter, she wears the "look of a lioness bereft of her young" (201).

Having learned the painful lesson of the powerlessness of a black woman in the United States, she adopts a new, white identity and strives to identify with the National Father. After heroically surviving her fall into the Potomac River, she proceeds to survive her fall from the grace of white society. She makes her way across the United States to California, where she supports herself as a waitress in a San Francisco resort, meets the very rich Zenas Bowen, and, in a feminized version of the American ideal of the self-made man, becomes—through marriage—a wealthy woman. Renewing her youthful interest in the nation's colonial beginnings and the pleasure she took in being "the belle of every assembly" during her wedding trip to Washington with her first husband (44), Hagar-cum-Estelle fashions her new self strategically, with an eye to the long-range goal of occupying an elevated place in the nation. Her marriage to Zenas Bowen forwards this plan beautifully. She encourages him to go into politics (81–82), a position he may not be entirely cut out for. Although the novel assures us that Bowen is no fool, he appears to be naïve, as his unquestioning trust of General Benson and the broader political scene demonstrates: "The government, my dear, gives him its confidence by placing him in a responsible position. That is enough for me. Uncle Sam never employs rascals to transact his business" (139–40). Hagar helps to protect him from this type of naivety. Using her wifely influence, sanctioned by nineteenth-century domesticity as a suitable way for a woman to participate in politics, she subtly facilitates Zenas's success: "Thanks to her cleverness, he made no mistakes and many hits which no one thought of tracing to his wife's rare talents" (82). Now, passing as white and married to a rich senator, she revises the story of the biblical Hagar, undoing the exile foisted upon her by identifying with the National Father and thus establishing her place in the nation.

Hagar's endeavor to choose the Father over the Mother does not, however, work out as she hopes. As we saw in *Contending Forces,* the African-coded "occult arts" play a small but significant role in the story, suggesting the Mother's ongoing presence (199). Shortly after Enson and Hagar's marriage, their slave, Aunt Henny, procures a charm from another slave, "Unc' Demus," to protect Hagar from bad luck. Unc' Demus makes a bag of rattlesnake skin and fills it with a rabbit's foot, a snake's tooth, a scorpion tail, and graveyard dust. This he ties up in one of

Hagar's handkerchiefs, provided by Aunt Henny. Unc' Demus promises great things from the charm: "'Long as yer mistis keep dis 'bout her, trouble'll neber stay so long dat joy won't conquer him in de end" (41). Although the novel says nothing hereafter about the charm, its promise eventually comes true, suggesting that Hagar's African heritage remains with her, drawing her back to the joy of her maternal relationships, both personal and national. The early story of the charm invites readers to attribute her survival, her success in marriage, and her remarkable reunion with her family, to the African occult power conjured by Aunt Henny and Unc' Demus.

Ironically, then, Hagar's attempted journey away from motherhood takes her back to her identity as a mother just as her denial of the Mother puts her into a situation that facilitates her reclamation. She does not know that Zenas Bowen's daughter, Jewel, is, in fact, her lost child, but she feels drawn to her, and with her marriage to Zenas she becomes "a mother to the motherless child" (81). So begins her maternal redemption. Hagar's choice of husband proves to be another fateful element of her redemption. Certainly, as the guardian of her lost daughter, Zenas plays an important role in her journey. Although he has the wealth and political connections she needs to pursue her national entitlement, he is also good in ways that contrast starkly with the National Father. A man of "sterling worth in business and morals" (81), Zenas stands as "one of those genial men whom the West is constantly sending out to enrich society" (80). He differs from General Benson in that he exhibits the nineteenth-century ideal of manliness: when, as a newly rich man, he meets Hagar, a waitress, he does not use his fortune to take advantage of her, but instead exhibits appropriate sexual restraint and honorably proposes marriage. Moreover, with the "hair and skin of an Indian" (80) he has an ambiguous racial identity. While he embodies the Emersonian ideal of the self-reliant American who has tried and succeeded at a variety of professions—mate on a Mississippi steamboat, soldier, miner, and entrepreneur[24]—if he is a Native American, he is also a member of a disenfranchised race. So as the Washington insider that Estelle needs, Zenas is also an outsider, and as such he unwittingly pulls her in the direction of the Mother.

These factors combine to prepare Hagar for maternal redemption. After spending time in Washington's high society, as she had longed to do, she discovers its true character, and she becomes convinced that her quest for the Father through the establishment of her place in the nation has compromised her character as well. In response to Jewel's brave choice to marry Cuthbert Sumner, a show of faith in him despite his arrest for murder, Hagar confesses, "once, perhaps, I should have acted and felt as you do. . . . [But] now, my child, I am of the world—worldly" (193).[25] Hagar recognizes the damage done by her association with the nation's capital and wishes to leave it: "Perhaps it is well that we do not return to Washington next fall. I am glad your father has so decided" (142). Persuaded of the detrimental effect of seeking the Father, Hagar is prepared to reclaim the Mother, and in the courtroom at Cuthbert's trial, she gets her opportunity. When Ellis Enson abandons his assumed identity and declares himself to be General Benson/St. Clair Enson's supposedly dead brother, Hagar springs to her feet to reclaim her identity as Hagar Enson, former slave and Ellis's lost wife (conveniently, also the widow of the recently deceased Zenas Bowen). The emotional avowal of her identity, her abdication of her quest for the National Father and claiming of her affiliation with the National African Mother, brings about Hagar's redemption. Yet, it costs her dearly. Her newly exposed identity destroys the national status she had worked for when Washington society rejects her as a member of the "mongrel race" (266). Nevertheless, redemption brings happiness to Hagar, the happiness promised by Unc' Demus's charm: "She was happy—happier than she had ever hoped to be in this life. True, no callers begged admittance into the grand mansion, no cards overflowed the receivers in the spacious entrance hall, since the sensational items disclosing her identity had appeared in the columns of the daily press; that fact did not disconcert her in the least" (273–74). Hagar's maternal redemption becomes complete when, like Sappho, she can reclaim her identity as mother. Discovering that her stepdaughter, Jewel, is in fact the daughter she believed she lost in the Potomac, Hagar becomes the mother who yearns for her child (279–80).

Jewel's redemption poses more of a challenge than does Hagar's. Certainly, she needs it: in Hopkins's rewriting of the biblical Hagar story, Jewel may be fatherless—like Ishmael—but the real tragedy is her motherlessness. As Hagar's lost daughter, Jewel unknowingly follows the condition of her mother, even to the point of replicating her mother's previous "condition" as a black woman unknowingly passing for white. Unaware of her connection to Mother Africa, Jewel inadvertently passes and, as the daughter of a U.S. senator, seems to enjoy uncontested access to identification with the National Father—indeed, the novel's representative of the nation, General Benson, woos her. Jewel does not welcome this attention, however. She feels repulsed by Benson, in spite of his outward kindness and charm, and experiences an inexplicable sense of apprehension: "She took herself to task for her growing dislike of him. Why should she be so ungenerous to one so kind? Why should she shrink from him with a loathing she could not repress?" (137).[26]

Not only does Jewel dislike General Benson; she senses that he brings disaster for her: "There has been an adverse fate at work since General Benson crossed my path. There has been a train of unfortunate circumstances attending our whole acquaintance. It is absurd to suspect him I know, but I cannot help it" (189–90). Of course, Jewel's revulsion at General Benson and his romantic overtures is not at all absurd. Unknown to any of the characters at this point in the novel, General Benson is Jewel's uncle, and a sexual relationship between them would amount to incest, an inversion of the oedipal drama's incest taboo. Here, and as we saw in *Contending Forces,* the Father—not the Mother—presents the threat of incest, a twist that fits into the general tenor of sexual immorality that the novel ascribes to the nation's capital. Jewel's "absurd" or inexplicable feeling of dis-ease with Benson, then, points to her subconscious awareness of her motherlessness and her maternal heritage.

Jewel's motherlessness is further found in a periodic haunting sensation that she lacks something, a feeling of melancholy that strikes a dissonant chord in contrast to her otherwise charmed existence: "A sense of horrible loneliness, of grief, apprehension, and the weight of some unknown calamity weighed her young heart down. Young, beautiful, well-born, and wealthy, surrounded by every luxury money could purchase or a cultivated taste long for. Jewel was supremely wretched" (199). The privileges of wealth and luxury that derive from passing as Senator Bowen's daughter—and from identifying with the National Father—do not bring her happiness. Instead, Jewel feels the loneliness and grief of the motherless child. She has experienced positive glimmers of her relationship with the Mother, as well. Upon her first meeting with Hagar since being separated from her as an infant in the Potomac, Jewel felt naturally drawn to her, holding her arms out to Hagar as if recognizing her as her mother. Years later, when Jewel seeks help with Cuthbert's arrest, she feels herself moved by a "hidden force" (186) that leads her to her unknown father, the man who will ultimately reunite her with her mother, Hagar, and the National Mother that Hagar represents for her.

These suspicions and premonitions prepare Jewel to begin a redemptive journey to the Mother. Ironically, General Benson is the engine behind this journey. When he abducts Jewel and makes her a prisoner in the now empty Enson Hall, he intends to bring her into his power. We might expect this gothic setting to be just the place to frighten a young woman into compliance. The once idyllic estate has become rundown and decrepit. The "extensive gardens" are now filled with "the ruins of what must once have been buildings and offices of a large plantation. The once well-kept walks [are now] overgrown with weeds, and a heavy growth of trees [obstruct] the view in all directions" (214). Like the fate of the biblical Eden, the machinations of the devilish St. Claire Enson/General Benson have caused the expulsion of the "daughter of Eve," Hagar, leaving the house motherless. Without a mother, the domestic space becomes a gothic shadow of its previous manifestation: "Enson Hall reminded one of an ancient ruin. The main body of the stately dwelling was standing, but scarcely a vestige of the once beautiful outbuildings remained." However, this ruin also bears "an uncanny reputation": "The Negroes declared that the beautiful woods and the lonely avenues were haunted after nightfall. It had grown into a tradition that the ghost of Ellis Enson 'walked,' accompanied by a lady who bore an infant in her arms" (228). The fate of this plantation replicates the fate of the African American family under slavery, broken and separated. The gothic setting decries the motherlessness of the post-Reconstruction African American community, particularly its unwitting members like Jewel, who do not recognize the Mother who haunts them. Nevertheless, this gothic setting also figures as an ideal place for Jewel's journey in that it is haunted with memories of her mother.

This abandoned plantation therefore provides the perfect place for Jewel to encounter her Mother, and she inadvertently makes steps to do precisely that. Locating what she believes will be an avenue for escape, she follows it and finds herself experiencing rebirth. The scene is rife with classic gothic set pieces—hidden passages, secret entrances, and closed doors, all pointing to an encounter with the subconscious, the return of the repressed:

> She took the lamp in her hand. . . . Scarcely waiting to widen the aperture, she crept through, and soon stood, covered with dust, trembling shaken with emotion, in the dark passage. . . .
>
> . . . It had evidently led to the servants' quarters at the back of the house when mirth and gaiety held high revel in the glorious old mansion. . . .
>
> She shaded her lamp with one hand and with fascinated gaze took in, in one brief instant, the contents of the room. . . . on the bed lay a woman of dark brown complexion and wrinkled visage; about her head was wound a many-hued bandanna handkerchief. (215–16)

Jewel undergoes a metaphorical rebirth as she makes her way through a narrow opening and down a dark passage. This birth canal leads to the former slave quarters, home to the race community she still does not recognize as hers, and ultimately promises to return her to her Mother and her lost racial heritage. When she meets an African American woman, Jewel addresses her as "Auntie," a title of respect for an elderly African American woman but also a title signifying kinship, often the role of "othermother." In other words, Jewel's journey of rebirth ushers her into the presence of a metaphorical National Mother.

If Jewel cannot identify with the National Father, her identification with her maternal heritage does not come easily either, leaving her in the liminal position Frantz Fanon attributes to the black child educated in the perspectives of white privilege (*Black Skin* 145–49). Her meeting with Aunt Henny lays the groundwork for her redemption, but the process remains incomplete. The novel highlights Jewel's failed redemption by contrasting it with Hagar's reception of Jewel. When Hagar discovers that Jewel is her daughter, she eagerly anticipates their reunion. She pleads with her husband to speed the moment that will complete her maternal redemption: "I beseech you, lose not a moment, bring her to me—bring my Jewel, my daughter, to my arms" (279). Their emotional moment of physical closeness will bring about Hagar's maternal redemption—the reinstatement of her identity as mother—and it seems that the embrace has the same effect for Jewel: "Clasped in her mother's arms . . . Jewel doubted not that she was Hagar's daughter" (280). And yet, the discovery of her mother does not bring about redemption for Jewel. Indeed, when Jewel encounters the truth of her racial identity—her connection to both her natural mother and National Mother—her response resembles Hagar's initial response of twenty years earlier. Because Jewel has adopted the racist views of white superiority that mark her society, her new identity brings about self-loathing: "She loved her mother . . . but feelings engendered for twenty years were not to be overcome instantly. It was horrible—a living nightmare" (280). While this recovery of identity should be redemptive, the narrator acknowledges that even the comfort of the mother fails to heal some kinds of trauma: "Ah! children who have not needed it yet, believe that the wound must be mortal that cannot be soothed by parental balm and oil. Those dear ones have the power to restore self-respect though they may be powerless to restore happiness" (137–38). Both women find self-respect with their revealed identities, but happiness remains elusive for Jewel, as the maternal redemption available to her is undermined by the power of the National Father over her own opinions and those of her new husband.

In stark contrast to Ellis Enson's unconditional acceptance of his wife Hagar's racial identity, Cuthbert Sumner's racism exacerbates Jewel's suffering. Cuthbert left his family's Massachusetts manufacturing business and came to Washington to work for General Benson. His name may have reminded Hopkins's readers of Charles Sumner (1811–1874), the Massachusetts abolitionist whom Hopkins admired. She was one of the speakers at a Boston celebration commemorating the one hundredth anniversary of his birth.[27] An outspoken advocate for African Americans, Charles Sumner worked tirelessly during Reconstruction for their civil rights. If Hopkins intended to evoke Charles Sumner with the character Cuthbert Sumner, however, she undoubtedly intended to draw a contrast between them. Cuthbert appears to be a good soul, but he bears the traits of Washington men and so remains vulnerable to corruption. He shares General Benson's sexual appetite, having been "in love with the [female] sex, more or less, since the day he left off knee-breeches" (84). The novel signals Cuthbert's vulnerability to the influence of General Benson by highlighting their similarities: they both, over time, have pursued many of the same women. Cuthbert had been attracted to Elise Bradford, the woman whom Benson had seduced, and, like Benson also, has had an affair with Aurelia. During the novel's action, he finds himself competing with Benson for Jewel's affection. And yet he differs from Benson also. Conflicted in his moral posture, Cuthbert feels both revulsion and attraction for General Benson's example. He knows about Benson's scheming and expresses concern for any woman connected to the "reformed rake seeking to re-instate himself in society by a high political position and a rich marriage." Nevertheless, moments later he cannot help but cast an "admiring glance" at the general (150).

If Washington has corrupted Cuthbert's morality with regards to women, it has also done nothing for his views on race. When confronted with the information that Aurelia, his former fiancée, is an "octoroon," he feels "unnerved," shouting and declaring the information to be "too horrible" (158–59). Readers have little doubt that Cuthbert's horror resides not in what her identity means for her, but in the fact that he has had a relationship with her. Later, at the discovery of Hagar's racial identity, he breathes a sigh of relief, believing that Jewel, now his wife, has no blood relation to her, and he makes plans to extricate Jewel from her relationship with Hagar immediately (265). He tells Enson that he could not marry a black woman because the vision of the "grinning, toothless black hag that was her foreparent" would squelch any sexual desire he had for her (271).

Cuthbert's corruption points to the power of the Father that undermines the maternal redemption in *Hagar's Daughter.* In spite of St. Clair Enson/General Benson's defeat—he fails to get the Bowen money, is arrested for the murder of Elise Bradford, and dies while attempting to escape from prison—we know that the values he represents will continue to flourish in the nation's capital. Moreover, we see that black women have no power or place in the novel's version of the nation. The novel marks in several ways the nation's refusal to acknowledge Hagar and Jewel as its children. For example, it denies credence to the voice of the black woman. When Aunt Henny gives her eyewitness account of Elise Bradford's murder, testimony that will prove the innocence of Cuthbert Sumner and the guilt of General Benson, the outraged prosecuting attorney dismisses her: "On what would you base such an unheard of precedent?

On the evidence of a Negress? Would you impugn the honor of a brilliant soldier, a brave gentlemen [*sic*]—courteous, genial, standing flawless before the eyes of the entire country?" (257). The courtroom explodes with support of these sentiments, asserting, "This is a white man's country yet!" and refusing to take the word of a black woman. The conflict resolves only when Ellis Enson appears in the courtroom. (He, too, has taken a new identity and now serves as the chief of the Secret Service.) In a dense four pages, Ellis confirms all that has been said in defense of Cuthbert and against General Benson. Because he is a white man working for the government, Ellis Enson's voice is doubly validated, providing the needed authority to confirm the testimony of Aunt Henny, who remains on the margins of the nation.

The fate of Aurelia—another motherless child in the novel—provides further evidence of the nation's denial of its black "children." The final scene with Aurelia recalls her comparison to Camille earlier in the novel. In Dumas's story, Camille's young lover punishes her by exposing her. Finding her at a large ball, surrounded by members of high society, he gives her an envelope full of money, making public her role as a courtesan. After this exposure, she dies alone, poor, and abandoned. Replicating the tale of Camille, Cuthbert threatens to expose Aurelia: "I warn you; do not try me too far. You will act wisely if you drop this whole matter and leave Washington and the society where you have queened it so long under false pretenses, for solitude and seclusion where you may escape the scorn of the world" (237). Cuthbert's threat does not concern Aurelia's sexual exploits—those, as we have seen, are not damning in Washington—but exposure of her racial identity will end her access to social and national privilege. Well aware of this, she attempts in her court testimony to maintain her connection to the nation by denying her relationship with the mother: "I do not remember my mother—I never saw her. I know nothing of her" (245). Aurelia denies both her biological mother and, by extension, the African National Mother. Therefore, she never experiences maternal redemption. She has felt shame at her African heritage all her life, and when her racial identity becomes public, she maintains that opinion, accepting the judgment and rejection of the Father—here represented by Cuthbert—and removes herself from "public view" (272).

"The sin is the nation's"

Much of *Hagar's Daughter* is highly entertaining. Appealing to her serial readers, Hopkins fills the story with cliffhangers and excitement. Benson arranges Jewel's abduction, keeping her captive in an abandoned plantation home where, after several weeks, she discovers a mysterious old woman, also a captive. The unflappable Venus, a former slave on the Sargeant plantation and Isaac's daughter, disguises herself as a boy as part of a scheme to rescue Jewel and the old woman, who turns out to be Venus's grandmother, Aunt Henny. The suspenseful courtroom drama meets readers' expectations, revealing hidden identities, reuniting separated lovers, answering long unanswered questions, and sending villains to jail. But this is not enough to heal the deeper problems raised in the novel. Thanks to the far-reaching influence of the National Father, maternal redemption is impossible for Jewel, and her motherlessness, it seems, remains unaddressed. Rather than resolution, the novel turns to the jeremiad, concluding with critique and warning.

Although Cuthbert's racist views can be held accountable for the novel's sentimentally unsatisfying conclusion, Hopkins removes blame from Cuthbert—insisting on his "noble nature" and attributing his faults to "environment and tradition" (265)—and places it on the National Father. This displacement of guilt from the individual to the nation transforms this sentimental story into a jeremiad. Sacvan Bercovitch famously described the American jeremiad, based on the laments and warnings of the Old Testament prophet Jeremiah and manifest in John Winthrop's *Model of Christian Charity*. According to Bercovitch, the jeremiad as it developed in American letters held community behavior against a moral or spiritual standard and found it wanting. It offered warnings of future destruction if current behavior was not modified, while at the same time holding out hope for improvement. Hopkins joins this tradition in *Hagar's Daughter* as she places the blame for Hagar's and Jewel's hardships squarely on the nation. Cuthbert and Jewel both adopt the language of sin to describe Jewel's racial identity, indicating their acceptance of the Father's assessment of the Mother. Cuthbert determines that he is "ready to overlook and forgive all" (282)—presumably extending forgiveness for Jewel's blackness. Similarly, in a letter to Cuthbert, Jewel describes her situation in terms of God's judgment. Invoking another Old Testament heroine, she compares herself to Miriam, the sister of Moses, who criticized her brother for marrying an Ethiopian woman, Sephora: "My sin, for it is a sin to hold one set of God's creatures so much inferior to the rest of creation simply because of the color of the skin, has found me out. Like Miriam of old, I have scorned the Ethiopian and the curse has fallen upon me, and I must dwell outside the tents of happiness forever" (281–82). Miriam was cast out from the community tents because God made her white with leprosy (Num. 12). And yet in Jewel's adaptation of Miriam's story, blackness becomes her "curse." There is no indication that she ever changes her opinion of her African heritage and experiences redemption. Cuthbert—and the novel's readers—learn of Jewel's death suddenly, by coming across her tombstone at the Enson plantation. But if Jewel's maternal redemption fails, her death prompts Cuthbert to see differently. Rather than attributing the sin and the need for forgiveness to Jewel, he arrives at the same conclusion as Hopkins: "the sin is the nation's" (283).

With the rediscovery of her daughter, Hagar's maternal identity is restored and her redemption is complete. Jewel's experience is not so positive, however. In her case, the novel shows the power of the National Father to impact her feelings about her mother, to the point that her race-based self-loathing precludes any possibility of redemption. Jewel's surprising death from Roman fever emphasizes the sentimental nature of her unresolved motherlessness. With this outcome, Hopkins complicates the national ideal of American exceptionalism by equating "father Abraham," the biblical originator of the chosen nation of Israel, with the immoral and unscrupulous St. Clair Enson as the novel's representative of the National Father. *Hagar's Daughter* alerts readers to the danger and reach of the National Father who has been the cause of the community's motherlessness.

CHAPTER THREE

"SOMETHIN'S GWINE HAPPEN"

National Warning in *Winona*

> People will never forget that my mother was an American Negress even if I forget.
>
> —*Winona*

FROM THE NATION'S CAPITAL, Pauline Hopkins moves to another site crucial to the nation's mythos and to the construction of American identity: the frontier. Hopkins may have begun to form her ideas about the possibilities of the West as she wrote *Hagar's Daughter,* where the West figured—albeit marginally—as a place of renewal and character building. In the West, Hagar finds the freedom to create a new identity, Zenas Bowen develops the character that made him stand out in Washington, and Jewel grows up experiencing the West as a place of wildness and freedom. Like Washington, D.C., or the colonial period that Hagar dreamed of, the West functions as a locus for one of the nation's founding myths of the American character which, according to Frederick Jackson Turner, formed on the frontier: a romanticized hybrid of civilized and savage, exhibiting coarseness, strength, inventiveness, inquisitiveness, restlessness, and individualism. Hopkins explores—and debunks—this idyllic notion of the West in *Winona,* demonstrating that it is the West's other legacy, a legacy of conquest and fraught race relations, which proves to be most formative for Winona, the novel's heroine.

Winona's main action occurs during the 1850s in the Kansas territory, a nascent region of the nation whose status as a free or slave state had yet to be determined. This setting allows Hopkins to take a close look at the volatile and ultimately violent national debate over the Kansas-Nebraska Act of 1854, one of the important stepping stones toward the Civil War. In this struggle the analogue for the National Father, the United States, is divided against itself as it fights for more slave territory, thus further entrenching its denial of the African American "child's" rights to national entitlement ostensibly available through identification with the Father. Like *Hagar's Daughter*—and serialized in the *Colored American Magazine* almost immediately after that novel[1]—*Winona* abounds with adventure, disguises, suspense, and romance. In the end, the villains get their comeuppance and the heroine gets her hero. But beneath the drama, danger, and happy ending, the novel raises questions about black women's status in the nation and condemns the violence of the National Father. As we saw in *Hagar's Daughter,* the power of the Father makes for extreme conditions of motherlessness and severely undermines the novel's hope for maternal redemption. Unresolved until just months before the start of the Civil War, the havoc over Kansas's statehood boded ill for the nation, and Hopkins treated it—along with Winona's story—as a portent of the impending disaster for the nation and potential good for the African American community, so long abused by the National Father. Reserving the novel's strongest representative of the African National Mother to the end, she lets the maternal Aunt Vinnie announce the promise of change: "somethin's gwine happen."

Motherless in the "Unfrien'ly World"

The novel begins in the wilds of Buffalo, New York, in the early 1850s with Judah and Winona, two children who live in the care of White Eagle, a man of mysterious origins. When White Eagle is murdered, Warren Maxwell, a British lawyer who has come to investigate White Eagle's background, volunteers to take the children back to England with him after he has finished some business in the southern states. Upon his return to Buffalo to collect the children, however, he learns that they have been identified as runaway slaves and, thanks to the recently passed Fugitive Slave Law, returned to a southern plantation. Two years later, Maxwell discovers the children on a plantation where he conducts business for an English client. He orchestrates their escape with help from the historical figure of John Brown and his "army." This association plunges Judah, Winona, and Maxwell into the violent history of "Bleeding Kansas," the battle between the proslavery settlers from Missouri and the free state settlers, or Free Soilers, who sought to establish the new territory as a free state. Against this violent backdrop, two important plot lines develop. Maxwell and Winona discover their love for one another, and Maxwell confirms the information he had come to investigate: that White Eagle had been the heir to an estate in England but, being framed for murder, fled to the United States. As we learn, the plantation owner and his overseer who enslaved Judah and Winona had committed the murder in England and then murdered White Eagle in Buffalo as part of a plan to inherit his fortune. With both those men now dead—casualties of the Kansas battle—Winona inherits the Carlingford estate. She, Judah, and Maxwell agree to leave the United States and make their home in England.

Winona opens with a complex treatment of motherlessness. In many ways, the mother's absence is palpable, starting with the appearance of Judah and Winona, two "helpless children" (337). Judah's mother died as she journeyed north with her young son to escape slavery. Winona's mother—"a handsome well-educated mulattress" and also a fugitive slave—died shortly after Winona's birth (290). The two motherless children grew up in the care of Winona's father (Judah's adopted father), White Eagle. Although we never see White Eagle directly, due to his murder early in the novel, all accounts declare him to be a kind man and a loving father. Unlike St. Clair in *Hagar's Daughter,* however, White Eagle cannot be read as a representative of the National Father in terms of a national oedipal narrative. According to the model at work in this study, the National Father represents the United States and the institutionalized racism that calls for the exclusion of African Americans from citizenship based on their identification with the African National Mother. White Eagle's national alliances connect him to England and to the marginalized population of American Indians, both of which have vexed relationships with the United States. As his name suggests, when he left England, he became part of a Native American community in Buffalo. He created a multiracial family for himself by marrying an escaped slave, having a child with her (Winona), and adopting another escaped slave (Judah). After the death of Winona's mother, Nokomis, an older Native American woman whom he had brought into his home as a housekeeper, served as caregiver for the children. He also settled in a community that the novel pointedly describes as racially mixed.

The western town of Buffalo in its 1850 setting features a "mixed community of Anglo-Saxons, Indians and Negroes" (287). The narrator indicates that such a community would trouble the modern world, which relies on clear divisions between the races. Hopkins had pointed out the nation's desire for such separations in *Hagar's Daughter,* where Hagar's years of successful passing gave the D.C. society pause. As the press commented about that case: "This story, showing, as it does, the ease with which beautiful half-breeds may enter our best society without detection, is a source of anxiety to the white citizens of our country" (266). *Winona* speculates further on that anxiety. If faced with the Buffalo found in *Winona,* "the world [would] stand aghast and try in vain to find the dividing line supposed to be a natural barrier between the whites and the dark-skinned race" (287). The novel's narrator ventriloquizes the voice of this opinion, referring to the mixing as "mischief" (287).[2] The "world" here seems a clear reference to the dominant white U.S. society, the National Father, whose laws—the "one drop rule," to name one example—exist to keep the racial "dividing line" intact and visible. Native Americans populate this region, people who even in the early twentieth century were associated with nature and widely classified as "uncivilized." And yet, the narrator pointedly ascribes to these Indians in Buffalo qualities readers would recognize as "civilized" according to the standards of a European American middle class. Unlike those who migrated farther west to the Black Hills "before the on-sweeping Anglo-Saxon," explains the narrator, Native Americans who remained in New York adopted Christianity, sent their children to white schools, and pursued farming and other "arts of civilized life," all the while "cultivating the friendship of the white population about them" (287). These forms of assimilation do not eradicate the ties to their culture, however; the Native Americans keep their traditional lifestyles, including their style of dress, allowing one to see at a glance the diverse quality of the region. "Negroes" also populate the area. Again, the narrator editorializes: the inhabitants of Erie County did not have such a "thirst for power" that they curtailed the liberty of others; "the free air of the land of the prairies was not polluted by the foul breath of slavery" (288).

If the peaceful cohabitation of race communities marks the sophistication and civilization of this region, the fluidity of racial identities extends that characterization. White Eagle, a British aristocrat by birth, identifies himself with Native Americans, who adopted him into their tribe. The tribe's chief, Red Eagle, gave him a Native American name, and White Eagle lives and practices medicine among them. As a result of their upbringing in this hybrid community and the influence of their Native American caregiver, Nokomis, Judah and Winona both exhibit a number of behaviors and traits that the novel stereotypically classifies as Native American. Judah ably handles canoes, tames wild horses, and stoically bears pain. Winona is called a "pretty squaw" and is assumed to have a taste for warfare (375, 405). And their longtime friend and protector, Ebenezer Maybee, a rough-spoken, western character, calls them "Injin-niggers," attributing to them, through derogatory epithets, a hybrid racial identity (311). The mixed population of Buffalo, its "shifting panorama" of people (288), and its liberal position on slavery, all mark it as an ideal place where Judah and Winona live in blissful ignorance of their supposed racial inferiority. The physical description of their home echoes its socially idyllic quality: "The transparent shadows, the sifted light that glimmered through the trees, the deer-paths winding through the woods, the green world still in its primal existence in this forgotten spot brought back the golden period unknown to the world living now in anxiety and toil" (291). The "primal" and "forgotten" quality of Judah and Winona's childhood home, recalling as it does an "unknown" "golden period," identify it as the pre-oedipal state in their national oedipal narrative, a state of close identification with their National Mother, broadly defined in the dark-skinned, friendly community they inhabit. In this way, White Eagle, the children's father, has given them a home that keeps them close to their Mother.

Clearly, White Eagle does not constitute the typical father of the oedipal narrative as this study has theorized it. He does not intervene between mother and children; rather, he participates in and fosters a community to which his children belong and with which they are encouraged to identify. His acceptance of the children's racial heritage and his own racial alliances exhibit as much fluidity and hybridity as the town of Buffalo. In this way, White Eagle functions as a representative of the National Mother, and Judah and Winona identify with him in this role almost completely. Indeed, in this early, pre-oedipal, portion of the novel, White Eagle so effectively fills the gap of motherlessness that Winona thinks only of him with apparently no glimmer of the longing for a lost mother that we have seen in Hopkins's earlier novels. At his death, she mourns, "I wanted no one else but papa, and now he is gone" (313).

Nevertheless, we do find a trace of Winona's deeply repressed identification with and longing for the Mother, not simply her representative. To see it, we must first note that in its efforts to show the mixing of the races—characteristic of Hopkins's lifetime commitment to the cause of "humanity" and her deep investment in the notion that all people are "of one blood"—the novel treats African and Native American identity collectively on several occasions.[3] Having first described the members of the Buffalo community by breaking them into three groups, "Anglo-Saxons, Indians and Negroes," the narrator goes on to explain that one has difficulty locating the supposed "natural barrier between the whites and the dark skinned race" (287). With the use of the singular "race" rather than "races," the narrator combines Indian and black identity as one "dark-skinned race." Following that pattern, on one occasion when Winona insists upon identifying with her caregiver and othermother,[4] the "dark-skinned" Native American Nokomis, we understand this as embedding a reference to her maternal, "dark-skinned" heritage. Nokomis has taught Winona traditional Native legends about flowers, which Winona adopts wholeheartedly. Such stories recall the marginalized, non-Western epistemologies associated with African heritage and represented by Madam Frances in *Contending Forces* (199) or Unc' Demus in *Hagar's Daughter* (40–41). Judah insists that Winona must give up her adherence to Nokomis's traditional knowledge and predicts that she will do so when she attends the Catholic school to which her father plans to send her: "In school you learn not to believe all the silly stories that we are told by the Indians" (292). Unwilling to abandon the maternal Nokomis's nontraditional epistemology, however, Winona expresses her plan to defy her father's wishes: "Papa cannot make me. I will not" (293).

At the start of the novel, then, Winona and Judah live in an idyllic community, "a primal life" where they have "not a thought of racial or social barriers" (376). They identify primarily with their father, but their father often represents the Mother. He has welcomed and encouraged their identification, so Judah and Winona believe themselves to be citizens entitled to full membership in their community and nation. They do not realize that the nation, on the whole, marginalizes their maternal heritage and bars them from the rights of citizenship on the basis of that heritage. They find themselves, therefore, on the cusp between the preoedipal relation with the Mother and the intrusion of the National Father that will thrust them into the world where they come to understand their motherless condition. Maybee articulates the difficulty of their situation: "White Eagle taught [Judah] to speak like a senator"; that is, he taught him to speak as a rights-bearing citizen capable of holding government office and entitled to that position. "Truth is," Maybee continues, "neither of them two forlorn critters realizes what 'bein' a nigger means; they have no idee of thar true position in this unfrien'ly world" (310). And he's right.

Colonel Titus and his overseer, Bill Thomson, represent the Father in Judah and Winona's oedipal narrative. Like White Eagle, they hale from England, but unlike White Eagle, they have wholeheartedly identified with the National Father of the United States, choosing to own and run a Missouri plantation worked by slaves. Their removal of the children from their "primal" home, then, figures as the Father's intrusion into Judah and Winona's relation with the Mother. Their move out of the civilized and racially fluid world of Buffalo into the slave-holding society of the southern United States marks their fuller induction into the paradoxical motherlessness that insists on their identification with the Mother of African heritage while robbing that maternal figure of power, thus giving them an abject national status. This transition, marking a crucial stage in the oedipal crisis, as we have seen, resembles that of the tragic mulatto, but in this case, the tragic quality of their transition arises not from the discovery of their racial heritage, but from the discovery of the nation's denigration of that heritage. Like the slave child who after the blissful ignorance of childhood discovers what it means to be a slave, Judah and Winona find out, in their new setting, their status through the Father represented by the nationally sanctioned institution of slavery and their masters, Colonel Titus and Bill Thomson.

At Magnolia Farm, the Missouri plantation, Thomson sets about re-educating Judah to understand his true position in the "unfrien'ly world." When, on one such occasion, Judah acts "without a shade of servility," forgetting "his position as a slave" and bearing himself, momentarily, "as a free man" (323), Thomson orders him whipped:

> "Now, Judah, this is a taste of wholesome discipline you're getting. You've got to be brung down. I'm going to do it if I have to have you whipped every month for a year. I'm goin' to break your spirit and teach you a nigger's place. . . . No more high-head carryin,' gentlemanly airs, and dictionary talk. . . .
>
> "You've got to learn to say 'massa.'" (328)

A white man wielding the phallic whip, Thomson stands as representative of the National Father and in that position gives Judah instruction. Judah must learn that, unlike White Eagle, the National Father will not allow him to speak like a senator. Indeed, he will attempt to strip Judah of the self-possession and confidence reserved for subjects who identify with the Father. Judah must learn that, as a colonial subject, he must identify with the Mother, but that the impoverished status of the African Mother in the United States offers none of the rights and privileges available to a white American citizen. As Thomson inscribes this lesson on Judah's back with the lash, Judah comes to understand his motherlessness.

Winona's motherlessness takes the form of childlike passivity and vulnerability. Readers notice early on that, for a title character, Winona has very little to say and engages in surprisingly little action. Following her removal, with Judah, from their ideal home of Buffalo to the slave state of Missouri, Winona's silence becomes more noticeable. When Maxwell discovers Judah and Winona after they have spent two years on the plantation, Judah approaches and speaks to Maxwell while Winona appears only once, silently doing her work, and quickly becoming "invisible" (333, 334–36). References to Winona primarily take the form of other characters' observations of her and actions upon her, as we see on the steamboat trip that was supposed to take Judah and Winona to the slave market but will turn out to be the means of their escape. The boat's "passengers were moved by [Winona's] beauty." She "bore herself like a young princess" and cast an "appealing glance" at Maxwell. But through it all, she remains silent (341, 342). In the escape scene, in spite of Maybee's claim that Winona has "the pluck of a man," she affects the role of inanimate cargo as Maxwell throws her overboard and Judah catches her (348, 344).

We understand Winona's silence and inaction as deriving from the vulnerable situation she finds herself in. Although Judah asserts that Titus and Thomson have "educated her to increase her value in the slave market," her virtual silence gives readers scant evidence of her education. When it comes to marketable traits, the novel most consistently highlights Winona's sexual attractiveness. The purpose of this trip, therefore, becomes clear: Winona is to be sold as a sexual commodity. In this context, the notion of Winona's "education" becomes sinister, as Judah's statement suggests: "If help does not come I have sworn to kill her before she shall become slavery's victim. It is impossible for me to put in words the fate of a beautiful female slave on these plantations; the torture of hell cannot surpass it" (335). It seems, then, that Winona's passivity and silence derive from the sexual vulnerability which in turn, as we will see, derives from her motherlessness.

Winona, who has "passed from childhood to womanhood in two years of captivity" (319–20), exhibits signs of awakening sexual desire, but this state is marked by idealism, indicating her naivety and vulnerability. The narrator describes Winona's attraction to her rescuer, William Maxwell, punctuating this description with language of danger: "Winona was only sixteen, and she was dreaming the first enchanted dream of youth. She did not attempt to analyze the dazzling happiness it was to once more meet and be remembered by the one object of the pure-hearted and passionate hero-worship of her childish soul; but in which, alas! for her lay the very seed of the woman's love, that must now too surely spring up into full life, forcing her presently to know it by its right name" (355). Like a lovesick school girl with thoughts marked by sentimental hyperbole, Winona appears to be oblivious to the danger the narrator alludes to with language of fear ("alas!") and violence ("forcing"). Moreover, Winona's dream causes her to pay little attention to the treacherous task at hand, namely her escape from slavery. Instead, she travels with her escape party "in a waking dream," thinking only of Maxwell (356). Typically a natural and special time in a young woman's development, Winona's first experience of love becomes dangerous for her because of her status as a slave. Her beauty, youth, and occasional frailty and helplessness combine to mark her as particularly vulnerable to sexual exploitation and abuse. The novel directs its readers to understand this aspect of Winona's character as a reflection of her motherlessness: "In the life she had led as a slave, this poor child had learned things from which the doting mother guards the tender maidenhood of her treasure with rigid care; so the girl thought of marriage or its form, with the utmost freedom" (356). A mother protects her daughter from sexual knowledge until she reaches the age at which such knowledge is appropriate. A motherlessness child, Winona has become knowledgeable about sex to the point that she thinks of marriage and "its form"—sex—equally. Even if she is not raped, she may make foolish and—according to the terms of domesticity and ideal womanhood in her day—morally wrong decisions that will impact her life negatively.[5]

Winona seems to comprehend her sexual vulnerability. An extreme sign of this awareness, she appears to have secured a promise from Judah to kill her if it appears that she will become "slavery's victim" (334).[6] Moreover, she notices and appreciates instances when she feels free from danger. After Maxwell has been injured and imprisoned, Winona assumes the disguise of a male nurse, Allen Pinks, in order to be near him and to provide him medical attention. Although this disguise serves the specific purpose of getting her into the jail, it has the added and unexpected benefit of providing her with a sense of security she has not experienced as a woman. She feels "purely and proudly glad" in her assumed male identity (404), and her sense of safety enables her to speak frequently and with confidence. On one occasion, when the loud voices of other prisoners threaten to disturb Maxwell's sleep, she tells them to be quiet "in a low tone of authority" (387), a departure from her typical behavior. She also uses her assumed male identity to express physical affection by kissing Maxwell on the cheek without the risk that the physical encounter will go any further. The safety afforded her by an assumed male identity empowers her to act and to speak with confidence.

Winona further registers her motherlessness by seeking a return to the womb. During her escape from slavery, she slips away from the group to find a setting that will replicate her pre-oedipal home, where "the woods calmed her" and she heard "their whisper of a secret that has lasted from the foundation of the world" (376), the secret, perhaps, of a life-giving force, of the "desire of the mother [which] is the origin of everything" (Lacan 283). Motivated by instinct, Winona locates and retreats to a womblike space in the natural setting: "Some impulse of the wild things among whom she had lived drove her to a hole in under [*sic*] the bluff. It was necessary to descend to find it. Presently she was in a tunnel which led into a cavern. She made herself a divan of dried moss and flung herself down at full length to think. . . . She had come upon the eternal now as she lay in a sweet stupor until forced to arouse herself" (375–76). Winona discovers a hidden opening and vaginal tunnel leading to a womb-like cavern, where she enjoys a "sweet stupor" and the "eternal now"—an almost fetal consciousness. The imagery in this scene indicates her success in finding a return to the Mother whose absence she has felt since leaving her pre-oedipal home in Buffalo. This figurative womb in nature does not, of course, return Winona to her Mother nor does it address her sexual vulnerability. Judah reinscribes her motherlessness with romantic overtures that make explicit her womanhood and sexuality. He looks for her in the woods, "watch[ing] her with hungry eyes" (377), with the plan of declaring his love for her. Winona attempts to distance herself from sexuality by affecting the demeanor of a child, sitting on a rock, "folding her arms across her knees, [and laying] her forehead against them" (378). Nevertheless, she cannot avoid the fact of her womanhood, a fact that emphasizes her sexuality and heightens her vulnerability as a motherless child.

Bleeding Kansas and the Barbaric Nation

Winona offers a critique, not of the "unfriend'ly world," but of the unfriendly nation that enforces Judah and Winona's motherlessness by prohibiting their identification with the Father and thereby restricting access to citizenship in the nation while forcing their identification with a literally absent Mother who signifies marginalization and abjection. The critique resides in a two-pronged argument that develops over the course of the novel. The first part of this argument resembles the critique Hopkins instantiates in *Hagar's Daughter,* that the immoral character of the capital—embodied by St. Clair as the representative of the National Father—causes the nation's devolution. Here, instead of sexual immorality and excess, Hopkins points to the violence practiced by the Missouri settlers in Kansas that runs counter to accepted ideas about civilization and marks the nation as barbaric and immoral. In response to that immorality, the second part of the argument draws on the American tradition of the jeremiad. Hopkins casts the violence enacted in Kansas by John Brown and the Free Soilers as a justified response to the Missouri settlers. In *Winona,* Bleeding Kansas reads as a holy war, fought between virtuous and evil men, in which the stakes are not only Judah's and Winona's fates, but the fate of the nation.

Hopkins deliberately chooses the fraught period following the passage of the Kansas-Nebraska Act as the setting for *Winona.* Passed in 1854, the Kansas-Nebraska Act divided the Nebraska territory into two parts, repealing the Missouri Compromise of 1820, which had barred slavery in the Great Plains territories, and allowing Kansas and Nebraska to decide by popular vote whether they would be free or slave states.[7] There seemed little risk that the northern territory of Nebraska would opt for slavery, but the Kansas territory was up for grabs, inspiring a frenzy of attempts at control from both North and South. Eli Thayer of Massachusetts organized the New England Emigrant Aid Society, calling on New Englanders to settle the Kansas territory as a means of controlling the November 1854 vote that would determine the future of the state. Many heeded that call.[8] Southerners—largely from the neighboring state of Missouri and known as the "Border Ruffians"—responded by flooding into Kansas to participate in the impending vote.[9] The southerners' plan succeeded, and the election went to the proslavery contingent, who quickly established a proslavery legislature. At the March 1855 vote to select delegates to the new legislature, Missourians again swarmed the polls, "armed," historian Elizabeth R. Varon explains, "marching to drumbeats in virtual battalions," and ultimately intimidating many Free Soilers, thus preventing them from voting. Territorial governor Andrew

Reeder denounced the vote as fraudulent and called for new elections in a number of districts. While proslavery Missourians ignored the new results, Free Soilers formed their own government, holding a constitutional convention in Topeka in October 1855 (Varon 260). The federal government, represented by proslavery president Franklin Pierce, "denounced the Topeka movement as treasonable and threatened military intervention to keep order" (266). Considerable violence accompanied these events, primarily on the part of proslavery men, who tarred and feathered, kidnapped, and killed Free Soilers. May 1856 brought "the sack of Lawrence," in which a group of proslavery men stormed the town of Lawrence, destroying newspaper offices, businesses, and homes, including that of the free-state governor (266).

Hopkins's historical romance foregrounds this fight for the Kansas territory, situating most of the novel's action in May 1856. After the murder of White Eagle and the capture of Winona and Judah, the young people find themselves in Missouri, slaves on a plantation overseen by Bill Thomson, a fictional leader of the proslavery efforts in Kansas. Judah and Winona's friend from Buffalo, Ebenezer Maybee, has answered Eli Thayer's call to stake a homesteader's claim in Kansas, only to have his house burned down and his cattle driven off by proslavery vigilantes. He recounts for Warren Maxwell a number of brutal attacks on Free Soilers, including the "sackin' o' Oswatamie [*sic*]" (338).[10] After Maxwell and Maybee help Judah and Winona escape from Magnolia Farm, they all join forces with John Brown and his company in exchange for aid in Judah and Winona's escape, a twist of plot that allows Hopkins to offer an up-close depiction of this national event.

Whereas *Hagar's Daughter* castigates the National Father's sexual immorality and failure of sexual self-control, *Winona* focuses on another failure in self-control: the failure to control violence. Depicting the violence of the Border Ruffians, Hopkins again highlights the failure of the nation—and the National Father—as an exemplar of civilization and progress. She emphasizes the barbarity of the proslavery forces' violence by linking it to lynching, a topic receiving much attention in the press at the time of *Winona*'s publication. With this link she supports the assertion she had made in the preface to *Contending Forces*, that "mob-law is nothing new" (14). More, it allows her to deploy a successful rhetorical strategy she may have learned from Ida B. Wells's anti-lynching campaign in the 1890s.[11]

According to Gail Bederman, Wells effectively reworked common rhetoric that constructed white Americans as civilized and self-controlled. The press deployed this rhetoric routinely in the justification of lynching, pitting the manly and self-controlled white man against the savage black man who could not control his sexual passions. By this logic, lynching black men—accused of raping white women in increasing numbers from 1880 into the twentieth century[12]—became the duty of civilized whites, "paragons of disciplined, self-restrained manliness" who did their work with moderation and self control (Bederman 50). For example, according to the *Providence Journal*'s description of an 1893 Louisiana lynching, "three Negroes were lynched in a quiet, determined manner by a mob of white men on Friday night. . . . The lynching was one of the coolest that has taken place in this section" (qtd. in Bederman 50–51). Such reporting cast brutally violent events as duty calmly carried out by the superior race, transforming the white mob into "manly defenders of civilized values" (Bederman 51).

Ida B. Wells, however, dismantled the familiar rhetorical link between white masculinity and civilization. In her 1893 and 1894 tours of England, Wells cast her argument as an "appeal from one civilized race to another for protection from violent white barbarians" (Bederman 60). She characterized lynching as an uncivilized abomination in which victims were sentenced, tortured, and killed without a trial. "By refusing to try accused African Americans in a court of law," Bederman explains, "and by engaging in the most horrific of tortures, lynch mobs and the Americans who tolerated them exposed themselves as unmanly barbarians" (61). The success of Wells's strategy became clear in the British press, which endorsed her condemnation of American violence against blacks as animalistic. The *Birmingham Daily Gazette* pointedly remarked, "The American citizen in the South is at heart more a barbarian than the negro whom he regards as a savage. . . . Either [Americans] mistrust their legal institutions or they murder in wantonness and for mere lust of blood" (qtd. in Bederman 67). *Winona* evokes these British opinions through the voice of Warren Maxwell, the British lawyer who comes to the United States to settle an estate matter and gets caught up in Judah and Winona's plight.

Hopkins's inclusion of a British character pointedly recalls Wells's successful work. As Maxwell becomes intimately acquainted with the situation in the South, the narrator repeatedly describes his dismay: "What a travesty the American government was on the noblest principles! Bah! it made him heartsick" (381).

The novel characterizes the violence enacted in Bleeding Kansas as a "lust for blood" to be found at the base of human nature, controlled only by the forces of civilization or, in Freudian terms, by the development of the superego. In this, Hopkins anticipated psychologist William James's 1903 critique of lynching, in which he describes the behavior of fanatics in a lynching crowd as "a kind of 'reversion,' which civilization particularly requires to extirpate" (172).[13] Even the kind-hearted Ebenezer Maybee notices a proclivity toward violence in himself and insightfully expounds upon its source: "It beats all nature how fightin' jes' grows on a man once he's had a taste. Mr. Maxwell, do you know anythin' about the transfiguration of souls that some college fellars advocates? Dad gum it, I believe mos' of us must have been brutes once" (338). A white American himself, Maybee functions as a reliable spokesperson for the flaws of the nation and of the white man's psyche. He shows himself to be, at least in some measure, civilized in his ability to recognize and rise above his "brute" desire for violence.

The violence of this period reached beyond Bleeding Kansas to the nation's capital with one rather startling event. In May 1856, Charles Sumner—an abolitionist senator from Massachusetts and possibly the source for the name of Cuthbert Sumner in *Hagar's Daughter*—became a victim of violence.[14] Sumner delivered in the Senate a powerful speech, "The Crime against Kansas," in which he accused proslavery senator Andrew Butler of South Carolina of choosing as his "mistress" the "harlot, Slavery." In retaliation, Butler's nephew, Congressman Preston Brooks, found Sumner in the Senate chamber after it had emptied and attacked him at his desk, beating him some thirty times with a cane and leaving him bleeding and unconscious (Varon 268–71). In a lithograph depicting the event shortly after its occurrence, *Southern Chivalry—Argument Versus Clubs,* artist John L. Magee shows the northern Sumner wielding a pen in defense against Brooks's far more threatening cane, indicating the brute efforts of the South in comparison to the civilized—educated, peaceful—efforts of the North.

Southern Chivalry—Argument versus Clubs, lithograph by John L. Magee, 1856
The Library Company of Philadelphia

Although Hopkins does not refer directly to this event in the novel, she draws an oblique line from it to *Winona.* Colonel Titus, the murderer of White Eagle, the captor of Judah and Winona, and a strong advocate of Kansas's becoming a slave state, makes an aggressive speech for this cause, charging his listeners to identify any abolitionists they can find "and exterminate them" (316). Hopkins took Titus's speech from an address made by Border Ranger Benjamin Stringfellow and quoted by Sumner in the speech that prompted Preston Brooks's attack.[15] It is not surprising that Hopkins would use this event to neatly make her case for the South's uncontrolled violence. The occurrence of such an event in the Senate chamber extends the attribution of violence beyond Kansas, and allows the reader to understand Hopkins's critique of barbarism as indicative of the national character.

Winona repeatedly and pointedly contrasts the civilized and moderate behavior of abolitionists and Free Soilers to the bloodthirsty violence of the Border Ruffians from Missouri. For example, we learn of one woman who gave the details of the Osawatomie battle to her family and the Massachusetts newspapers. To punish her and make her a warning to others, the Ruffians tied her by her tongue to a tree and left her to die. Drawing on the familiar stereotype of Native Americans as uncivilized, the novel compares Bill Thomson's tactics with those used by the "savage" Indians. Maybee explains that Thomson requires his men to "carry hatchets so as to skulp the foe like Injuns do" (339). When Thomson and his men capture Maxwell and bring him to Missouri, the mob takes over, demanding the opportunity to beat, hang, and burn Maxwell, tactics that readers would undoubtedly recognize and deplore for their similarity to lynching. Indeed, speaking directly to her contemporary reader, the narrator seems to refer specifically to the phenomenon of lynching: "They who speak or think lightly of a mob have never heard its voice nor seen its horrible work" (368). Faced with the opportunity for violence, the crowd devolves into a pack of animals, a "bestial party" (343):

> It was not the voices of human beings, but more like the cries of wild animals, the screaming of enraged hyenas, the snarling of tigers, the angry, inarticulate cries of thousands of wild beasts in infuriated pursuit of their prey, yet with a something in it more sinister and blood curdling, for they were men, and added a human ferocity.
>
> On they rushed . . . , eyes aflame, faces distorted, the brute latent in every human being coming out from his lair to blot out the man, the awful cries, waning, waxing. (367–68)

Here, the white Ruffians exhibit the regression that had been expected of African Americans after emancipation when they were no longer under the supervision and control of whites.[16] *Winona* counters this theory. In stark contrast to the animalistic and retrogressive violence of the white Border Ruffians, Judah practices the restrained "manliness of self-defense" (374). As we saw in the previous chapter, in nineteenth-century usage, the term "manly" "referred to traits which civilized men had, [while] 'masculine' referred to traits which savage men and civilized men both possessed" (Bederman 253n24). The novel characterizes Judah's actions as civilized—indeed, he feels "the sheer repulsion from . . . butchery" (423)—while the Ruffians and proslavery southerners appear increasingly barbaric.

With its discussion of "savagery" and "civilization" in the West, *Winona* invokes Frederick Jackson Turner's famous report delivered ten years prior to the novel's publication, which declared the West and the frontier to be the site of the formation of the true American character. Turner describes a cycle of regressing and advancing civilization—"perennial rebirth"—as the frontiersman approaches and crosses the line of the frontier, the "meeting point between savagery and civilization" (32). Here, he argues, the civilized easterner meets with primitive conditions on the frontier, a setting inhabited and tended—if minimally—by the uncivilized Native tribes. This wilderness transforms the easterner: "It strips off the garments of civilization and arrays him in the hunting shirt and the moccasin. It puts him in the log cabin of the Cherokee and Iroquois. . . . Before long he has gone to planting Indian corn and plowing with a sharp stick; he shouts the war cry and takes the scalp in orthodox Indian fashion" (33). The influence runs both ways, however, and eventually the easterner transforms the frontier, but not entirely. Remnants of the wilderness—the wild—remain.

Hopkins reflects this thesis to some extent in her portrayal of Buffalo's hybrid condition. The Indians show the effects of European influences in the form of Anglo religion and education, while Europeans like White Eagle, and by extension Winona and Judah, have adopted the dress and lifestyle of Native Americans. Hopkins acknowledges and works within the categories of "civilized" and "savage," describing the Indians' adoption of Anglo habits as a move toward "civilized life" (287).[17] Although it focuses on cultural rather than biological hybridization, Turner's thesis resonates with theories of amalgamation voiced by African American intellectuals in Hopkins's day and adopted to some extent by Hopkins herself. As one example, Charles Chesnutt's 1900 "The Future American" posits racial mixing as the solution to the race problem: "If it is only by becoming white that colored people and their children are to enjoy the rights and dignities of citizenship, they will have every incentive to 'lighten the breed' that they might claim the white man's privileges as soon as possible" (qtd. in Wallinger 126). Placing racism in the context of its nationalist implications, Chesnutt identifies the conflicts inherent in barring African Americans from identification with the National Father, and he argues that racial mixing offers the solution. If distinct racial divisions constitute the grounds for racism, the elimination of those divisions through amalgamation would, in theory, end racism.

Hopkins did not unreservedly adopt Chesnutt's theory of amalgamation as a remedy for the injustices experienced by the African American community. She makes a number of references to the effects of racial mixing, especially in *Contending Forces,* but she tempers her optimism for its benefits with concerns over the quality of blood to be mixed. Employing popular theories of evolution, she imagines positive outcomes in cases where the "best" blood is added to the black race:

> Man has said that from lack of means and social caste the Negro shall remain in a position of serfdom all his days, but the mighty working of cause and effect, the mighty unexpected results of the law of evolution, seem to point to a different solution of the Negro question than any worked out by the most fertile brain of the highly cultured Caucasian. Then again, we do not allow for the infusion of white blood, which became pretty generally distributed in the inferior black race during the existence of slavery. Some of this blood, too, was the best in the country. (87)

Mixing the "best [blood] in the country" with the blood of African Americans can remedy what Hopkins seems to accept as a tendency among African Americans toward poverty and a permanent ranking among the working classes. However, Hopkins also anticipates negative consequences of amalgamation when the added blood is of poor quality. For example, in *Contending Forces* Hopkins attributes John Langley's selfishness and disloyalty to just such an infusion of inadequate blood: "Natural instinct for good had been perverted by a mixture of 'cracker' blood of the lowest type on his father's side. . . . This blood . . . vitiated his moral nature and left it stranded high and dry on the shore of blind ignorance, and there he seemed content to dwell, supinely self-satisfied with the narrow boundary of the horizon of his mental vision" (221). Here Hopkins credits African American blood with a lofty moral nature which, in Langley, has been tarnished by "cracker" blood. The notion that "low" blood can compromise the "best" blood returns us, oddly, to Turner's thesis, which posits that "civilization" and "wilderness" blend as part of the "perennial rebirth" of the easterner on the frontier. For the most part, Hopkins accepts the argument that the mixing of races—either biologically or culturally—strengthens the human race, building understanding and community among diverse people. Her depiction of Buffalo at the beginning of the novel, as we have seen, reads as an application of Turner's thesis to the nation's race problem and posits the superiority of such a community.[18]

Turner's celebratory description of "rebirth" on the frontier and its resulting American character, however, downplays the violence that typically occurs in the encounters he describes. With its treatment of the violence of Bleeding Kansas, *Winona* challenges this lacuna in Turner's thesis much as historian Patricia Limerick would do in her study, *The Legacy of Conquest: The Unbroken Past of the American West.* According to Limerick, the frontier's significance lies not in its status as the site of the nation's developing character but rather in its legacy of conquest so central to the American West. While Turner's study deemphasizes conquest in the evolution of the American character, Limirick argues that conquest is the real story of interest. "Conquest," she asserts, "forms the historical bedrock of the whole nation, and the American West is a preeminent case study in conquest and its consequences" (27–28). Richard Slotkin, author of *Gunfighter Nation: The Myth of the Frontier in Twentieth-Century America,* agrees. Violence, he posits, has been "the means to our achievement of a national identity, a democratic polity, an ever-expanding economy, and a phenomenally dynamic and 'progressive' civilization" (10). So, according to Limirick and Slotkin, violence has been a cornerstone of the national identity, the character of the National Father. Furthermore, and important for our purposes, the conquest central to the American West has been, largely, racially motivated conquest. As Slotkin explains, "The Anglo-American colonies grew by displacing Amerindian societies and enslaving Africans to advance the fortunes of White colonists. As a result, the 'savage war' became a characteristic episode of each phase of westward expansion" (11). Certainly, as a fight over the slave status of the new territory, Bleeding Kansas constitutes the type of "savage war" Slotkin describes. Hopkins casts this battle as, in Turner's words, a "meeting point between savagery and civilization" (32), but turning that binary on its head, she portrays the Euro American proslavery fighters as savage and the Free Soilers—composed largely of advocates for African Americans—as civilized.[19]

Hopkins's treatment of this episode in U.S. history functions as a meditation on the character of the nation, and ultimately, the character of the National Father. If the violence of the West were responsible for the building of national character, the novel seems to ask, what kind of national character did this violence build? *Winona* answers this question in several ways. First, it is a nation that prohibits free speech. With the establishment of the proslavery government in Kansas, legislators passed "a series of deliberately provocative laws that made it a felony to criticize slavery" (Varon 261). The novel refers to this silencing as Maybee sarcastically warns Maxwell not to speak his abolitionist opinions too loudly, sarcastically referring to a freedom the nation proudly claims: "Them's dang'rous opinions to hold onto in free Ameriky" (337), he warns. The story of the woman who was murdered for telling her story serves as one example. Again sarcastically, Maybee opines, "Them's our leetle ways o' doin' things in free Ameriky. . . when other folks talks too free or dares to have opinions o' thar own without askin' our permission to so think contrairy agin us" (337–39). As we saw in *Hagar's Daughter, Winona*'s white characters offer their critique of the nation and thus question the value of citizenship in that nation. Maybee exclaims, "I never befo' felt ashamed of bein' an American citizen" (314). And Parson Steward, a minister in Kansas who fights with John Brown's troops, declares, "I hate the laws that make this country a nursery for slavery" (351). By holding up John Brown, who would eventually be convicted of treason, as more truly American—"more in-dependent-like" (339)—than those approved by the nation's president, *Winona*'s white characters provide a damning "self-impeachment" of the nation.[20]

As a second answer to the question of what type of national character developed through violence, Hopkins shows that this nation not only limits free speech, but it also transforms the law from a tool of justice into a tool of corruption and violence. When the Missouri Rangers capture Maxwell, they invoke the law to justify their treatment of him: "In the fus' place you are found' guilty of associatin' with northern abolitionists; . . . the law mus' take its course" (364). As in *Contending Forces,* Hopkins demonstrates how the law—the Law of the Father—can be invoked to condone actions that maintain racial hierarchy. Here, the Border Ruffians manipulate the law to punish and eliminate one who tries to thwart their efforts in Kansas. They hold a mock trial for Maxwell in which only one side tells its story and the jury makes its decision in a matter of moments without leaving the room (382–83). Such a perversion of the law further demonstrates the nation's corruption and failure according to its own ideals of freedom. The abdication of national ideals—not only by the nation's president who sides with the Ruffians but by the proslavery forces more generally who deny freedoms and use excessive, barbaric violence—solidifies the novel's portrayal of an inadequate National Father.

"A Holy War"

Of course, the violence in Kansas was not one-sided; the Free Soilers and abolitionists did their share of fighting and killing. John Brown engaged in very violent tactics, most notoriously in his brutal slaughter of five people at Pottawatomie. Hopkins uses the trope of the holy war to justify Brown's violence. Thus, where the novel depicts the South's violence as barbaric, it casts the violence of the northerners as the "manliness of self-defense" (374), necessary retaliation in a holy war. Drawing on the literary tradition of the jeremiad, *Winona* becomes a story of the battle fought between good and evil.

Hopkins took her cue from history as she cast the violence in Kansas in religious terms. In 1854, three thousand clergymen from the North signed a petition against the passage of the Kansas-Nebraska Bill, which stated that by considering this bill, "Congress had exposed the 'beloved Union' to the 'righteous judgments of the almighty.'" In 1856, George Thacher delivered an antislavery sermon in which he asserted that efforts to make Kansas a slave state were akin to "joining forces with Satan to fight against God" (Varon 256, 252). And Henry Ward Beecher, the well-known minister, provided rifles for the New England settlers to Kansas, weapons that came to be known as "Beecher's Bibles," underscoring the perceived holiness of the mission.[21]

So, in addition to characterizing southerners in evolutionary terms as barbaric and uncivilized, the novel depicts them in moral terms as evil, the allies of Satan in a holy war. Bill Thomson, the leader of the Kickapoo Rangers, resembles Satan—the "Foul Fiend himself"—with his "devilish face" and his direction set for "Hell" (322, 362).[22] Angry at Judah's ability to tame a horse he himself could not manage, Thomson wears "an evil look distorting his face into a grin of malice and fury" (326). Moreover, he surrounds himself with equally devilish characters. The men who capture Maxwell are "a motley crowd of Southern desperadoes, men who stopped at nothing in the line of murder and rapine" (362), and the Missouri mob that calls for Maxwell's hanging is no better. Their faces become "distorted like demons with evil passions" (367). Thomson's co-conspirator, Colonel Titus, shares in Thomson's evil deeds. Together they killed Winona's father and, prior to the action of the novel, his brother as a means of gaining his inheritance. Colonel Titus recognizes his deeds and "sin" and recalls with fear the biblical text that decreed that "evil deeds shall be visited upon the progeny of the doer unto the third and fourth generations" (318).[23]

In contrast, the novel depicts the Kansas settlers and abolitionists as religious and righteous. Maxwell describes them as "rough but kindly" folks who live by the biblical injunction to love one another (352). With this characterization, the novel lays claim to American exceptionalism and uses a model practiced in Puritan texts of interpreting events as part of their spiritual journey and signs of their election.[24] Maybee offers a prayer for a thunderstorm to cover their escape: "O Lord, ef we'd only get such a thunder storm as we had the night White Eagle was murdered, it'd be the makin' of this expe—dition [*sic*]. It's been threat'ning all afternoon. Lord, let her come" (341). When the storm appears as requested, the narrator editorializes: "Surely God was with them" (344).[25] Parson Steward exhibits "holy wrath" (350) straight out of the Old Testament, and he punctuates their battle with shouts of biblical language: "'Behold, the uncircumcised Philistine,' he cries as he fights; "how he defies the armies of the living God'" (412).

Perhaps the most glaring rhetorical strategy for casting Bleeding Kansas as a holy war resides in the likening of Maxwell's captivity, torture, and near execution to the crucifixion of Christ. In references far from subtle, Thomson divides Maxwell's clothes among his men and then subjects him to the collective will of a rabid crowd who beats him and demands that he be taken to the "cross-roads" where they will execute him (362, 367). And in case her readers have missed her cues, Hopkins announces, "There came to [Maxwell] then a realizing sense of all the Immortal Son must have suffered on His way to Golgotha" (369).

In her depiction of this holy war, Hopkins may have found something of a challenge in John Brown's portrayal. Brown orchestrated the attacks that came to be known as the Pottawatomie Massacre. Frustrated by the nonviolent abolitionism of the free staters, he organized an attack in which he and his men called several proslavery men out of their homes during the night and killed them (Etcheson 107–11).[26] In an effort, perhaps, to make John Brown's history more palatable, Hopkins rewrites this event in *Winona,* transforming Brown's victims into prisoners of battle who have already committed atrocities against the free staters. With this change, Brown's execution becomes retribution, in the spirit of "an eye for an eye." And while Brown originally intends to execute all the prisoners, Maxwell persuades him to release "most of them" (423). In this retelling, Brown's massacre becomes justified and even somewhat merciful. Hopkins distances her readers from the violence. The scene is not dramatized; instead, Maybee, Maxwell, Winona, and Judah hear from a distance "the crack of rifles . . . that carried death to the last of the captured Rangers." The narrator's comment evokes Judgment Day in keeping with the portrayal of Bleeding Kansas as a holy war: "Guilty soul joined guilty soul in their flight to Eternity" (429).[27]

If Hopkins sought to soften Brown's violence in her portrayal of him, she was not alone. Many hailed him as a hero and—after his hanging for the Harpers Ferry insurrection—a martyr.[28] Hopkins's portrayal of Brown follows this trend. In contrast to the barbaric and evil forces of the South, Brown leads the holy war, guided by "deep religious convictions," convictions evident in the statement credited to him prior to his death: "I am about God's work; He will take care of me" (373–74). Already established via Maybee's testimony as more truly American than representatives of the National Father in his respect for individual rights and independence, Brown emerges as a benevolent parent figure, a poignant contrast to the violent Father Nation supporting the Missouri Ruffians. The Brown camp, where Judah and Winona stop during their escape to Canada, recalls the Quaker settlement that serves as a utopian stopping point for Eliza and George in *Uncle Tom's Cabin.* Like the maternal Rachel who reigns with love over her family, Brown appears as a gentle patriarch: "In the Brown camp the great family of fugitives dwelt together in guileless and trusting brotherhood" (373).[29] His camp resembles a family, and under his guidance, "one soul of harmony and love was infused into each individual dweller" (373). His "gentleness and self renunciation" inspire the love and respect of those around him (374). Countering any perception of Brown as a perpetrator of unnecessary violence, Hopkins marks him as an agent of peace in *Winona*. When Judah has Bill Thomson—whom he believes murdered White Eagle—in his power and prepares to kill him, it is Brown who urges Judah to "spare him!" (393).

The depiction of Brown as peaceful and gentle is not entirely a product of Hopkins's wishful thinking; it comports with at least one popular portrayal of him in the press following his death. John Greenleaf Whittier, whom Hopkins revered and paid tribute to as "the friend of the negro" in an essay by that name in the *Colored American Magazine*, immortalized Brown's gentle nature in a poem published in the New York *Independent* on December 22, 1859, just weeks after Brown's hanging. Whittier's "Brown of Ossawatomie" dramatized a fabled event in which, on his way to the gallows, Brown was greeted by a slave woman with her child:

> John Brown of Ossawatomie, they led him out to die;
> And lo! a poor slave-mother with her little child pressed nigh,
> Then the bold, blue eye grew tender, and the harsh face grew mild,
> And he stooped between the jeering ranks and kissed the Negro's child!
> (lines 5–8)

This event, erroneously reported in the New York *Tribune*, became widely accepted as fact, thanks in part to Whittier's poem.[30] It went on to be immortalized in numerous illustrations, including one by Louis L. Ransom in 1860, which was copied by Currier and Ives in 1863 and published in such high-circulation periodicals as the *Atlantic Monthly* and *Harper's Weekly*.[31] One rendition of the scene served as an illustration/frontispiece for Whittier's 1866 collection of poems, *National Lyrics*.

Thomas S. Noble's 1867 painting, titled *John Brown's Blessing*, depicting Brown with his hand on the head of the child, supported explicitly Hopkins's depiction of Brown as a holy man and a leader in a holy war.

Brown of Osawatomie, unsigned woodcut in John Greenleaf Whittier's *National Lyrics,* 1865

All of these illustrations draw upon the iconic figure of the African American mother with child, a representation of the African American community for whom Brown fought and an image that would undoubtedly have resonated with Hopkins. The association of Brown with the slave mother and, by extension, with the National Mother to the motherless child, supports Hopkins's portrayal of the holy war and righteous mission of the abolitionists. More, it links this holy war to her broader project of denouncing the nation's rejection of the African National Mother and her children and offering maternal redemption as the hope for the African American community's motherlessness.

John Brown's Blessing, by Thomas S. Noble, 1867,
oil on canvas, accession no. 1939.250
Collection of The New-York Historical Society

Hopkins buttresses her portrayal of Bleeding Kansas as a holy war with the fitting literary trope of the jeremiad. As we saw in the previous chapter, the jeremiad measured a community against a standard for moral or spiritual behavior and, finding it wanting, delivered grave warnings of future destruction. The jeremiad had been deployed before in polemic writings by African Americans. Frederick Douglass offered severe warnings to the audience of his Fourth of July speech; Nat Turner drew his sermons most often from the "Scriptures of prophecy and apocalypse" and typically blended the prophetic with the language of revolution

(Douglass, "Meaning of July Fourth" 201; Sundquist 58). Hopkins draws on this tradition in *Winona* as several characters issue warnings or interpret events as God's retribution for evil deeds. Maxwell cautions, "Your government cannot long survive under a system that thrusts free-born people into slavery as were those helpless children" (337), and Colonel Titus interprets his daughter's handicap as punishment for his sins (318). Most dramatically, Parson Steward hails Judah as a prophet when, as if under the influence of a prophetic vision, he warns of the impending Civil War as the punishment of God:

> "The storm," said Judah with wild exultation in his voice, "the storm is but gathering force. These bloody happenings which are convulsing Missouri and Kansas are but the preliminary happenings to a glorious struggle which will end in the breaking of every chain that binds human beings to servitude in this country."
>
> Warren regarded him in astonishment.
>
> "Why do you think so, Judah?"
>
> "I cannot tell. But I feel that the sin will be punished in a great outpouring of blood and treasure until God says it is enough. The day of deliverance of the Negro is at hand." (351–52)

Taking this prophecy further, the narrator—speaking from the vantage point of the early twentieth century—declares that the punishment of the Civil War was not "enough." She expresses her own warning, which extends the prophecy to the racism of the twentieth century and the violence of lynching that the novel evokes with its description of the mob's barbaric behavior: "The liberties of a people are not to be violated but with the wrath of God. Indeed, we tremble for our country when we reflect that God is just; that His justice cannot sleep forever; that considering natural means only, a revolution of the wheel of Fortune, an exchange of situation is among the possibilities" (385–86). The prophetic warnings lend an ominous tone to the novel's conclusion, as did Cuthbert Sumner's recognition that the nation's sin laid the foundation for Jewel's death in *Hagar's Daughter.* Although Winona and Judah successfully escape slavery, leave the scene of violence unhurt, and travel to England, where they will no longer suffer the threat of slavery and racism, the novel leaves the reader with no doubt that they are still motherless.

Motherless Child . . . Still

Winona's multiple observations of the barbarity that characterizes the National Father effectively convince her to abandon any hope of identifying with that Father as well as any desire for that identification. However, separated from her pre-oedipal home and community, as well as from her father and Nokomis, the only people who raised the possibility of identifying with the Mother and her African heritage in any way, Winona has not developed a connection with the Mother either, even if she has sought that connection by returning to a figurative womb. She expresses her feelings of national alienation to Warren Maxwell: "'Which is my country, I wonder? Judah says that he will not fight for the Stars and Stripes if war comes—the flag that makes the Negro a slave. This country mine? No, no! The fearful things that I have seen—' she broke off abruptly. 'My father's country shall be mine'" (406). Winona actively rejects the United States, but she neither considers nor even acknowledges her African heritage as a possibility. She declares with apparent confidence and certainty that she will identify with England, a national heritage she received from White Eagle. Her choice seems to be less about her father, however, than it is about her romantic attraction to Warren Maxwell. Just moments earlier in the same conversation, she makes a far less adamant statement about her father's nationality to Maxwell: "Oh, your country! Do you know, I believe my dear papa was of the same?" (405). Winona declares her national alliance, therefore, only after she recalls Maxwell's nation—"Oh, your country!" she says, as if the fact has just occurred to her. Similarly, her failure to think of her maternal heritage follows closely on her experience of fear that Maxwell scorns that heritage: "His reply fell upon her ear like a reproach—a reflection upon her Negro origin" (405). In response, perhaps, she determines to forget the "condition of the mother" and worries that others will not do the same: "People will never forget that my mother was an American Negress even if I forget" (407).

Even had she hoped to link herself to her maternal heritage, she would have had scant support. By the conclusion of the novel, Winona's mother, if not forgotten, has been effectively erased. With the end of the fighting in Kansas, Winona and Judah return to Buffalo, where Maybee produces papers given to him by White Eagle and intended for Winona. These papers provide official documentation of her relation to White Eagle and ensure her inheritance of the Carlingford estate in England. They also confirm Winona's motherlessness. Apart from a briefly mentioned "certificate of marriage," White Eagle's papers comprise only documents that tell his story: "a record of happenings after the fugitive from justice had arrived in America . . . ; jeweled family portraits, including one of Captain Henry [White Eagle] when a young man; also a ring bearing the family crest. Nothing was missing—the chain of evidence was complete" (433). The exclusion of Winona's mother from White Eagle's narrative goes largely unnoticed—"nothing was missing." Winona registers this lacuna, however, in spite of her wish to forget her mother. She evinces the same sense of loss or absence that we have seen in other of Hopkins's characters as she ponders a "cherished, never forgotten memory" along the lines of the Lacanian sense of loss or absence (Lacan 355–56), but she attributes that space not to her missing mother but to Warren Maxwell.

In terms of Winona's quality of life, adopting her father and Maxwell's country as her own represents a wise choice. While England suffered from its own class struggles, its antislavery sentiments and policies earned it a reputation for liberality among members of the African American community. In England, Winona would have property, love, and—most important—she would enjoy freedom from "American caste prejudice" (435). At the time of the novel, England would far more readily welcome and accept a person of African heritage than would the National Father of the United States. Indeed, with this bright future ahead of Winona, we might judge the novel to end happily. But Winona's attraction to Maxwell—her selection of his national identity as hers and her substitution of him in the empty space left by her mother—recalls the sexual vulnerability that characterizes her motherlessness and gives the reader cause to doubt her future happiness.

The novel remains strangely noncommittal on the subject of Winona's sexual knowledge and experience. As we have seen, on one of the rare occasions that the novel mentions her motherlessness explicitly, the comment links it to sexuality. Without the protection of a mother, Winona has become prematurely knowledgeable about sex (356). Just how knowledgeable, the novel leaves unclear. According to Maxwell's perception, the "noisome things that creep and crawl about the life of the bond chattel [have] fallen away from her" (404), Winona refers to the "degradation of the two years" she spent as a slave (406), and in his deathbed confession, Bill Thomson admits, "I done the girl worse'n dirt." While we are tempted to read the "noisome things" and "degradation" as rape—certainly, a historically supportable conclusion—we also learn that Judah believes she has not yet been raped. As we have seen, he tells Maxwell: "I have sworn to kill her before she shall become slavery's victim. It is impossible for me to put in words the fate of a beautiful female slave on these plantations; the torture of hell cannot surpass it" (334–35). Judah refers to the sexual victimization experienced by the "beautiful female" and he believes that Winona has not yet suffered this fate. He does not say whether he has sworn to himself or to Winona, however, again leaving some uncertainty. If he has sworn to himself, he could be mistaken about Winona's experience; if his resolution comes at her request, we would have more definitive information.[32]

The reader's uncertainty replicates Maxwell's. He does not know the details of her experience in her two years at Magnolia Farm, and this uncertainty seems to increase his attraction to her: "She was unique: a surprise every day in that she was innocence personified and yet so deliciously womanly" (404). If the uncertainty of her sexual experience makes her more attractive, it also makes her more vulnerable. Although she understands the sexual dangers posed by her enslavement and may have asked Judah to help her avoid rape, she shows less discernment about more benevolent predators. We most clearly see the relationship between motherlessness and sexual vulnerability in a moment of danger during the fighting, when the alarm sounds to announce an attack by the proslavery forces. Startled, Winona nearly falls over a cliff, but Maxwell catches her: "For a second he held her in a close embrace, she clinging to him in affright. There was extraordinary gravity in both look and tone as he leaned his cheek against the cropped curly head that nestled close to his throat like a frightened child" (408). Both Maxwell and Winona read Winona's childlike behavior as romantic attraction, and he goes on to declare his love for her.

Given Maxwell's heroics during the fighting in Kansas and the apparent happiness he brings to Winona, readers long to see the good in this relationship. For example, Martha H. Patterson argues that Maxwell's promised marriage to Winona represents his "transfiguration." Because he has fully adopted the "John Brown ethic," she asserts, their marriage affirms their "shared African racial roots" and "rejects the dominant history of miscegenation in the white press, a history of black men raping white women" (456). Nevertheless, one cannot help but feel discomfort at the depictions of Maxwell's attraction to Winona and note the domination that characterizes their relationship. The novel refers to both Winona and Judah as children in the early part of the novel (308, 337), and upon first seeing her, Maxwell notices Winona's youth, "a girl not more than fourteen, but appearing younger" (302). He also notices her beauty. In fact, Maxwell seems to identify Winona's youth as her primary source of beauty: "Warren . . . entered the room where he had left Winona. She lay on the bed where he had placed her [after fainting at the news of her father's murder], still unconscious, her long hair lank with the rain, streamed about her face; her lips were lightly parted, even younger and more beautiful than he had at first thought; and as he remembered her story and the position that the death of her father placed her in, his soul went out to her in infinite pity" (307–308).

The "position" in which White Eagle's death puts Winona is one of abject vulnerability, and not only because of her youth. As a mixed-race girl in the antebellum United States connected to neither father nor mother, her socially vulnerable position is illustrated by her physical position, prone and unconscious on a bed. Maxwell responds to her vulnerability by planning to take over the guardianship of Judah and Winona, something his privilege as a white man and their proscribed citizenship as African Americans allow him to do with no more legal process than his assertion of intent. Although he plans to take both children, he thinks only of Winona:

> Maxwell rowed over to the island to tell Winona of his departure and the arrangements made for her welfare. He laughed softly to himself as he thought of his own twenty-eight years and his cool assumption of the role of Winona's guardian. Yet he was not sorry. Upon the whole, he was glad she had been surrendered to his care, that there would be no one to intrude between them; and he felt that the girl would also be glad;

> she appeared to rely upon him with childlike innocence and faith. How could he fail to see that the brown eyes clouded when he went away, and brightened when he approached? (312)

Maxwell revels in the promise of his future control over Winona with "no one to intrude between them." Throughout the rest of the novel, his attentions focus almost entirely upon her appearance: her "girlish figure"; her "appealing glance"; her appearance as she "sat on her horse with ease and held the reins with no uncertain hand"; her "same graceful form" from two years before, "now so rounded"; her "white throat" and "supple figure" accented by a "poor gown"; her "exquisite complexion" (341, 342, 356, 359, 396).

With her depiction of Maxwell's attraction to Winona, Hopkins invokes the legacy of violence against black women in the United States. His attraction to her youth displaces the real source of his attraction—her vulnerability as a mulatta and a slave. Judah appears to have more sophisticated judgment; he questions Maxwell's love for Winona, knowing as he does "the worth of a white man's love for a woman of mixed blood" (357). Lauren Berlant expresses similar suspicions of such a match:

> For dark-skinned "black" women this [sexual] form of exploitation involved rape and forced reproduction. These conditions applied to mulatta women too, but the lightness of these women also provided material for white men's parodic and perverse fantasies of masking domination as love and conjugal decorum. (554–55)

Maxwell's relationship with Winona enacts such a parody. Their courtship and projected marriage solidifies this power differential, providing a parody of "conjugal decorum." The novel attempts to assuage its own discomfort with this situation with the elevation of Maxwell to a Christ-like figure, as we saw earlier. Nevertheless, Winona's motherlessness and vulnerability to Maxwell come through clearly in her loss of identity and voice. We hear little from her throughout the novel, leading the reader to wonder why she figures as the titular character (Patterson 445). By the end of the novel, she is silenced entirely. As the characters gather to read White Eagle's papers, Winona gives the papers to Warren Maxwell to read rather than performing this duty herself. Meanwhile, she stands in "silent self-repression" (433). As her friends express their joy at her inheritance, Winona remains silent, and the narrative offers no description of her reaction. We never hear from her again. In the end, the reader cannot help but feel that as the silent Winona travels to England with Maxwell to become his wife (and, conveniently, his point of access to the Carlingford fortune), she has lost all hope of finding her Mother, her African heritage, her self.

"Somethin's gwine happen": Having the Last Word

The story neatly wraps up according to the conventions of the domestic novel tradition. Winona has her (ostensibly) happy ending in the form of a promise of marriage and fortune in a safe and welcoming environment. Like *Contending Forces,* however, this novel figures as a romance in the quest tradition. Winona seeks her Mother, not marriage, but this quest has barely been undertaken, much less achieved. Marriage and fortune will not solve the problem of motherlessness. In a nation governed by a corrupt, barbaric National Father—a National Father who will stop at nothing to bar the citizenship rights and paternal identification of his African American children—the motherless child is left vulnerable. Winona, the novel's representative motherless child, is reduced almost entirely to her body. The resultant sexual vulnerability puts her into the care of Warren Maxwell and effectively terminates her quest for the Mother.

Hopkins imbues the novel's troubling conclusion with an element of hope, however. Situating Winona's future in England, she revisits the positive associations with that nation seen in her previous novels. Ida B. Wells's activism in England seems relevant here. As Bederman explains, Wells's campaign in England stirred up American sentiment so successfully because "many white Americans felt a pleasurable sense of racial kinship with the English, whom they saw as fellow Anglo-Saxons, the most manly and civilized of all races" (61). *Winona* draws upon this sentiment, subtly associating its African American heroine with England by repeatedly figuring her as royal. As a child, we are told, "Winona was queen of the little island" with her father and Judah as loyal subjects

(290). As she grows up, the novel repeatedly compares her to a "young princess" and credits her with queenly behavior (341, 359, 377). Judah, too, exhibits a majestic bearing (335). Thus, surrounded by barbaric southerners making a bid for control of the nation, Winona and Judah emerge as more highly civilized and more deserving of the privileges of citizenship because of their similarity to Anglo-Saxon royalty. Perhaps in England, the queenly figure of Winona will be in a position to exercise some power over—to rule over—Maxwell and amend the disturbing power imbalance in their relationship.[33]

Winona's relocation to England figures as triumphant to the African American community in Buffalo, and this success prompts a return to the novel's jeremiad thread. Judah's prophecy had carried the promise that the power would soon shift in the nation. The prophetic voice this time belongs to Aunt Vinnie, a black cook in Maybee's hotel. Although readers have seen Vinnie (431, 432), we have never heard her speak. The fate of Winona, it seems, empowers her to find her voice and offer a "short sermon on the fate of her race" (436). She blends African American "folk" speech with the jeremiad form as she and her companions read omens of future recriminations for the nation in such quotidian events as a mule kicking three times or a rabbit running across a path. All are perceived as signs that "somethin's gwine happen" (437): "Glory to God, we's boun' to be free. Dar's dat gal, she's got black blood nuff in her to put her on de block in this forsaken country, but over dar she's a lady with de top crus' of de crus.' Somethin's gwine happen" (436). Finally, Aunt Vinnie sings a slave song promising freedom. This traditional voice offers a prophetic promise that things will turn around and that the National Father is heading for a fall. As we have seen, early in the novel Winona expresses an attachment to the traditional wisdom of the Native American woman Nokomis, that wisdom being the closest thing to Winona's African heritage in the form of non-Western epistemology. By giving the last word of the novel to Aunt Vinnie, whose voice similarly registers an alternative epistemology, Hopkins takes the focus away from Winona's motherlessness, and turns instead to a woman speaking in the folk language of African American culture, pointing to the still extant hope of reclaiming the African National Mother.

With *Winona,* Hopkins continues her campaign against the National Father, the source of the African American community's motherlessness. Linking the violence of lynching, a crisis at the time Hopkins wrote the novel, to the historic violence of Bleeding Kansas, she heaps up evidence against the character of the National Father as barbaric and unworthy of the community's identification. She gives the final prophetic words to a black cook who invokes African American tradition and, through that tradition, the voice of the African National Mother. Speaking from the 1850s, Aunt Vinnie foretells the Civil War that will bring emancipation and the constitutional amendments granting citizenship and civic rights to freed slaves. Writing in 1902, a year in which eighty-five African Americans would be lynched,[34] Hopkins knows that these things did not bring the change African Americans hoped for. Nevertheless, Aunt Vinnie's message still rings with hope, and she speaks her words of comfort directly to Hopkins's *Colored American Magazine* readers, promising that although things are bad, they will get better. "Somethin's gwine happen."

CHAPTER FOUR

FINDING MOTHER AFRICA

Of One Blood and Hopkins's National Vision

> Ever since I was a child these songs have stirred me strangely. They came out of the South unknown to me, one by one, and yet at once I knew them as of me and of mine.
>
> —W. E. B. DU BOIS, *Souls of Black Folk*

IN *HAGAR'S DAUGHTER,* when the title character discovers that the child she thought she had lost is alive, she pleads with her husband: "I beseech you, lose not a moment, bring her to me—bring my Jewel, my daughter, to my arms" (279). *Of One Blood; or, The Hidden Self* similarly imagines a mother longing for her children, but rather than a personal, biological mother like Hagar, it is the National Mother—Mother Africa—who pursues her children and draws them to her. This novel provides an appropriate conclusion to this study. Motherlessness and the recovery of the pre-oedipal and National Mother are most explicitly depicted in *Of One Blood,* Hopkins's last complete novel.[1] The missing mother is strangely present, a ghostlike force who guides her children and actively draws them to her. Making explicit the quest motif that more subtly appeared in Hopkins's previous novels, *Of One Blood* reaches highs and lows heretofore unseen in her novels. It imagines the pinnacle of Stuart Hall's notion of a "glorious past" featuring Ethiopianism—the belief that Ethiopia is the true source of Western civilization—as the backdrop for its plot in which the protagonist rediscovers the African National Mother and is crowned king of Ethiopia.

Motherless Child

Set in the 1880s, *Of One Blood* tells the story of Reuel Briggs, a medical student passing for white. Reuel's gift in the arts of mysticism and mesmerism enables him to restore the beautiful soprano Dianthe Lusk to consciousness after her apparently fatal injury in a train wreck. He marries Dianthe and then sets off on an archaeological expedition to Africa in order to earn money to support his bride. While there, he discovers the thriving lost city of Meroe, evidence that Ethiopia is the true source of civilization. Meanwhile, Reuel's duplicitous friend, Aubrey Livingston, uses his own gifts of mesmerism—along with blackmail—to seduce Dianthe. Hearing of Aubrey's betrayal, and learning that he, Dianthe, and Aubrey are all siblings—the offspring of the slave, Mira, and her master, Aubrey Livingston Sr.—Reuel returns to the United States to save Dianthe, but too late. Having poisoned Dianthe, Aubrey takes his own life, and Reuel returns to Meroe to marry Queen Candace and fulfill his destiny as king.[2]

As we have come to expect of Hopkins's oeuvre, in its focus on the search for the missing mother, *Of One Blood*'s governing ethos is motherlessness, located primarily in the novel's protagonist, Reuel Briggs. A morose character, Reuel distances himself from his fellow medical students, who speculate on his origins and find him mysterious with "apparently no relatives" (444). The key missing relative is, of course, his mother. By passing, Reuel has followed the oedipal directive of denying his mother, Mira, a former slave and the source of his "black blood," in hopes of identifying with the National Father of dominant white society. Denying his personal mother, he thereby also denies the National African Mother. Outwardly he distances himself from his heritage, expressing to Aubrey his "horror of discussing the woes of unfortunates, tramps, stray dogs and cats and Negroes" (449).

He seeks instead identification with the National Father, indicated by his longing for the approval of the medical men at Harvard. When Dianthe arrives at the hospital, critically injured in a train accident, Reuel eagerly desires to help the injured woman, yet his desire is not entirely altruistic. He recognizes this as an opportunity to demonstrate to his colleagues and superiors his ability to "reanimate" the patient whom all doctors agree to be beyond hope (464). He runs the reanimation session much like a magic show, asking each doctor present to "individually examine the patient" and offer a diagnosis before he restores Dianthe's consciousness, to the amazement of his audience (467). His performance has the desired effect. Word of his success spreads quickly through the white medical community:

> The scientific journals of the next month contained wonderful and *wondering* (?) [*sic*] accounts of the now celebrated case,—reanimation after seeming death. Reuel's lucky star was in the ascendant; fame and fortune awaited him; he had but to grasp them. Classmates who had once ignored him now sought familiar association, or else gazed upon him with awe and reverence. (472)

With this approval and respect, Reuel has achieved a measure of the identification he seeks.

As further evidence of his quest for the National Father's approval, Reuel adopts the imperialistic values associated with the United States. When presented with the opportunity to participate in an expedition to Africa, he agrees to go for purely financial reasons, sharing the goal of the other "capitalists" of looting ancient Meroe and the pyramids of Ethiopia (507, 496). With these aspirations, Reuel adopts the imperialistic leanings of the National Father evidenced in such late nineteenth-century jingoist adventures as the annexation of Hawaii, the war in Cuba, and the seizing of the Philippines from Spain. Charlie Vance, a member of the expedition, speculates on the possibility of turning the African setting into a circus: "Arabs, camels, stray lions, panthers, scorpions, serpents, explorers, etc., with a few remarks by yours truly, to the accompaniment of the band—always the band, you know, would make an interesting show—a sort of combination of Barnum and Kiralfy. . . . There's money in it" (514).[3] Evoking P. T. Barnum and Imre Kiralfy, two turn-of-the-century masters of the crowd-drawing, money-making spectacle, Charlie positions himself and the other members of the expedition to profit by casting Africa as exotic. He takes his exploitative intentions to ridiculous extremes, alerting readers to the author's likely assessment of these financially driven goals.

While Reuel engages in a determined oedipal quest for the Father, his rejection of the Mother brings about a distinct sense of dis-ease, melancholy, and loss, outcomes we have seen throughout this study as inevitable consequences of the oedipal directive. If Reuel has consciously committed his life to pursuit of the National Father, he subconsciously spends his life trying to fill the gap left by the denied Mother. Unsatisfied by the successes achieved in his medical pursuits, he seeks more by trying to delve beyond the intricacies of the body into the soul: "You know as well as I," he tells Aubrey, "that the wonders of a material world cannot approach those of the undiscovered country within ourselves—the hidden self lying quiescent in every human soul" (448). Reuel believes that unlocking the secrets of the soul and the soul's destination after death—"whither life tends"– would lead to a true knowledge of the unknown, of the "Divine Essence from whom comes all life" (463–64). His attraction to this life-giving—motherly—force leads Reuel to develop a fascination with death, and he comes to believe that the "most marvelous thing to watch is the death of a person" (463). As he explains, "if we could but strengthen our mental sight, we could discover the broad highway between this and the other world" (459).[4] In his study of mysticism Reuel finds what he believes to be the best link between "this and the other world," life and afterlife.

Reuel's interest in mysticism or spiritualism and the afterworld indicates more than a desire to distinguish himself in the fields of medicine and psychology, however. His mother apparently dead and making ghostly visitations to him periodically, Reuel's wish to bridge the gap between life and afterlife registers a deeper longing to reconnect with the mother he denies.[5] Even his contemplation of suicide, prompted by discouragement over his lack of success in this intellectual quest, points to his wish for something that would take him to the afterlife and, presumably, to his mother. Moreover, he believes that the key to his quest lies with his "occult powers" (443), powers he inherited from his mother, although he does not acknowledge her as their source at this point in the novel. As we saw in *Contending Forces* and *Hagar's Daughter,* Hopkins associates occult abilities with African heritage, touting them as "once the glory of the freshly imported African" (*Contending Forces* 199). Reuel's use and development of his mystical prowess, then, grow out of his repressed desire to address his motherlessness, his sense of loss, and his inability to find the meaning he seeks.

Missing his mother, Reuel is haunted by her, resembling Jacques Lacan's description of the subject haunted by its pre-oedipal closeness to the mother. The only time that Reuel experiences ease, it seems, occurs when his mother appears to him. The source of Reuel's occult powers, Mira had also been gifted with mysticism. While she was a slave, her master—Aubrey Livingston Sr.—had routinely brought her out at parties to entertain his guests with her abilities, a parlor trick Reuel unwittingly replicates when he performs Dianthe's reanimation for the doctors. After one of these spectacles, in which Mira horrifies her audience by describing the inevitable results of the coming Civil War—death, widowhood, poverty, and so forth—the elder Livingston sells her and she seems never to be heard from again. Now, although presumably dead, Mira continues to exert her mystical powers. Just as Reuel longs for his absent mother, his mother pursues him, truly the "Other that it is impossible to forget" (Lacan 71). And while Reuel seeks the "broad highway between this and the other world," his mother travels that road routinely. Her visits do not alarm Reuel: quite the opposite. She comes to Africa to warn him of danger, but he experiences no surprise or fear at her ghostly presence. Rather, "it was as if a familiar and welcome visitor had called upon him" (522). Indeed, her presence brings about a "dreamy ecstasy of a past time" (522), the pre-oedipal time of wholeness and plenitude.

Equipped with supernatural abilities that enable her to guide and protect her children, this powerful pre-oedipal mother becomes the most concrete depiction of the idealized mother figure found in all of Hopkins's novels. Since his childhood she has functioned for Reuel as both the personal, biological mother and the National Mother. In one of Reuel's memories, which comes to him while on the expedition in Africa and may be prompted by that locale, he recalls his childhood relationship with his mother and its national implications: "The nature of the mystic within him was, then [in childhood], but a dreamlike devotion to the spirit that had swayed his ancestors; it was the shadow of Ethiopia's power. The lotus [mark] upon his breast he knew to be a birthmark [indicating his royal lineage]. Many a night he had been aroused from childhood's slumbers, to find his mother bending above him, candle in hand, muttering broken sentences of prayer to Almighty God as she examined his bosom by the candle's rays" (558).[6] As a child, Reuel had begun the process of suppressing his national identity and destiny to a shadowy, "dreamlike" state. Nevertheless, Mira's double function as both a personal mother who watches while he sleeps and a National Mother from whom he inherits his royal lineage remains clear to him in memory. It is in this shadowy pre-oedipal realm that he will most readily rediscover his Mother.

If supernaturalism offers a means for Reuel to pursue his Mother, so too does his relationship with Dianthe, the woman he reanimates through his mystical capabilities. When he meets Dianthe, he feels drawn to her as that which "he had vaguely sought and yearned for all his forlorn life" (465). Similarly gifted in mysticism, Dianthe had appeared to him prior to their physical meeting, and has therefore built a relationship with Reuel similar to the one his mother develops with him through her other-worldly appearances.[7] Revealing herself to him first through the window of his medical school residence and then on a dark, presumably haunted road, Dianthe solicits Reuel's help, foretelling the train accident in which she will be injured and thus preparing him for the restoration he will provide. As with his mother's appearances, Reuel feels not fear but "delight" at seeing the ghostly Dianthe (461). Later, after he has brought her back from near death, Reuel misinterprets his feelings as romantic love, but since, as we later learn, Dianthe is his sister, his attraction to her can be read as a displaced desire for his mother through the family he lacks. That he apparently never consummates his relationship with Dianthe, postponing their marriage until minutes before he departs for Africa, further suggests an affection based not on passion but rather on their familial connection.

Like Reuel, Dianthe too suffers from the dis-ease of motherlessness. A soprano with the Fisk Jubilee Singers, Dianthe appears to have no family. Several weeks prior to her accident, she leaves the choir—a possible surrogate family and a representative of her racial "family"—to work for a mesmerist. Her attraction to this woman with mystical powers indicates her search for the psychically gifted mother from whom she was separated in childhood. She leaves the mesmerist's employ just prior to her train accident, so when she meets Reuel (in the flesh rather than in a psychic visitation), she shares his lack of family. Reuel reinforces her motherlessness by taking advantage of her amnesia to suppress her black identity after he brings her back to life, essentially forcing her to pass for white as he does. Lacking a mother, she forms ties with representatives of the Father of white society. Her lack of family and her inability to recall her past leave her financially vulnerable, so the doctors at the hospital where she was treated contribute to her support, and she becomes the "dear adopted daughter of the medical profession" (489). Although she does not strive to please or identify with this Father to the extent that Reuel has done, she experiences a more concrete connection with that adoptive parent than with her forgotten mother. Her recollections of the pre-oedipal time of close attachment to the mother register merely as haunting or periodic eruptions of the subconscious.[8] She tells Reuel, "Do you know, I sometimes dream or have waking visions of a past time in my life? But when I try to grasp the fleeting memories they leave me groping in darkness" (499). Attempting to find her past, her Mother, Dianthe finds herself drawn to Reuel. Her attraction to him is far from passionate and, like his attraction to her, grows out of her oedipal longing. Rather than a romantic or passionate attraction to this man who had, in fact, performed the motherly act of giving her life—or rebirth—after her accident, she feels a familial attraction, one in which she occupies the position of a child looking for its mother. At Reuel's declaration of love, for example, she responds "with the sigh of a tired child and [creeps] into his arms" (492).

Fortuitously, just as Reuel's search for his mother leads him to Dianthe, his desire to secure his relationship with Dianthe takes him even closer to his mother via an expedition to Africa. Aubrey, aware of Reuel's hidden African heritage, manages to thwart all his attempts to find employment in the United States by leaking the secret of his racial identity to prospective employers. In this way, Aubrey makes the African expedition Reuel's only option to earn the money he needs to support Dianthe. Having developed his own attraction to Dianthe, Aubrey wishes to separate the lovers, and Reuel's absence on a two-year expedition to Africa suits his plans perfectly. Aubrey's deceitful plot ultimately works to Reuel's advantage, however, as it takes him not away from but, symbolically, closer to Dianthe and the mother to whom they both belong.

Long Ways from Home

Africa or African heritage figures centrally in all of Hopkins's novels, as we have seen, but in *Of One Blood* she intensifies this focus, taking her readers to Ethiopia to explore her themes more explicitly. With the move to Africa, Hopkins's interest in recovering the lost mother merges more pointedly with the postcolonial goal, described by Stuart Hall at the beginning of this study, of recovering a "glorious past." We saw the centrality of history to Hopkins's project in her first two novels, where she began the stories with their historical background, and in *Winona,* set entirely in the past. With *Of One Blood* she reaches farther back to the ancient past and connects her novel to Ethiopianism, a popular movement in her day.[9] Ethiopianism looked to both the past and the future. Looking back, the movement posited that Western civilization derived not from the Greeks, as popularly believed, but from Ethiopia. As Edward Blyden, mid-nineteenth-century adherent of Ethiopianism, argued, "African civilizations had once been great at a time when Europe was composed of barbarous tribes" (qtd. in Sundquist 556). Hopkins had described the Ethiopianist theory of civilization's evolution in the *Colored American Magazine* just a few months before *Of One Blood*'s first installment appeared. There she argued that the Anglo-Saxon race was not always the civilized race it is today; indeed, Caesar called it "the most degraded people I ever conquered" (Hopkins, "Famous Women" 130). Instead, she asserted, it acquired its civilization from Ethiopia:

> Rome got her civilization from Greece; Greece borrowed hers from Egypt, thence she derived her science and beautiful mythology. Civilization descended the Nile and spread over the delta, as it came down from Thebes. Thebes was built and settled by the Ethiopians. As we ascend the Nile we come to Meroe the queen city of Ethiopia and the cradle of learning into which all Africa poured its caravans. So we trace the light of civilization from Ethiopia to Egypt, to Greece, to Rome, and thence diffusing its radiance over the entire world. (130)

Looking to the future, Ethiopianism had a prophetic aspect that it derived from an Old Testament text: "Princes shall come out of Egypt, [and] Ethiopia shall soon stretch forth her hands to God."[10] Many interpreted this passage as a prophecy of divine deliverance from bondage for colonized Africa as well as the enslaved and oppressed African diaspora. Ethiopianism subscribed to a cyclical version of history, according to which the dominance of the white race was a temporary condition eventually to be replaced by the elevation of the African race as it once again assumed its ancient status. The prophecy suggests that this elevation would be brought about by a black redeemer from Africa or, some believed, from America.

Eric Sundquist points out that, in its day, Ethiopianism enjoyed a measure of respect as an important nationalist philosophy. He cites George Shepperson, who referred to Ethiopianism as "a significant, if overlooked, section of the 'glory road' of American Negro history" (qtd. in Sundquist 552). The need for glory was perhaps never greater. During the late nineteenth century, racist scientific theories seeking to prove their inferiority characterized Africans as naturally debased and "uncivilized." Jim Crow laws and cultural mores followed suit by institutionalizing their oppression (Moses 21). In such a context, beliefs that Ethiopia—which, Sundquist points out, generally stood for all of Africa (554)—founded civilization offered the African diaspora a source of racial pride and served as part of the project of revising and reclaiming history.

Hopkins's attraction to Ethiopianism comes as no surprise, combining as it does her dual interest in national pride and redemption through the reclaiming of the maternally figured Africa. In *Of One Blood,* then, Ethiopianism serves as a means of making prominent the theme Hopkins had pursued throughout her writing career: the restoration of the Mother as a means of building nationalism. Reuel's physical journey to Africa serves as the catalyst for his psychic journey to his mother, the Ethiopia W. E. B. Du Bois would later refer to as the "All-Mother of men."[11] Professor Stone, leader of the expedition to Meroe, repeats almost verbatim the legacy of Ethiopia as Hopkins outlined it in the *Colored American Magazine:* "It is a *fact* that Egypt drew from Ethiopia all the arts, sciences and knowledge of which she was mistress. The very soil of Egypt was pilfered by the Nile from the foundations of Meroe" (521, emphasis in original). Aware of his hidden African heritage, Reuel secretly delights at the words of Professor Stone, as indicated by the taunting tone of his remarks: "Your theories may be true, Professor, but if so, your discoveries will establish the primal existence of the Negro as the most ancient source of all that you value in modern life, even antedating Egypt. How can the Anglo-Saxon world bear the establishment of such a theory?" (520). His pleasure signals his shifting perspective on his race and the beginnings of the redemption that will take place in the course of his journey. In contrast to his earlier distaste for "negroes" as a topic of conversation, here he takes pleasure in his discussion with Professor Stone, doubtless because in this conversation, the "negroes" cannot be cast as "unfortunates."

Reuel's journey to Africa and his discovery of the hidden city of Telassar—a figuration of Reuel's repressed mother—are marked as a psychically charged journey, a "quest to uncover a repressed psychic prehistory."[12] This city, which became the "hidden city of refuge" after "Egypt rose in power and sent her hosts against the mother country" (529), has remained hidden for centuries, protected by walls, swamps, and other structures forming "an impassible barrier" (529). In spite of their efforts and a letter providing somewhat cryptic directions (a stock prop for the adventure tale genre to which the novel belongs), the expedition team has failed to gain access to Telassar. Falsely informed of Dianthe's death by the duplicitous Aubrey, Reuel feels again that sense of loss we saw at the novel's start. Again, he contemplates suicide: "He had no purpose, no sensation. Once he halted and tried to think. His love was dead:—that was the one fact that filled his thoughts at first. Then another took its place. Why should he live? . . . better to rejoin her where parting was no more. He would lose himself in the pyramid" (542). As they had at the novel's start, his thoughts of crossing the divide between life and afterlife again draw him to contemplate death. Losing himself in the pyramid refers metaphorically to connecting with his "hidden self," his African heritage, and his repressed emotional desire for his Mother. Indeed, the novel hyperbolically foregrounds the psychoanalytic content and the oedipal nature of this journey with Reuel's search for the sphinx within the pyramid (543–44).

Reuel's experience in the hidden city resembles a dream or hypnotic state as he "ramble[s] aimlessly" through the sepulcher of the pyramid with his "feeble light," the "moaning wind" calling to mind the "centuries marching by" (543). In this dreamlike setting he begins the process of redemption. When Reuel is on the verge of locating the entrance to the city, an unseen figure intercepts him, rendering him unconscious with chloroform. He awakens later from "profound unconsciousness" (544). Paradoxically, this physical awakening precipitates the unconscious state of discovery as the unreal, dream-like city of Telassar replicates the "dreamlike state" of the pre-oedipal period in the child's development in which the mother reigns. Reuel experiences a distinct sense of déjà vu as he tours the city, where "shadowy images of past scenes and happenings flitted across his brain like transient reflection of a past perfectly familiar to him" (551). He explains to the prime minister, Ai, "I am surprised to find that it all seems familiar to me, as if somewhere in the past I had known just such a city as this" (551). Not only Reuel's experience but the city itself emphasizes that this is Reuel's return to the Mother. Ethiopia has been referred to repeatedly as a mother country, and Telassar exhibits maternal qualities, as demonstrated by the reign of Queen Candace. Scholars believe the name "Candace" to be a title held by a succession of Meroitic queens, signifying a queen mother, possibly the mother to a reigning king.[13] Such signification brings another layer of meaning to the notion that the child follows the condition of the mother. This edict sought to keep the children of slave women from inheriting property from their landowning fathers; it further succeeded in preventing those children from inheriting the Father's national entitlement in the form of citizenship and the accompanying rights. In Meroe, the mother's "condition" is one of royalty, and it passes to Reuel, who has borne the mark of the king on his chest since birth.

Dana Luciano observes that although Meroe is ostensibly a masculine place, to be ruled by a king, Candace does wield power. She "claims" Reuel and—not surprisingly—exercises "magic influence" over him (*Of One Blood* 570–71). In this way, "the affective and maternal power that has maintained African American survival seems to continue, as it were, undercover" (Luciano 180). The maternal connections abound: Candace closely resembles Dianthe who, we have seen, metonymically represents the mother, Mira, and continues the matriarchal tradition established by Mira and her mother, Hannah (Luciano 180). Thus, this collection of women—queen, sister, mother, nation—merge in the city of Telassar.

As the climax of his journey, Reuel must acknowledge the nation's maternal quality and reclaim the mother he has denied. His participation in the discussions of Ethiopianism with Professor Stone has paved the way for this reclamation, and his introduction to the proud history and glorious culture of Telassar continues his preparation. In contrast to the poverty Reuel has known, the residents of Telassar display the city's luxurious appointments—vast rooms with marble columns and silk upholstery.[14] Reuel finds the beauty of the place "bewildering" (545). Based on the expectations formed from his own experience in a racist America, Reuel finds not only the setting but the residents of Telassar surprising, highly educated and bearing faces "perfect in the cut and outline of every feature" (545). As part of his tutorial, Ai questions Reuel on the status of blacks in the United States, seeming to apprehend Reuel's surprise at the state of things in Telassar: "Is it true that the Ethiopian there is counted less than other mortals?" (560). (Reuel needn't answer; Ai knows the answer to his question.) He goes on to point out the irony of racism in the United States, voicing the argument important to Hopkins's polemic: "And yet, from Ethiopia came all the arts and cunning inventions that make your modern glory. At our feet the mightiest nations have worshipped, paying homage to our kings, and all nations have sought the honor of alliance with our royal families because of our strength, grandeur, riches and wisdom" (560). His statement emphasizes the power and worth of the African Mother whom Reuel has denied in favor of the white Father. Still not entirely reformed, however, Reuel continues to think of his oedipal quest for identification with the Father: in the midst of his conversation with Ai, he wonders, "What would the professors of Harvard have said?" (576).

"Sometimes I feel . . ."

Thus far, Reuel's encounter with Africa through Telassar's history and culture has occurred largely on an intellectual plane. Like Sappho in *Contending Forces,* however, he must undergo an emotional response in order to complete his transformation and redemption. When Ai questions Reuel about his "isolation from our race" in the United States, Reuel responds emotionally: "Reuel bowed his head in assent, while over his face passed a flush of shame. He *felt* keenly now the fact that he had played the coward's part in hiding his origin" (560, emphasis added). Reuel makes the transition from the intellectual to the emotional, the flushing indicating a spontaneous, visceral response to Ai's question. The pinnacle of emotion for Reuel marks the final step in reclaiming both the personal mother and the National Mother, a step prompted by Mira herself. When the sound of a scream awakens Reuel one night in Telassar, he finds "the form of Mira" beckoning him. She leads him to Jim—Aubrey Livingston's lackey—who has been injured while looking for Reuel. Jim, who has been under instructions from Aubrey to kill Reuel, now seeks forgiveness before he dies. Formerly a slave at the plantation where Aubrey, Dianthe, and Reuel were all born, Jim has crucial information that becomes the novel's startling revelation: the three are siblings, children of the slave, Mira. Reuel virtually overlooks what should be disturbing information: that his wife is his sister. Instead, his primary concern is the confrontation with his racial heritage and his mother's identity, a revelation that precipitates his emotional catharsis: "Reuel stood for a moment, apparently struggling for words to answer the dying man's assertion, then fell on his knees in a passion of sobs agonizing to witness. 'You know then, Jim, that I am Mira's son?' he said at length" (593). Reuel responds powerfully to the disclosure of the information he has suppressed, physically brought to his knees by the force of his emotions. The novel invites readers to share his response as they "witness" this "agonizing" scene, becoming not simply passive viewers but active participants in Reuel's catharsis.

As Lacan indicates, Reuel's emotional response facilitates his "purification" and redemption (244). For Reuel, this purification takes the form of reclaiming both his personal mother and his National Mother, understanding Mira to be the source not only of his racial heritage but also of his national identity. Through this story of Meroe—maternally characterized as the "mother country" (529) and "Mother of ancient warfare" (557)—the novel enacts the project outlined by Stuart Hall, of "representing or 'figuring' Africa as the mother of these different civilizations" in order to "restore an imaginary fullness or plentitude, to set against the broken rubric of our past" (224–25). In Meroe, following the condition of the mother is not a social and national liability, but a source of honor and prestige. So, whereas at the opening of the novel, we find Reuel suffering from the poverty that keeps him from his intellectual pursuits, now he receives jewels and wealth beyond his wildest dreams. Where he had hidden his family heritage and dreaded his expedition to "that dark and unknown country to which Fate has doomed [him]" (496), he now—thanks to that same family heritage—finds himself king of a great civilization with a proud history.

Things do not turn out so well for Dianthe, however. At the end of the novel her character undergoes a symbolic reincarnation in the person of Queen Candace, but her agonizing death by the same poison she attempts to use on Aubrey registers a level of tragedy hitherto unseen in Hopkins's fiction. While Reuel's emotional climax encourages readers to share in his proud claiming of the mother, Dianthe's death leaves readers with an unresolved sense of despair. Nevertheless, Dianthe's complex story contains an element of victory. Prior to this dark end, the novel uses Dianthe to explore a far more optimistic and central aspect of Hopkins's racial uplift theory: the role of music in the African American's recovery of cultural roots and of past traumas. In *Of One Blood,* music becomes a vehicle of catharsis, facilitating insight and connection to the past, the community, and the lost Mother. True to the cathartic process, music performs painful work for Dianthe, revealing a past that she cannot live with. It also accompanies her ultimate healing via maternal redemption.

The Souls (and Songs) of Black Folk

Dianthe's past as a soprano for the Fisk Jubilee Singers serves a greater purpose than simply a plot device providing Reuel an opportunity—at a concert—to see her; music becomes the channel through which she will recover her identity, her past, and her mother. As we saw in the introduction, music had been an early passion for Pauline Hopkins, not just for its aesthetic pleasure but for its political promise as well. In *Of One Blood,* music figures as a vehicle for the catharsis that precipitates maternal redemption.

Hopkins's musical career followed closely on the heels of the rising popularity of the Fisk Jubilee Singers, a choir formed in 1867 to raise money for Fisk University, founded in Nashville in 1866 "for the higher education of the freed people" (Marsh 8). Hopkins had several opportunities to hear this powerful and popular choir, as it appeared regularly in Hopkins's home city of Boston. They had toured New England in their earliest forays in performing, and were invited to participate in the 1872 World's Peace Jubilee in Boston, where they enjoyed tremendous success (Wallinger 32; Lois Brown 72–75). According to J. B. T. Marsh's 1881 account, the group drew an enthusiastic and emotional response from the audience: "Twenty thousand people were on their feet. Ladies waved their handkerchiefs. Men threw their hats in the air, and the Coliseum rang with cheers and shouts of 'The Jubilees! The Jubilees forever!'" (41). The performers' emotional power derived, at least in part, from their personal experience as slaves. Henry Ward Beecher made this link explicit: "they make their mark by giving the 'spirituals' and plantation hymns as only they can sing them who know how to keep time to a master's whip" (qtd. in Marsh 30). The powerful emotional impact explicitly linked with the Jubilees' racial heritage and experience would make this group a perfect choice for inclusion in Hopkins's emotionally charged novel.

As the choir's popularity surged, it naturally sparked imitation. Other musical performers wanted to get in on this popularity, and Hopkins' Colored Troubadours were no exception (Andrew Ward 198–99).[15] The group used the term "Jubilee" in its advertising in August 1880, promoting a "Jubilee Concert" that would feature Hopkins' Colored Troubadours.

In 1882, the group advertised itself as "Hopkins' Colored Troubadours Guitar Players and Southern Jubilee Singers." Such wording apparently posed a danger of falsely claiming to be former slaves, however. The promotional materials carefully negotiate this potential landmine by linking Hopkins's group to the Jubilee Singers in spirit, if not in fact:

> This collection of talent brings together some of the best Artists of their race, from nearly all parts of the country, especially from the South, some of whom have felt the yoke of bondage, but we do not seek to deceive by advertising a band of Original Slaves, but promise only what the kind public may expect to see and hear—the best of our race, with native talent cultivated and refined, in a performance Rich in Harmony and Pure in Character.[16]

HOPKINS'

COLORED TROUBADOURS

Guitar Players and Southern Jubilee Singers,

Will give one of their Pleasing Entertainments, consisting of Jubilee Singing, the sweetest ever heard,

UNDER THE AUSPICES OF THE ROYAL ARCANUM,

At ARCANUM HALL, ALLSTON,

Friday Evening, Nov. 24, 1882.

Miss PAULINE E. HOPKINS, Boston's Favorite Colored Soprano.
Miss ANNIE PARKS, Washington City Favorite Contralto.
Mr. JAMES FREEMAN, Tenor.
Mr. JAMES HENRY, Bass.
Assisted by Mr. GEORGE TOLLIVER, Camp Meeting Songster.
Mr. W. A. HOPKINS, Guitarist and Vocalist.
Miss CARRIE ALDEN, Pianist and Vocalist.

Despite the unfavorable weather the Hopkins Colored Troubadours had a very good audience at the City Hall, last Sunday evening. The programme was an appropriate one, and excellent in all respects, consisting of solos, duets, piano and guitar renderings, and chorus singing by the entire company. The company has left behind a very good impression, and will be heartily welcomed whenever they choose to visit our city again.—*Maiden Press*, Jan. 28, 1882.

BOSTON, AUGUST 19, 1882.

Having employed the Hopkins' Jubilee Singers several times, I take pleasure in recommending them to societies, especially temperance organizations. No meeting of this kind is complete without good music. Miss Pauline E. Hopkins, the Soprano, has a sweet voice, and is a favorite wherever she sings,

JAMES H. ROBERTS.

PROGRAMME.

PART I.

1. OVERTURE, Piano, ...Miss Carrie Alden
2. "We are all hyar," ....Jubilee Singers
3. SONG AND CHORUS, "Sunny Home," ....Miss Hopkins and Quartette
4. "Blow Gabriel," ....Mr. Freeman and Jubilee Company
5. "I 'll be dar," ....Mr. Tolliver and Jubilee Company
6. SOLO, Selected, ...Miss Hopkins
7. "Yellow Rose of Texas," ....Mr. Freeman and Jubilee Company
8. DUET, "Whispering Hope," ....Misses Hopkins and Alden
9. "Moses," ....Mr. Tolliver and Company
10. "Water chilly and cold," ....Company

PART II.

1. "Live Humble," old fashioned Camp Meeting Hymn, Mr. Tolliver and Com'y
2. "Magnolia," ....Mr. Freeman
3. "Children I 'm gwine to shine," ....Mr. Freeman and Company
4. "Sweet Chiming Bells," ....Quartette
-. SPECIALTY, Exedus, ...Mr. Tolliver
'Ship of Zion," ....ver and Company

Doors ope

...ber of Society.

Flyer for Hopkins' Colored Troubadours performance, 1882

Fisk University Franklin Library Special Collections

By linking her performance to the Jubilee Singers, Hopkins accomplishes several things. First, she appeals to a white audience who, like Beecher, desires the spectacle of former slaves and may attend her show in order to see it. Second, she claims authenticity for her experience as an African American. Although she had undoubtedly felt the sting of racism in her life, neither she nor her parents experienced slavery firsthand. Third, and most significant, by invoking the Jubilee Singers, Hopkins lays the groundwork for an emotional response to her music. As we shall see, Hopkins valued this emotional response, depicting it in her work and seeking to inspire a similar reaction in her readers. Given her confidence in the political power of music, we should not be surprised to find a soprano as a central character in *Of One Blood*. Indeed, perhaps the surprise is that she waited so long to feature a musician in her fiction.[17]

Du Bois, too, believed music served an important function in the race community, as he explains in *The Souls of Black Folk*.[18] Du Bois begins with a description of the psychic condition of the African American community in need of uplift, the condition that he has famously dubbed "double consciousness": "an American, a Negro; two souls, two thoughts, two unreconciled strivings" (5). His extended description of this condition should sound familiar in its similarity to subjects making their way through the oedipal complex:

> The history of the American Negro is the history of this strife—this longing to attain self-conscious manhood, to merge his double self into a better and truer self. In this merging he wishes neither of the older selves to be lost. He would not Africanize America, for America has too much to teach the world and Africa. He would not bleach his Negro soul in a flood of white Americanism, for he knows that Negro blood has a message for the world. He simply wishes to make it possible for a man to be both a Negro and an American, without being cursed and spit upon by his fellows, without having the doors of Opportunity closed roughly in his face. (5)

Du Bois describes the conflict of needing to identify with the Father of white America—bleaching his Negro soul in a flood of white Americanism—but not wishing to deny the Mother of African heritage, the source of that "Negro soul."

He ends *Souls* with a discussion of the music that offers the antidote to this condition: the "sorrow songs" of the "olden days" (204). He indicates that the songs' presence throughout *Souls* in the form of epigraphs at the start of each chapter replicates their ongoing presence in his consciousness, "a haunting echo" of the songs that "have stirred me strangely" since childhood (204). Although he identifies a specific maternal source for these songs in his life—his great-great-grandmother, who "often crooned a heathen melody to the child between her knees" (207)—the music has a more fluid, mystical presence for him than his attribution to a specific ancestor suggests. As the epigraph for this chapter reasserts, for Du Bois the songs "came out of the South unknown to me, one by one, and yet at once I knew them as of me and of mine" (204). His recognition of these unknown songs recalls Sigmund Freud's notion of the uncanny—something simultaneously strange and familiar—and he recognizes them as one might recall something long forgotten.

His words also testify to the music's power to unify a disparate group of people—African Americans from various regions and economic classes—solely on the basis of their shared heritage, their shared Mother. Therefore, these songs carry not only individual significance for Du Bois, but also collective significance for his family's and his community's history: "Out of them rose . . . bursts of wonderful melody, full of the voices of my brothers and sisters, full of the voices of the past" (205). The songs further play an important part in Du Bois's claim to national belonging for black Americans, representing "the sole American music" and "the singular spiritual heritage of the nation" (205). With such a claim, he offers an antidote to the "double consciousness" that plagues him and other members of his community in that the sorrow songs offer an example of the successful merging of these two conflicting histories, African heritage recognized as a rightful and equal participant in and contributor to American identity and culture.

With the abundance of music in *Of One Blood,* Hopkins invokes the antidote Du Bois identifies. The emotional power of music enables characters to connect to the Mother of black ancestry and the national unity she facilitates. Toward this end, the novel codes Africa as musical. Throughout his journey, Reuel encounters groups who communicate their history and their current condition through song, his first experience of this occurring as the group travels through the desert toward Meroe. Here, as they journey on a string of camels, their local guides sing a song that fascinates Reuel because it describes his own feelings and experiences: "Ah, when shall I see my family again; the rain has fallen and made a canal between me and my home. Oh, shall I never see it more?" (515). The longing for family and home here recalls the sorrow song at the center of this study, "Sometimes I feel like a motherless child, a long ways from home," and speaks to Reuel's own sense of distance from his mother and the "home" she represents. Finding the hidden city of Telassar, Reuel discovers it to be replete with music. The prime minister, Ai, speaks in "musical language" (546). The inhabitants of Telassar, much like the chorus in a Greek tragedy, use music to tell Reuel their national history and his place in that story. Engaging in a dialogue between chorus and soloist,[19] they tell the history of Meroe—its early greatness and wealth, all ruled by Reuel's ancestors, and its eventual fall.[20] The music and its story move Reuel—"upon Reuel a strange force seemed working" (557)—affecting a change of heart that contributes to a shift in his perception of his heritage, from something to be hidden to a source of pride.

The music in Hopkins's Telassar undergirds the work of music throughout what would become a tragic tale in *Of One Blood*. The "strange force" that works on Reuel in Telessar points to the emotional power of music to affect its listeners, and begins the process of preparing Reuel to acknowledge his denied mother, a rectification the novel clearly treats as virtuous. We had previously seen music's potential to "develop virtue" at the Jubilee concert. When Aubrey invites Reuel to a "jubilee concert given by a party of Southern colored people" (449), Reuel hesitates, claiming (as we have seen) disdain for the stories of such "unfortunates" as "Negroes" (449), but perhaps actually wishing to avoid the music so relevant to his hidden identity. Once there, however, this music moves Reuel: it "soothed [his] restlessness" and eventually "Reuel was carried out of himself" (452, 454). The reference to "Reuel" and "himself" points to Reuel's double consciousness, a fragmented identity that he has pushed to extremes by passing. The further separating of these two selves—one being "carried out of" the other—suggests that Reuel begins to release his assumed white identity and move toward the virtuous embracing of his true racial identity.

Reuel is not the only one deeply affected by the Jubilees' performance; recalling the group's powerful performance in Boston during Hopkins's youth, the concert depicted in *Of One Blood* inspires an emotional response in its audience: "Some of the women in the audience wept; there was the distinct echo of a sob in the deathly quiet which gave tribute to the power of genius. Spell-bound they sat beneath the outpoured anguish of a suffering soul. All the horror, the degredation [*sic*] from which a race had been delivered were in the pleading strains of the singer's voice. It strained the senses almost beyond endurance" (453–54). Hopkins focuses on not only the empathy drawn from the listeners by the music, but also the music's ability to bring back to memory the suffering forced upon African Americans under slavery. Almost like a patient undergoing psychoanalytic hypnosis for the purpose of a cathartic recovery of repressed memories, the audience sits "spellbound."

Here we do well to look more closely at Freud's notion of the uncanny. According to Freud's formulation, the uncanny does not frighten us because it is unfamiliar or unknown. Rather, and paradoxically, the uncanny frightens because it is "familiar and old-established in the mind," "alienated . . . only through the process of repression" ("Uncanny" 421). Lacan's emotionally tinted description of the uncanny works particularly well for linking it to the emotionally charged pre-oedipal mother: Lacan describes the uncanny as "something strange to me, although it is at the heart of me" (71). Madelon Sprengnether has fittingly made explicit the connection between the uncanny and the oedipal requirement that the child reject the mother: "the mother's body becomes that which is longed for yet cannot be appropriated, a representative of both home and not home, and hence, in Freud's terms, the site of the uncanny" (9). The state of repression or concealment is crucial here. As Freud, drawing on the work of F. J. W. Schelling, asserts, the uncanny can be understood as "something which ought to have remained hidden but has come to light" (241). Freud, it seems, prefers to let sleeping dogs lie, so to speak, marking revealed secrets or shameful pasts as inevitably uncanny. Ella Sheppard, a Jubilee performer, shared his opinion. She said the Jubilee Singers' music was "associated with slavery and the dark past, and represented the things to be forgotten" (qtd. in Ward 110), but Hopkins clearly believed these events were things to be remembered. Indeed, as Valerie Rohy persuasively argues, "For Hopkins [Freud's] 'ought to' is the central injunction of white culture, which threatens to obscure both Africa's glories and America's crimes" (220). In other words, in the case of the repressed National Mother of African heritage and the African American past, to repress or forget serves the interest of the Father of dominant white culture. Hopkins seeks to undermine those interests by revealing this past. The performance of songs sung by former slaves, Hopkins suggests, brings to the surface the memory of the trauma experienced by black Americans at the hands of white slave holders and the American government.

Du Bois asserts that the sorrow songs themselves had been "forgotten," that "their memory [had] died" before the Fisk Jubilee Singers recovered them, singing "the slave songs so deeply into the world's heart that it can never wholly forget them again" (205). If the white "world" had forgotten these songs and the history they represent, the novel suggests that the turn-of-the-century African American community had forgotten, or repressed, not only the horrific abuse under slavery, but the effect of that abuse on its relationship with the Mother of African heritage. That Hopkins's novels all reach into the past to keep alive the abuses of African Americans under slavery indicates her belief in the need to remember and in the power to be gained from the emotional catharsis that leads to the recovery of the past.

Hopkins reveals her goal of uncovering the past through the mystical communication between Mira and Dianthe, mother and daughter. Mira appears to Dianthe, pointing to a biblical passage[21] that she intends as an important message: "For there is nothing covered that shall not be revealed" (506). Dianthe's amnesia and her lost ability to make music (491) are part of her motherlessness, the loss or repression of her past. Music's cathartic ability to recover the past works on Dianthe to effect her maternal redemption through the recovery of her mother. This is not an easy journey for Dianthe. Indeed, this recovery is entwined with the novel's tragic component. Recovery of the mother brings up the uncanny truth of her identity and the atrocities experienced by her mother and herself, not only in the past but also in Dianthe's present. So whereas Reuel's recovery of his mother brings about his redemption and ascendancy to his rightful place in the kingdom of Meroe, Dianthe's maternal redemption precipitates her death.

While the Jubilee Singers' music leaves its audience with an "echo" of slavery's horrors, Dianthe recovers much more specific and personal memories as music not only ushers in the memory of her past—where she came from, her racial identity—but also serves as the catalyst for the reenactment of her mother's experience as a slave—sexual exploitation at the hands of a powerful (ostensibly) white man. Reuel has naïvely entrusted Dianthe to Aubrey Livingston's care during his African expedition, so she now lives with Molly Vance, Aubrey's fiancée. In spite of his engagement to Molly and his feigned friendship with Reuel, and—like his siblings—ignorant as to his kin relationship with Dianthe and Reuel, Aubrey has developed an attraction for Dianthe and has committed himself to seducing her.[22] One evening, at a party at the Vance home, Aubrey—who enjoys the same mesmeric affinities as his siblings—uses his psychic power to compel Dianthe to the piano. Just as his father had coerced Mira to "perform" her ability to tell the future, Aubrey makes Dianthe sing the song she sang at the Jubilee concert, this time for his guests. Ironically, the supernatural performance is Aubrey's, as he uses his own mesmeric abilities to compel Dianthe to sing a sorrow song that will restore her memory:

> There was a strange rigid appearance about the girl that was unearthly. Never once did she raise her eyes. At the first sharp treble note the buzz in the room was hushed at stillness. Livingston moved forward and rested his arm upon the piano fastening his gaze upon the singer's quivering lips.
>
> Slowly, tremulously at first, pealed forth the notes:
>
> "Go down Moses, way down in Egypt's land,
> Tell ol' Pharaoh, let my people go."
>
> (501–502)

This song that powerfully pleads, "Let my people go!" recalls for Dianthe the horrors of enslavement and racism, the sexual vulnerability of African American women under slavery and after, and specifically her mother's vulnerability to Aubrey Livingston Sr. More—in a jarring repetition of that relationship—the memory anticipates her own coerced union with Aubrey Jr. Since Dianthe believes that Reuel is white and ignorant of her mulatta identity, Aubrey will use her racial identity against her to force her into a sexual relationship with him under threat of exposing her secret.[23]

Significantly, however, her mother appears to her at this moment, offering her support as Aubrey takes Dianthe into his power. Aubrey's guests hear her, "a weird contralto, veiled as it were, rising and falling upon every wave of the great soprano, and reaching the ear as from some strange distance" (502). Mira sings with a "veiled" voice, signaling her assistance to Dianthe in her desire to know the "powers and influences behind the veil" (475). Ultimately, the music conjures Mira both in her audible voice and in Dianthe's memory of the identity she inherited from her.

Through this cathartic return of the repressed mother, the novel points to the promise of restored plenitude. Simultaneously, however, it points to the promise of costly revelations as Mira both embodies and reveals the atrocities of slavery that will lead to Dianthe's tragic end. Later Hannah, the grandmother of Reuel and Dianthe and therefore an extension of Mira, reveals the blood relationship between the three siblings. The exposure of these secrets becomes a means of telling a story, of recovering a lost past, and of reminding readers of the atrocities that have resulted from slavery. According to Freud's figuration of the uncanny, the incestuous relationships brought about by the violence of slavery are things that "ought to" have remained hidden, serving the interests of the National Father. Mira's appearance and the telling of these stories become a means of undermining the tyranny of secrecy. In this way the pre-oedipal mother—the National Mother—emerges as source of power and promise.

Tragic Ends

Like *Hagar's Daughter* and *Winona, Of One Blood* ends with qualified optimism. The incest between Aubrey and Dianthe signals a deep problem that cannot easily be resolved. Motherlessness is both the effect and the cause of the destruction of the community, as the incestuous relationship poignantly illustrates. Although certainly a farfetched situation, the unknown relation between these characters—due to their unknown relationship with the mother—points to a possible reality for families divided by slavery. We have seen this before: Hopkins had raised the matter of incest in *Contending Forces* with Sappho's rape by her uncle, and in *Hagar's Daughter* with St. Clare Enson's attempt to seduce Jewel, whom he does not know to be his niece. In all three novels, the occurrence or threat of incest offers a dramatic reversal to Freud's oedipal model. In Freud's formulation, the father prohibits the boy's connection to the mother to prevent incest. In this way, the separation of the child from the mother is held out as beneficial to the family. In Hopkins's formulation, the father's separation of the child from his mother leads directly to incest and would, therefore, be responsible for the family's destruction.

The complex conclusion of Dianthe's story is anticipated by Mira's predicted revelations (506). The novel recovers the story of a glorious distant past as it reveals the city of Meroe, the source of civilization, but it also recalls the story of a horrific recent past. Dianthe's coerced relationship with Aubrey—like the parody of marriage anticipated by Maxwell and Winona—replicates her slave mother's relationship with her master, Aubrey's father, bringing to the surface what the narrator describes as "the accumulation of years of the foulest wrongs heaped upon the defenseless and innocent women of a race" (594). In this context, the sexually coded language used at the end of the novel to describe Reuel's fear of "the advance of mighty nations *penetrating* the dark, mysterious forests of his native land" (621, emphasis added) becomes even more menacing. The novel powerfully registers the ongoing threat posed by the Father, and we must concede that, in spite of Reuel's impressive legacy and the national pride the novel's Ethiopianist position inspires, Hopkins ultimately offers a qualified optimism for the power of the National Mother.

At the same time, we also find some hope here as Dianthe's tragic death accompanies her maternal—and heavily national—redemption. This redemption is anticipated by Dianthe's performance of "Go Down Moses." This song is weighted with pathos, recalling the painful history of slavery in the United States. In terms of the novel's plot, Dianthe's performance of this song that demands freedom ironically serves as the occasion on which she recovers her memory and becomes even more deeply entangled in Aubrey's power over her. At the same time, however, "Go Down Moses" ties her to American nationalism in that the song appropriates the "chosen people" rhetoric central to the soteriological project of the fledgling United States (Bercovich, *Puritan Origins* 31–32). As the Puritans had deployed the trope of God's chosen people, claiming that exceptionalism for themselves, so American slaves attempted to make use of the same trope as a means of harnessing the powerful rhetoric for their own bid for freedom. Singing the words of the Israelite, Moses, Dianthe stakes a claim not only to God's protection but also to the American tradition that uses the same tactic. Simultaneously, as her death approaches, the novel focuses on Dianthe's privileged position in the nation of Ethiopia. Upon first meeting her grandmother, she recognizes her from "a description of an African princess" that she had read "somewhere" (603)—a vague memory that points to the pre-oedipal memory we have seen throughout this study. Her grandmother's royal status, like the figure of Candace in Telassar, gives new, proud meaning to the edict of following the condition of the mother, while the mark on her skin—not scars from whips or pigmentation randomly demonized, but the same lotus lily that marks Reuel—further identifies her as a member of the royal line (606). Finally, "strains of delicious music" play as Dianthe dies, audible not only to her but also to the town at large. A regal encore of the Jubilee concert earlier in the novel, the music crescendos, augmented by "thousands of voices swelling in rich, majestic choral tones": "it was the welcome of ancient Ethiopia to her dying daughter of the royal line" (615). While the National Mother draws Dianthe to her, her personal (grand)mother holds her as Dianthe realizes the wish expressed in the sorrow song, "Bright Sparkles": "Mother, rock me in the cradle all day." Both tragedy and triumph mark Dianthe's death, and in this way her death reminds readers of Uncle Tom, whose violent death is in some measure softened, according to the terms of the novel, by his deliverance to the destination he has been traveling toward, namely heaven. Hopkins secularizes Harriet Beecher Stowe's vision, making the salvation available to her character not spiritual but national. Dianthe's redemption transports her not to heaven, but to Africa.

In spite of Dianthe's redemption and Reuel's coronation, this novel ends on a somber note. The final description of Reuel places him on the throne of Meroe, doing good works and surrounded by faithful subjects. But the "shadows of great sins darken his life" and undermine his peaceful existence. While his quest for the National Mother has been realized, he continues to be haunted by the pre-oedipal "memory of past joys," and he fears the threat of the intrusion of the National Father—"the advance of mighty nations penetrating the dark, mysterious forests of his native land" (621).

In *Of One Blood,* Hopkins weaves together the major threads of her four novels. She establishes the motherlessness of the novel's children, Reuel and Dianthe, showing their experience of melancholia and disconnection, both from the community they deny and, in Reuel's case, from the community that denies him. With the journey to Africa, the discovery of Telessar, and the discussion of Ethiopianism, she recovers Africa's glorious past, a point of origin credited as the source of civilization. With their return to the National Mother, Dianthe through death and Reuel through his assumption of the throne, she offers extreme manifestations of maternal redemption. And with Reuel's final meditation on the ongoing threat of the "mighty nations," she acknowledges that the oedipal drama is still not resolved, that the National Father still both requires and forbids rejection of the Mother and identification with him. Nevertheless, with the final scene of Reuel on the throne, the novel leaves readers with a vision of triumph and ultimate maternal redemption for the African American community.

CODA

I RETURN, IN CONCLUSION, to the song lyrics that this book is built on:

> Sometimes I feel like a motherless child
> Sometimes I feel like a motherless child
> Sometimes I feel like a motherless child
> A long ways from home
> A long ways from home

The haunting, melancholy quality of this song spoke powerfully to its intended audience of African American slaves in the antebellum period, and it has continued to speak to a broad range of listeners in the twenty-first century. It has been recorded by such diverse artists as Paul Robeson, Louis Armstrong, Ike and Tina Turner, Van Morrison, and Darius Rucker of Hootie and the Blowfish.[1] If the theme of this song has struck a chord with musicians over the years, it has similarly spoken to—and been spoken by—writers. From Frederick Douglass to Countee Cullen to Alice Walker and beyond, motherlessness and the longing for the mother have been expressed in the memoirs, poetry, and fiction of African Americans. Although Hopkins never explicitly invokes this sorrow song in her work, her novels point to the many voices that have sung the refrain, "Sometimes I feel like a motherless child."

Hopkins's writings have garnered significant attention in recent years, and for good reason. Hopkins was a woman writer and recognized as the first African American woman playwright (Bernard Peterson 125).

She belonged to the thriving Boston community of race activists. She participated in and spoke before women's clubs and literary circles, work she felt qualified for by virtue of her early career as a singer, actress, and playwright. Her reputation in her community earned her invitations to speak at such important public events as "The Two Days of Observance of the One Hundredth Anniversary of the Birth of Charles Sumner" and the "Citizens' William Lloyd Garrison Centenary Celebration."[2] As editor of and frequent contributor to the popular *Colored American Magazine* from 1900 to 1904, she helped shape one of the leading voices in race politics at a crucial time in African American history.

Hopkins's political message has been the focus of most of the scholarly attention directed at her work, while the recurring theme of motherlessness has received scant attention. In this study, I have argued that motherlessness emerges in Hopkins's novels as a coherent and consistent theme that addresses the personal but also the public and national condition of African Americans. I have focused on the long works of one author to illuminate her literary importance, but also to establish a pattern and develop a model for identifying and analyzing texts that participate in this literary tradition—which we can, at this point, call motherless child literature.

In *Contending Forces, Hagar's Daughter, Winona,* and *Of One Blood,* motherlessness takes a variety of forms: from an individual character missing her or his biological mother, to a mother separated from her children and therefore from her rights and identity as a mother, to a community of slaves exhibiting the melancholy that comes from being taken from its Motherland and made virtual orphans in a country that withholds the rights of citizens, to post-emancipation African Americans whose ties to African heritage have been made the grounds for exclusion from the full rights of American citizenship. As these various forms suggest, the trope of motherlessness can speak to both the individual and the community experiences. It can describe both the personal and the political aspects of individuals' lives. It can represent the experiences of first-generation slaves, abducted from Africa and sold into slavery, as well as the experiences of later generations born into the condition of slavery. Grounded in the sentimental tradition, the trope of motherlessness tells an emotional story, portraying the condition of melancholia and facilitating catharsis.

Motherlessness depicts the national upheaval, family fragmentation, and civic alienation that took place first under slavery and, later, in the institutionalized racism of the post-Reconstruction era. Representing their common experiences, motherlessness draws together the African American community in the recovery of its "glorious past" and the retelling of its history.

To accommodate the individual and collective levels at which the model of motherlessness functions, I have drawn on two theoretical models to inform these interconnected lines of inquiry. First, attending to the individual or personal trauma of this experience, I have looked to Freudian and Lacanian psychoanalytic theory, arguing that the recurring expression of loss in Hopkins's characters signifies the Lacanian notion of lack that results from the end of the pre-oedipal connection between mother and child, the separation Sigmund Freud touted as crucial to the subject's development. The father's intrusion into and prohibition of the child's close relationship with the mother ushers the child into the Symbolic Order that assigns social roles and dictates proper behavior in society, including the repression of both the original desire for the mother and the plenitude that the child derived from that relationship. Separation from the mother has the effect of making the mother impossible to forget and endows the figure of the mother with heightened importance. Looming large in the subject's psyche, "the desire of the mother," says Jacques Lacan, "is the origin of everything" (1959–1960, 283).

Taking the Freudian oedipal narrative as my starting point, I have sought to tease out the national ramifications of motherlessness in the context of American slavery and institutionalized racism. Recasting Freud's "family romance," I position dominant white society, or the United States, in the role of the Father—the National Father who insists that the African American subject must identify with him and reject the Mother—or, for the purpose of this study, African heritage—in order to become a fully formed subject and to enjoy the rights of citizenship that accompany that identification or allegiance. Freud cited the shift in identification from mother to father as crucial to the child's proper development. However, in the case of the collective subject, the African American community, the racist climate of the late nineteenth and early twentieth centuries made such a shift in alliances impossible. The antebellum edict, *partus equitur ventrem,* dictated that the child follow the condition of the mother, and while emancipation put an end to the legal power, or "letter," of this edict, its spirit lived on into the twentieth century, supported by the well-known "one drop rule" and enforcing the ongoing identification with the marginalized Mother. This identification became a source of national exclusion.

To address this national aspect of the African American subject's experience, I have drawn on postcolonial theory, and specifically the work of Stuart Hall and Frantz Fanon. Fanon has argued that under colonialism the colonial subject is robbed of its history and its legacy. In "On National Culture," he explains that "colonialism is not simply content to impose its rule upon the present and the future of a dominated country. Colonialism is not satisfied merely with hiding a people in its grip and emptying the native's brain of all form and content. By a kind of perverted logic, it turns to the past of the oppressed people, and distorts, disfigures and destroys it" (*Wretched* 210). As we saw in the introduction, Hopkins made a similar observation in the *Colored American Magazine:* "To the Negro is denied the stimulus of referring to the deeds of distinguished ancestors, to their valor and patriotism. He is distinguished only as the former slave of the country" (qtd. in Pamplin 174). Like Stuart Hall, who believes that the recovery of this history is "always constructed through memory, fantasy, narrative and myth" (226), Hopkins looked to storytelling and narrative for the purpose of recovering a "glorious past," as we saw most recently in *Of One Blood.* By envisioning the National Mother as a source of power rather than as a source of marginalization, Hopkins's novels rediscover a proud past and recapture that pre-oedipal plenitude identified by Lacan, thus imposing, in Hall's words, "an imaginary coherence on the experience of dispersal and fragmentation" (224). Hopkins's novels identify the mother as the crucial focal point in racial uplift politics. Her novels constitute her effort to reconnect with the mother—both personal and national—as a means of creating a proud history and acquiring national entitlement.

Part of the significance of this study resides in its depiction of the trope of motherlessness as it functions in African American literature. I have suggested that we will find the trope of motherlessness widely used in writings from the African American community in the nineteenth and twentieth centuries. With its discussion of the breadth of plot and polemic possibilities attached to this trope, this study offers a preliminary foray into this literary tradition and, I hope, has laid a foundation for further study of how this model has been—and continues to be—deployed in African American cultural productions. A brief survey of the ongoing literary treatment of the motherless child in the twentieth century shows its lasting hold on the African American imagination. I end this study, then, with some further examples of motherless child literature. With these examples, I hope to provide a brief look at how this genre has developed since Hopkins's writing and to call for further study in this area.

Countee Cullen's 1925 poem, "Heritage," depicts the speaker's powerful tie to a motherland that is very distant—both geographically and temporally. The speaker appears to be haunted by a powerful and relevant question: "What is Africa to Me?" He puzzles that although he is "three centuries removed" from the "Women from whose loins [he] sprang" (lines 7, 5), he still has a palpable tie to that heritage. Drawing on images of nature and of tribal groups signifying Africa, he portrays the conflicted psyche characteristic of the subject going through the oedipal divide between mother and father. For example, the speaker longs for the sound of "wild barbaric birds" (line 13) associated with his Motherland even as he tries to follow the National Father's directive to deny that Mother by blocking out (with fingers in ears) the sound of "great drums throbbing through the air" (line 22). Marking this conflict between National Mother and National Father, he feels, simultaneously, "pride," "distress, and joy allied" over his dark skin (lines 23–24). Africa is "unremembered" (line 33) since he has never experienced it firsthand. Nevertheless, he describes the imago, the ideal image of a Motherland to which he has deep, undeniable ties—ties as systemic as his blood:

> So I lie, who find no peace
> Night or day, no slight release
> From the unremittent beat
> Made by cruel padded feet
> Walking through my body's street.
> Up and down they go, and back,
> Treading out a jungle track.
> (lines 64–70)

He describes his relationship to this Mother as deeply and irrevocably physical. His heart beats an "unremittent beat" as his blood courses through his veins—his "body's street"—in the form of marching African feet, blood that defines him as holding a place of limited privilege in his country of birth, his Fatherland. Nevertheless, he responds to this conflict with a resolution to "quench" and "cool" the longing for the Mother.

> All day long and all night through,
> One thing only must I do:
> Quench my pride and cool my blood.
> (lines 117–19)

His condition is volatile, ready to burst into flames, but he must control himself "Lest a hidden ember set / Timber that I thought was wet / Burning like the dryest flax" (lines 121–23).

The speaker is conflicted between his identification with the African Mother, the source of his connection to the "jungle," and his attempt to identify with the National Father, the source of civilization. His body betrays him, linking him to his Mother, his African heritage, failing to understand his connection to the Father:

> Not yet has my heart or head
> In the least way realized
> They and I are civilized.
> (lines 126–28)

Like Hopkins's Reuel, the poem's speaker has denied—figuratively killed—the Mother in his determination to identify with the Father, and to claim the "civilized" status long associated by Americans with Anglo-Saxon heritage. His hot blood threatens to start a fire that will restore the Mother he has denied and sabotage his attempts to claim the rights and privileges entitled to the Father-identified American citizen.

Nella Larsen portrayed the motherless child in *Quicksand* (1928) in the form of Helga Crane. The pattern differs slightly here: Helga's biological mother is white and her black father figures as the source of her "colored" identity. (Scholars have noted that Larsen seems to create Helga out of her own experience—the similarities are many—but in her own mixed-race heritage, it was Larsen's mother who was black.) Larsen invites readers to link Helga's experience to the more common lineage, opening the novel with a poem by Langston Hughes:

> My old man died in a fine big house.
> My ma died in a shack.
> I wonder where I'm gonna die,
> Being neither white nor black?

Her mother having died, Helga experiences motherlessness as she senses that she is not accepted by the white, middle-class community. She exhibits the traits of melancholia that we have seen in Hopkins's novels, an unidentifiable but clearly felt sense of loss or lack, comparable to the lack experienced by the child after the break with the mother. Helga breaks the pattern, however, in that rather than a longing for either the Mother or the National Father, Helga seems to be repulsed by or resentful of both. After a series of attempts to fit in somewhere, including leaving behind both the National Father and the African Mother by relocating to Denmark for a time, Helga finally chooses to identify with her African heritage by moving to a primarily black community in Alabama. She throws herself into the lifestyle there and attempts to address her own motherlessness by having several children. It seems, however, that the black community to which she has committed herself, and the maternal figures that populate that town, represent for Helga an unsatisfying Mother image, one that leaves little room for freedom or self-definition. Neither the setting nor the experience of motherhood ends her own motherlessness, however. Ultimately, Helga's is a case of irresolvable motherlessness because she fails to find a suitable representative of the Mother with which to identify. The novel's conclusion finds her trapped in a setting from which she cannot escape, soon to be a mother again but still motherless.

In 1946, Ann Petry portrayed the hardships of the mother who tries, and ultimately fails, to protect her child from the fate of motherlessness. Written largely from the perspective of the mother, Lutie, the novel portrays Lutie's own motherlessness and the economic conditions that threaten her ability to mother her son, Bub. Echoing the corruption Hopkins had attributed to the National Father in *Hagar's Daughter* and *Winona, The Street* depicts a cruel, naturalistic setting that repeatedly undermines her best efforts. Despite her willingness to identify with the National Father by modeling herself after Ben Franklin and trying to claim the American Dream's promise that hard work will result in prosperity (43, 63–64), everything works against this mother as she tries to raise her son. She does not prosper as a result of her work. Rather, her material conditions require that she leave her son motherless while she looks after her employer's child: "Sometimes she took Little Henry Chandler to the postoffice with her and she couldn't help thinking that it wasn't right. He didn't need her and Bub did. But Bub had to do without her" (29). Ultimately, her disconnection from the National Father, which takes the form of alienation from the legal system, leads her to criminal action. She abandons her son to protect him, leaving him motherless and, ironically, a ward of the state.

In Alice Walker's *The Color Purple* (1982), the layers of motherlessness are dizzying. Celie's mother dies in the second letter of this epistolary novel. Her relationship with her own motherhood is destroyed on the novel's first page when her father begins a routine of raping her, eventually impregnating her. He takes her children from her, killing one, selling the others. He causes enough physical damage to her to leave her sterile. He eventually gives her, like so much property, to a man whose first wife has died, leaving his three children motherless. Celie thus becomes a mother and motherless simultaneously and under duress. A connection with Mother Africa proves to be Celie's salvation, taking the form of letters from her sister who has relocated to Africa, where she is charged with the care, remarkably, of Celie's estranged children.

The hopeful end to *The Color Purple,* a century after the post-Reconstruction era, makes a fitting answer to Hopkins's penultimate novel, *Winona.* Recall that, at the novel's conclusion, the titular character silently listens to William Maxwell read her late father's account of her family history, a history that erases Winona's slave mother and, therefore, her African heritage. But Aunt Vinny comes in with the novel's last word. She insists on hope with the prediction, "somethin's gwine happen." This is the work that Hopkins's motherless child literature does: mourns the loss, fills the gap, and re-centers the National Mother.

NOTES

INTRODUCTION

1. There have been a number of important and informative studies on the maternal ideal in domestic ideology. See Nina Baym, *Woman's Fiction;* Jane Tompkins, *Sensational Designs;* Ruth Bloch, "American Feminine Ideals in Transition"; Elizabeth Ammons, "Stowe's Dream of the Mother Savior"; Mary P. Ryan, *Womanhood in America;* Lora Romero, *Home Fronts;* and Linda K. Kerber, *Women of the Republic.* Several scholars have coined terms to characterize a particular aspect of the mother's role, similar to Ryan's "mothers of civilization." See, for example, Kathryn Kish Sklar's "qualitative mothering," Bloch's "moral mother," Ammons's "mother savior," and Kerber's "republican motherhood."

2. "The promotion of motherhood as a full-time occupation for women conveniently emerged at just the time that a fundamental change in the traditional pattern of female dependence might have occurred" (Ammons, "Stowe's Dream of the Mother Savior" 159).

3. American poet William Ross Wallace (1819–1881) expressed this sentiment in his 1865 poem: "For the hand that rocks the cradle / is the hand that rules the world" (7–8). The ongoing currency of this well-known phrase—serving as the source of the title for the 1992 thriller, *The Hand That Rocks the Cradle,* directed by Curtis Hanson—indicates the tenacity of aspects of domestic ideology.

4. Women also used this empowering domestic role to take their influence beyond the bounds of the nation and to join the project of American imperialism. See Amy Kaplan's "Manifest Domesticity" and Vincent L. Rafael's "Colonial Domesticity."

5. Ammons discusses the presence of the "mother savior" in work by women writers into the 1920s.

6. Carolyn Dever observes this pattern in Victorian-era British novels in *Death and the Mother from Dickens to Freud,* but little work has been done on this phenomenon in American literature.

7. I refer here to the following novels: Harriet Beecher Stowe, *Uncle Tom's Cabin;* Susan Warner, *The Wide Wide World;* Maria Susanna Cummins, *The Lamplighter;* E. D. E. N. Southworth, *The Hidden Hand; or, Capitola the Madcap;* Elizabeth Stuart Phelps, *The Story of Avis;* Edith Wharton, *The House of Mirth.*

8. Romero asserts that one nineteenth-century African American writer "found Anglo-American domestic ideology appealing because it provided a model for writing women into the leadership of nationalist movements" (63). See Romero, *Home Fronts*, her chapter entitled "Black Nationalist Housekeeping: Maria W. Stewart."

9. Kerber describes this phenomenon in her chapter, "Republican Motherhood," in *Women of the Republic*.

10. See Nell Irvin Painter for the biography of Sojourner Truth. For discussions of the stereotypes of black women during and after slavery, see Deborah Gray White, *Ar'n't I a Woman?*; Patricia Hill Collins, *Black Feminist Thought*; Herbert G. Gutman, *The Black Family in Slavery and Freedom, 1750–1925*.

11. I refer here to Claudia Tate's *Domestic Allegories of Political Desire*, Ammons's *Conflicting Stories*, Hazel V. Carby's *Reconstructing Womanhood*, and Deborah McDowell's *"The Changing Same."* The tenets of True Womanhood were outlined by Barbara Welter in *Dimity Convictions* (1985).

12. In her excellent analysis of Hopkins's critique of True Womanhood ideology, Gloria T. Randle argues that Hopkins "couches her generally more progressive views within conventional forms and language, attempting a delicate balance between palatable, acceptable content and perspectives that, at the same time, critique the very status quo she presents" (204).

13. Allison Berg's *Mothering the Race*, Eileen Boris's "The Power of Motherhood," and Geoffrey Sanborn's "Mother's Milk" represent notable exceptions in this scholarship, making important contributions to the study of motherhood in African American women writers.

14. Stuart Hall identifies two separate but related conceptions of "cultural identity": the first based on a shared culture and ancestry, as Wilson Jeremiah Moses describes here, and the second based not on similarities but on differences resulting from history's impact since the period of shared heritage. Although I will discuss the interplay between these two types of cultural identity later in this chapter, it is important to note here that race activists of Hopkins's era—such as those active in the Pan-African project and black nationalism—focused primarily on a conception of identity based on "oneness," or common heritage, and it is within this context that I locate Hopkins's work.

15. See, for example, Gutman, *The Black Family in Slavery and Freedom, 1750–1925*; White, *Ar'n't I a Woman?*; Blassingame, *The Slave Community*; and Carby, *Reconstructing Womanhood*.

16. The southern periodical, *American Cotton Planter*, offered this advice: "Well treated and cared for, and moderately worked, [female slaves'] natural increase becomes a source of great profit to their owner. Whatever therefore tends to promote their health and render them prolific is worthy of his [the owner's] attention" (qtd. in Gutman 76).

17. Mary Wollstonecraft observed that in order to "rise in the world," women "must marry advantageously, and to this object their time is sacrificed, and their persons often legally prostituted" (151). Sarah M. Grimké critiqued the tendency to deprive women

of intellectual pursuits. Such a tendency pushed a woman to "occupy her talents in the pursuit of those employments which will enable her to regale the palate of her lord with the delicacies of the table, and in every possible way minister to his animal comfort and gratification" (39). And in *Women and Economics,* Charlotte Perkins Gilman observed: "We are the only animal species in which the female depends on the male for food, the only animal species in which the sex-relation is also an economic relation" (5).

18. See Harriet Jacobs's chapter, "The Jealous Mistress."

19. Hortense Spillers, citing social anthropologist Claude Meillassoux, expands: "Under conditions of captivity, the offspring of the female does not 'belong' to the Mother, nor is s/he 'related' to the 'owner' though the latter 'possesses' it, and in the African American instance, often fathered it, *and,* as often, without whatever benefit of patrimony. . . . [T]he offspring of the enslaved, 'being unrelated both to their begetters and to the owners . . . , find themselves in the situation of being orphans'" (Spillers 74, emphasis in original).

20. Eric Foner 82. See also Leon F. Litwack, *Been in the Storm So Long.* Frances Ellen Watkins Harper dramatizes this post-emancipation search for families in her 1892 novel, *Iola Leroy.*

21. Ralph Ellison, in *Shadow and Act,* describes the blues this way: "The blues is an impulse to keep the painful detail and episodes of a brutal existence alive in one's aching consciousness, to finger its jazzed grain, and to transcend it, not by the consolation of philosophy but by squeezing from it a near-tragic, near-comic lyricism. As a form, the blues is an autobiographical chronicle of personal catastrophe expressed lyrically" (78–79).

22. Spillers refers to the removal of names as "a metaphor of displacement" (73).

23. See Tate's analysis of the suppressed racial discourse of psychoanalysis in "Freud and his 'Negro.'"

24. Introductory Lectures: 21st lecture on Oedipus Complex (16.330); 15.208 on castration complex; "New Introductory Lectures," 22.63 on identification; 22.116 and 128 on women, in *The Standard Edition of the Complete Psychological Works of Sigmund Freud,* trans. James Strachey, 24 vols. (London: Hogarth Press, 1953–1974).

25. David L. Eng and Shinhee Han, in their psychoanalytic study of the effects of racism, explain: "To the extent that the ideals of whiteness for Asian Americans (and other groups of color) remain unattainable, processes of assimilation are suspended, conflicted, and unresolved" (345).

26. Introductory Lectures 16.387, in *Complete Psychological Works of Sigmund Freud.*

27. According to Carby, one of Hopkins's goals is to "represent blacks as a colonized people" (134).

28. Feminist scholars have long noted Freud's problematic treatment of the mother in his theories of development. Placing Freud on the couch, a number of scholars have argued that his neglect of the mother indicates his own fear of castration. According to Estelle Roithe, "Freud's theoretical neglect of the mother in the early life of the child and his insistence on the centrality of the phallic, paternal power represents, apart from anything else, a denial of the profound importance of the two-person phase in infantile

life, the phase 'before' father when the infant is 'alone' with his mother. I believe that Freud's disturbed relationship to his own mother and thence to women in general was responsible, to a large extent, for this neglect" (qtd. in Sprengnether 2n2).

29. Here I should address Paul Gilroy's critique of two competing understandings of nationalism within black political discourse. Using the work of nineteenth-century black nationalist Martin Delany as an example, Gilroy critiques a conception of nationalism, informed by Euro-American modernity, which aspires "to acquire a supposedly authentic, natural, and stable 'rooted' identity" (30). He persuasively argues in favor of a more pluralistic nationalism "which affirms blackness as an open signifier and seeks to celebrate complex representations of a black particularity" (32). Although Hopkins's work has, in some respects, sought to "transcend both the structures of the nation-state and the constraints of ethnicity and national particularity," as Gilroy suggests (19) with her portrayals of transnational characters and travel, her vision of national identity shares the unified quality of Delany's, and does not achieve Gilroy's decidedly twentieth-century, poststructuralist position. This may be considered a weakness or naivety in her vision, but is probably understandable given her time period.

30. This quote comes from a short piece Hopkins wrote to promote her upcoming series, "Famous Men of the Negro Race" (*Colored American Magazine* 1 [September 1900]). It appears in Claire Pamplin 174.

31. Hanna Wallinger's and Lois Brown's biographies both include substantial coverage of Hopkins's musical background, and Daphne A. Brooks provides an insightful reading of music and performance in Hopkins's work, and especially of *Of One Blood,* in *Bodies in Dissent.* Eric Gardner's collection, *Major Voices,* has reprinted Hopkins's musical, *Peculiar Sam; or, The Underground Railroad, a Musical Drama in Four Acts.* See also Bernard L. Peterson's entry on Hopkins in *Early Black American Playwrights and Dramatic Writers.*

32. In my use of the term "race progress," I refer specifically to the racial uplift movement and its attention to the progress of the African American "race" within the context of nineteenth-century racialist theories. See Kwame Anthony Appiah's "Race" for a discussion of nineteenth-century theories of race and nationality.

33. First published as a pamphlet copy of a talk given before the Brooklyn Literary Society in 1892.

34. Boris cites a similar sentiment voiced by a mothers' club member at a meeting in Arkansas: "we must have good mothers before we can develop a good race of people" (224).

35. For more on the development of mothers' clubs in the National Association of Colored Women, see Boris (224–27).

36. See also Barbara McCaskill's discussion of African American women's use of motherhood rhetoric (78–83).

37. These philosophies are found, in various forms, throughout Gilman's extensive oeuvre. For her comparison of women's tendency toward life and men's tendency toward violence, see *His Religion and Hers* 11–14. For the use of mothering as rhetorical strategy, see Seth Koven and Sonya Michel, *Mothers of a New World;* Molly Ladd-Taylor, *Mother-Work;* and Berg, *Mothering the Race.* Berg identifies the concept of the "race mother" as a theme

shared by black and white women alike "not only to reinforce woman's traditional reproductive role but also to articulate mothers' vital role in racial and national progress" (16).

38. See Berg's insightful discussion of mother rhetoric among black and white women in *Mothering the Race* (43).

1. "THE BLESSED RELIEF OF TEARS"

1. Hopkins never strove for simple entertainment, it seems. Her first known piece of writing, an essay at the age of fifteen, addressed "the evils of intemperance." Her musicals, though humorous and romantic, told the story of a band of slaves escaping via the underground railroad. (See *Peculiar Sam; or, The Underground Railroad, a Musical Drama in Four Acts,* reprinted in Gardner.)

2. Nira Yuval-Davis and Floya Anthias offer five ways that women participate in nationalism: "as biological reproducers of the members of national collectivities; as reproducers of the boundaries of national groups (through restrictions on sexual or marital relations); as active transmitters and producers of the national culture; as symbolic signifiers of national difference; as active participants in national struggles" (7).

3. One barely need mention Nathaniel Hawthorne's now famous dismissal of the "damned mob of scribbling women." Although Hopkins wrote after the peak of the domestic novel's popularity, this form continued to influence and inform writers at the turn of the twentieth century. For a discussion of the ways nineteenth-century women's writing was devalued, see Baym's "Form and Ideology of Woman's Fiction" in *Woman's Fiction.*

4. Hopkins's treatment of race in her work vacillates from a pseudo-scientific theory of the effect of measures of Anglo blood on the abilities of individuals to a more modern understanding of race as a fiction. See Appiah's "Race" for the history of the term and its resulting consequences.

5. David J. Denby's description of the misfortune central to the sentimental plot resembles Sigmund Freud's theory of melancholia. Denby explains that, while the misfortune may result from the direct agency of a villain, it may also reflect a more general and unidentifiable "situation of insufficiency or lack" (72).

6. Boston enjoyed a reputation for its anti-racist sentiment, but this reputation was not without its detractors. Nevertheless, Hopkins would later praise New England as giving great benefits to her "persecuted race" and, presumably, to her personally ("Famous Women of the Negro Race" 130). See Wallinger for a discussion of Boston's complicated reputation (24–26).

7. Hopkins announces this intention in her preface: "I have introduced enough of the exquisitely droll humor peculiar to the Negro (a work like this would not be complete without it) to give a bright touch to an otherwise gruesome subject" (16).

8. Madam Frances has her home and fortunetelling business in the "Negro quarter" of the city (275), further solidifying the link between her art and African heritage.

9. The location of Langley's office, in contrast to Madam Frances's location in the "Negro quarter," underlines his attempt to identify with the Father.

10. Hopkins participated in, and won, an essay contest at the age of fifteen, receiving her prize from William Wells Brown. As an aspiring writer and acquaintance of Brown's, it is likely that she would have read his novel. Moreover, as we shall see in the following chapter, her second novel, *Hagar's Daughter,* seems to draw quite specifically on *Clotel.*

11. Carolyn L. Karcher argues that in her treatment of Grace's rape, Hopkins follows the conventions of the sentimental novel, which dictated the exclusion or elision of sexually explicit material, in deference to the sensibilities of its delicate female readers (Karcher 58). Carby, too, reads this scene as a thinly veiled rape scene (132).

12. The uncle refers here to the stereotypes of the sexual lasciviousness of black women, the "jezebel," according to Patricia Hill Collins, which was used to justify rape. See Collins (77–78) for a discussion of this stereotype.

13. Scholars are divided in their analysis of Mrs. Willis, seeing her as either a negative character whose ambition the novel views critically, or judging her to be an example of Hopkins's successful woman ideal. Alisha R. Knight convincingly argues that the narrator, who voices criticisms of this figure, should not be equated with Hopkins. Thus, Knight reads Willis as a character that Hopkins admired, much as she admired Josephine St. Pierre Ruffin, the Boston-based club woman and race activist upon whom Mrs. Willis's character was based. For the purposes of my argument, it is clear that Sappho perceives Mrs. Willis's motherly qualities and is drawn to them.

14. Richard Wright 79. Anne Anlin Cheng acknowledges potential dangers in talking about the "'melancholia' of racialized peoples." Namely, she notes that it "seems to reinscribe a whole history of affliction or run the risk of naturalizing that pain." As she rightly goes on to argue, however, "it is surely equally harmful *not* to talk about the history of sorrow" (14).

15. José Esteban Muñoz's project focuses on activism surrounding AIDS, describing the transformation of mourning for individuals into the productive activism of melancholia, which he refers to as "communal mourning." That is, he employs the terms "individual mourning" and "collective mourning" to describe the Freudian distinction between "mourning" and "melancholia."

16. The voice goes on in prophetic style, reminding her readers, perhaps, of the apocalyptic vision described in the biblical book of Revelation: "Time was no more. I stood there gazing at the approaching forms of matchless beauty advancing toward the judgment seat of God. And I asked a question; 'Who are these arrayed in white?' And one of the elders answered: 'These are they who come out of great tribulation!'" (*Contending Forces* 332). We will examine Hopkins's deployment of the jeremiad in chapter 3.

17. As one of his examples of the blues novel, Steven C. Tracy points to Langston Hughes's *Not without Laughter,* specifically Hughes's deployment of the "proverbial motherless child of the spirituals" and the way the novel seeks to address that motherlessness through a number of mothering characters ("The Blues Novel" 129–30).

18. Frantz Fanon, *Black Skin, White Masks,* 147. Fanon describes the experience of a black child raised in the Antilles to think of "our ancestors, the Gauls," and learning to think of himself or herself as a member of the dominant society. When this child grows up and finds himself a "Negro in France, which is his country, [he] will feel different from

other people" (145–49). Certainly, this effect is heightened if the child grew up assumed to be white, as is the case with the "tragic mulatta" figure.

19. Several scholars have offered an analysis of Hopkins's engagement with and resistance to American imperialist efforts. Kevin Gaines argues that the racial uplift rhetoric used by Hopkins and other African American activists closely resembled the rhetoric of the "civilizing mission" commonly deployed in defense of imperialistic missions, a similarity that undermines her antiracist efforts. Colleen C. O'Brien counters Gaines's argument in "'Blacks in all Quarters of the Globe.'" See also Carby (133–36).

20. The history of the Klondike gold rush also has its share of racial tensions, increasing its relevance for *Contending Forces.* Gold was initially discovered by Native peoples of Canada, Skookum Jim (Keish), a member of the Tagish nation, his sister, Kate, and her husband, George Carmack. Although Skookum Jim was the one to discover the gold, the three decided to put it in Carmack's name out of fear, motivated by strong racist attitudes of the day, that white miners would not recognize a claim made by a Native, nonwhite miner. See Charlene Porsild, *Gamblers and Dreamers* 3–4, 35–37.

21. For this argument, see Sandra Gilbert.

22. Patricia Hill Collins cites Harper's *Iola Leroy* as an example of community othermothing in literature (130). Barbara Christian refers to this type of mothering as she sees it in Alice Walker's *Meridian,* in which the title character goes "beyond the society's narrow meaning of the word *mother* as a physical state and expand[s] its meaning to those who create, nurture, and save life in social and psychological as well as physical terms" (242).

23. Stowe had constructed a link between the domestic activity of sewing and spiritual growth with Aunt Ophelia's questioning of Topsy. Ophelia asks two questions in close succession: "Have you ever heard anything about god?" and "Do you know how to sew?" (263). What appears as a jarring transition becomes clear when understood in the context of domestic ideology. The vision of Hopkins and her contemporaries replaces the spiritual with the political, linking the domestic with racial uplift.

24. Gilroy makes much of the image of the ship in *The Black Atlantic* as he seeks to broaden the understanding of nationalism from the narrowly defined English and American nationalism to the black Atlantic.

25. William Carlos Williams would point to the inextricability of the history of slavery and the national story: "Poised against the *Mayflower* is the slave ship." Williams, *In the American Grain,* 208, quoted in Carl Pedersen 43.

2. MOTHERLESSNESS IN THE NATION'S CAPITAL

1. Hopkins's work at the *Colored American Magazine,* especially the end of her tenure there, has been the subject of much scholarly discussion. See Jill Bergman, "Everything We Hoped She'd Be" and "'A New Race of Colored Women'"; C. K. Doreski, "Inherited Rhetoric and Authentic History"; and biographies by Hanna Wallinger and Lois Brown. Hopkins's contributions to the *Colored American Magazine* have been reprinted in Ira Dworkin, *Daughter of the Revolution.*

2. For a discussion of Hopkins's use of pseudonyms at the *Colored American Magazine*, see Wallinger 60–70.

3. *Hagar's Daughter* also draws on William Wells Brown's *The Escape; or, A Leap for Freedom* (1858). See Wallinger 41–42.

4. Readers familiar with William Wells Brown's *Clotel; or, The President's Daughter* will recognize Hopkins's debt to the novel. Clotel, too, is a mulatta figure married to a white man with whom she has a daughter. When her identity is discovered, she is taken by a slave trader named Dick Walker. To escape her fate, she takes her own life and that of her child by jumping into the Potomac River.

5. For information on the pastoral tradition and the Eden trope in American literature of the South, see Lewis P. Simpson, *The Dispossessed Garden*, and J. Lee Greene, *Blacks in Eden*.

6. Hopkins joins a tradition developed by African American authors and outlined by Greene, which constituted "in large part a direct response to Anglo-Americans' use of the Eden trope as a blueprint for American society" (5).

7. Hopkins draws her quote from the following lines by Milton:

> Mean while the winged Haralds by command
> Of Sovran power, with awful Ceremony
> And Trumpets sound throughout the Host proclaim
> A solemn Councel forthwith to be held
> At Pandæmonium, the high Capital
> Of Satan and his Peers
>
> (*Paradise Lost*, lines 752–57)

8. Janet Gabler-Hover examines the Hagar myth as it appears in nineteenth-century novels and notes that Hagar typically functioned as a synonym for the "fallen woman" in women's novels (141). Here Hagar does not "fall" from moral purity but rather from national entitlement.

9. As I will discuss in the following chapter, Gail Bederman observes that, in her anti-lynching campaign, Ida B. Wells capitalized on the American judgment of England and the English as the height of Anglo-Saxon civilization by courting the acceptance of and forming close ties with British reformers, and then describing those relationships in her columns published in American periodicals. These columns earned her a great deal of positive attention in the United States. By linking Hagar with England, Hopkins engages in a similar strategy. For a fuller discussion of Wells's strategy, see Bederman 45–76.

10. Rogers M. Smith 54–55. Smith traces this ideology to the Tudor and Stuart eras, when subjects appealed to the "ancient constitution of the sturdy Anglo-Saxon ancestors" to justify, among other things, their "political and religious liberty" (48). Such claims proved useful to Americans, whose dominant culture continued to think of itself, after the Revolution, as British (Appiah 283).

11. Genesis 12:2; 16:1–16. The characters undergo a name change in the course of the story. God renames Abram and Sarai as Abraham and Sarah. I have used the latter names to avoid confusion.

12. This poem, by Eliza Piotevent Nicholson, appeared in the November 1893 issue of *Cosmopolitan* (Gabler-Hover 131–32).

13. According to Gabler-Hover, Charles Winslow Hall portrays "Hagar's emblematic significance as a biblical model of African American empowerment" (129). For a fuller discussion of Hall's essay and accompanying illustrations, see Gabler-Hover, 127–30.

14. Significantly, Ellis Enson took Hagar to Washington on their honeymoon (44), an event that prefigures her sexual vulnerability as his property.

15. The Library of Congress website provides helpful information about the slave code in Washington, D.C.: "When the District of Columbia was established in 1800, the laws of Maryland, including its slave laws, remained in force. Additional laws on slavery and free blacks were then made by the District, and by Southern standards its slave codes were moderate. Slaves were permitted to hire out their services and to live apart from their masters. Free blacks were permitted to live in the city and to operate private schools. By 1860 the District of Columbia was home to 11,131 free blacks and 3,185 slaves. . . . Slavery in the District of Columbia ended on April 16, 1862, when President Lincoln signed a law that provided for compensation to slave owners. An Emancipation Claims Commission hired a Baltimore slave trader to assess the value of each freed slave, and awarded compensation for 2,989 slaves" (www.loc.gov/exhibits/treasures/trm009.html).

16. Established by Congress in 1865, the Freedman's Bank failed just nine years later due to "mismanagement, abuse, fraud, and other economic factors." As a result, "tens of thousands" of black citizens lost their savings. "The Freedman's Savings and Trust Company" www.archives.gov/research/african-americans/freedmans-bank.html.

17. "Willard Hotel," www.nps.gov/history/nr/travel/wash/dc36.htm.

18. Although a man of scrupulous honesty, Grant as president accepted handsome presents from admirers. Worse, he allowed himself to be seen with two speculators, Jay Gould and James Fisk. When Grant realized their scheme to corner the market in gold, he authorized the secretary of the treasury to sell enough gold to wreck their plans, but the speculation had already wrought havoc with business (www.whitehouse.gov/history/presidents/ug18.html).

19. O'Brien, in "Race-ing Toward Civilization," makes a similar argument about Hopkins and author Alice Rollins: "They prescribe standards for civic duty and civilization that apply to the nation as a whole, challenging doctrines of Anglo-masculine supremacy by associating sexual exploitation with Anglo-American political and economic power" (119).

20. Such ideas were articulated in the popular press. One article on lynching put it this way: "But a little way removed from savagery, 'Negroes' are incapable of adopting the white man's moral code, of assimilating the white man's moral sentiments, of striving toward the white man's moral ideals. . . . They are, in brief, an uncivilized, semi-savage people, living in a civilization to which they are unequal, partaking to a limited degree of its benefits, performing in no degree its duties" (qtd. in Bederman 49). On the other hand, Bederman notes that Ida B. Wells employed the discourses that merged civilization and manliness with sexual self-control. Her strategy may have informed Hopkins's depiction of General Benson in *Hagar's Daughter.*

21. These are the characters Hopkins had created so far in her novels. Still to come are Winona and Dianthe.

22. "[C]ivilization, as turn-of-the-century Americans understood it, simultaneously denoted attributes of race and gender. By invoking the discourse of civilization, many Americans found a powerfully effective way to link male dominance to white supremacy" (Bederman 23).

23. Hagar's choice to take her child's life in order to save her from a life of slavery recalls the fate of Margaret Garner, a slave woman who, in 1856, took her child's life during her attempted escape. Hopkins's contemporary, Frances Ellen Watkins Harper, retold this story in her poem, "The Slave Mother: A Tale of the Ohio."

24. In his treatise that calls for the rise of the ideal American, Ralph Waldo Emerson praises the "sturdy lad . . . who in turn tries all the professions, who teams it, farms it, peddles, keeps a school, preaches, edits a newspaper, goes to Congress, buys a township, and so forth, in successive years, and always, like a cat, falls on his feet" ("Self-Reliance" 26).

25. I have corrected an error in the text in this quotation, replacing "wordly" with worldly."

26. I have corrected an error in the text in this quotation, replacing "talk" with "task."

27. Hopkins's speech from this event is reprinted in Dworkin's *Daughter of the Revolution,* 358–60.

3. "SOMETHIN'S GWINE HAPPEN"

1. *Winona: A Tale of Negro Life in the South and Southwest* appeared in the *Colored American Magazine* from May to October 1902 (5:1–6).

2. Hopkins predicted correctly. In reaction to this novel, the magazine received a letter to the editor from Cornelia A. Condict expressing the very outrage at the interracial relationship that Hopkins anticipated. See Hopkins, "Letter from Cornelia A. Condict and Pauline Hopkins's Reply."

3. In an autographed photograph included in the Schomburg edition of *Contending Forces,* Hopkins inscribes, "For Humanity." The phrase "of one blood," found several times throughout her oeuvre, comes from the biblical text, Acts 17:24–28: "God that made the world and all things therein, seeing that he is Lord of heaven and earth, dwelleth not in temples made with hands; neither is worshipped with men's hands, as though he needed any thing, seeing he giveth to all life, and breath, and all things; and hath made of one blood all nations of men for to dwell on all the face of the earth, and hath determined the times before appointed, and the bounds of their habitation; that they should seek the Lord, if haply they might feel after him, and find him, though he be not far from every one of us: for in him we live, and move, and have our being; as certain also of your own poets have said, For we are also his offspring" (American King James Version).

4. See chapter 1 for a discussion of Patricia Hill Collins's term "othermother."

5. Jacobs describes this phenomenon as common among young slave girls: "For years, my master had done his utmost to pollute my mind with foul images, and to destroy the

pure principles inculcated by my grandmother, and the good mistress of my childhood. The influences of slavery had had the same effect on me that they had on other young girls; they had made me prematurely knowing, concerning the evil ways of the world. . . . But O, ye happy women, whose purity has been sheltered from childhood" (46). She portrays a conflict between the maternal forces that attempt to teach good values and to shelter girls from inappropriate information, on the one hand, and the forces of slavery that make girls "prematurely knowing," on the other.

6. I discuss the ambiguity of this information later in this chapter.

7. Not all advocates of Kansas's status as a free state opposed slavery. The antislavery Free Soil Party supported a gradual end to slavery, and was motivated largely by economic rather than moral concerns. According to historian Elizabeth R. Varon, the Free Soil Party "charged that the small oligarchy of slaveholders who had dominated national politics and, increasingly, the three branches of federal government, were determined to augment their power by spreading slavery into the Western territories" (10). Distinct from the Free Soilers' gradual approach to ending slavery, abolitionists advocated "radical immediatism." In other words, Varon explains, "all abolitionists were antislavery, but not all those who opposed slavery were abolitionists" (352n22). For further information on the history of the violence inspired by the Kansas-Nebraska Act, see Varon 260–71, and Nicole Etcheson.

8. Northern settlers came to Kansas for multiple reasons. Although some hoped to settle the question of slavery in the United States by making Kansas a free state, others wanted to protect their right to earn a living without competing against slave labor. Hopkins tends to conflate the Free Soilers—those who came for working rights or even with the racist motivation of keeping Kansas an entirely white state—with abolitionists in the novel. Her characters speak exclusively of abolition as their reason for migrating to Kansas.

9. "Border Ruffians" referred to Missourians who crossed the border only to vote or to "participate sporadically in Kansas affairs" but who did not intend to stay (Etcheson 31).

10. Osawatomie was a site of guerrilla warfare in Kansas in 1856. The actual events of this time are naturally more complicated than the novel suggests. Brown and his company attacked a settlement at Osawatomie on August 7, 1856, but they led the defense of the town against an attack by "proslavery guerrillas" several weeks later. Several free-state fighters died in this battle and were hailed as "martyrs to the liberty of Kansas" (Etcheson 121–23).

11. Martha H. Patterson's analysis of *Winona* also examines Hopkins's ideas about national progress, focusing on economics and management rather than violence.

12. In 1882, 49 black men were lynched in the United States; 10 years later, in 1892, that number increased to 161 (Bederman 47).

13. See Cynthia D. Schrager for a study of Hopkins's familiarity with the work of William James and the "new psychology" movement.

14. For more information on Sumner, see chapter 2.

15. Kansas State Historical Society, 126.

16. Historian Filipe Smith describes the postbellum belief that newly freed African Americans would regress to levels of savagery natural to them. According to this theory, "the postwar decrease of direct supervision of blacks meant less infusion of white blood through female concubinage (hence *somatic* regression) and less infusion of white civilization (hence *moral* regression)" (88, emphasis in original).

17. I use the terms "savagery" and "civilization" as terms informing the thinking at the time Turner and Hopkins wrote. In this, I follow the lead of Patricia Limerick, who insightfully points out that "the historian is obligated to understand how people saw their own times, but not obligated to adopt their terminology and point of view. That one may study how Westerners depended on the colt repeating revolver is not an argument for using a gun in professional debate" (25). Similarly, I read Hopkins's deployment of these concepts as a way to comprehend how she and her contemporary readers might have understood the text. The acceptance of religion and Anglophone education would have been read as marks of civilization, while the continued use of Native American dress would have signified the continued association with "savage" customs.

18. Hopkins voices a range of opinions on the topic of interracial relationships. In response to a reader's letter in the *Colored American Magazine* criticizing the interracial marriage depicted in her novels, Hopkins defends her plot choices and describes amalgamation as "designed by God for some wise purpose" (Hopkins, "Letter from Cordelia A. Condict and Pauline Hopkins's Reply" 594). She published an essay on this topic in the same issue under the pseudonym of her "more strident" persona, J. Shirley Shadrach (Dworkin 199). In "Black or White—Which Should Be the Young Afro-American's Choice in Marriage," Hopkins's advice to the "young Afro-American" who is undecided about amalgamation is simple: "Don't!" This firm directive follows a discussion of the complexity of the subject, however, a subject about which, she asserts, "no man can speak with certainty" (214, 208). She writes, as if to her disgruntled reader: "many Negroes are availing themselves of the privileges granted by our Northern States, to unite themselves with the Caucasian race; and this is more prevalent among men than among women. We find no fault in this if the Negro unites himself to one who is in all things his equal—morally and intellectually" (209).

19. O'Brien, too, sees *Winona* responding to the rhetoric of "civilization," and she links this aspect of the novel to Hopkins's nonfiction works: "*Winona* also provides a literary representation of African American resistance to white 'civilization'—slavery in Missouri—because its main characters fight alongside John Brown in Bleeding Kansas. Rhetorical and thematic similarities between *Winona* and Hopkins's more internationally focused works, such as the theme of insurrection and Hopkins's insistence that divine providence inspires and protects insurgents, connect her critique of Anglo-masculine civilization throughout the various genres she uses" ("'Blacks in all Quarters of the Globe'" 250).

20. The trope of "political self-impeachment," theorized by Lauren Berlant, is discussed in chapter 2.

21. Kansas State Historical Society, "Beecher Bibles," www.kshs.org/portraits/beecher_bibles.htm.

22. The Kickapoo Rangers were a northern division of the territorial militia. The historical leader of this group, David R. Atchison, seems to have shared the fictional Bill Thomson's violent tendencies. In a speech made at the time the novel is set, he reportedly said, "Boys, this day I am a Kickapoo Ranger. This day we have entered Lawrence with Southern rights inscribed on our banner, and not one abolitionist dared to fire a gun. And now, boys, we will go in again with our highly honorable Jones, and test the strength of that Free-State hotel, and teach the Emigrant Aid company that Kansas shall be ours. Boys, ladies should, and I hope will, be respected by every gentleman. But, when a woman takes upon herself the garb of a soldier by carrying a Sharp's rifle, she is no longer worthy of respect. Trample her under your feet as you would a snake. . . . If one man or woman dare stand before you, blow them to hell with a chunk of cold lead" (Carolyn Ward).

23. Hopkins's use of the archetypal evil of fratricide in both *Hagar's Daughter* and *Winona* points to her wish to invest the novels with prophetic weight.

24. See Sacvan Bercovitch, *The Puritan Origins of the American Self,* specifically his chapter "The Elect Nation in New England."

25. Similarly, Parson Steward recounts an attack on his church by the Missouri Rangers. Reading the event as a sign of God's approval, he asserts, "it was only by a special act of Providence that my congregation escaped massacre" (346). Steward classifies the Ruffians' actions as a "massacre," employing the civilized/savage binary common in Puritan captivity narratives and already in place in the novel. He recasts the role of the Native Americans—associated with barbarism and savagery in the captivity narratives—making the Rangers the perpetrators of the averted "massacre." See Richard Slotkin's chapter, "Israel in Babylon: The Archetype of the Captivity Narratives (1682–1700)" in *Regeneration through Violence.*

26. The rationale for the murders, circulated after the fact, was that these men posed a threat to the free staters, and killing them served as a preemptive strike.

27. In her essay on *Winona,* Patterson observes that Hopkins drew directly from the celebratory biography of Brown written by Franklin B. Sanborn in 1885 in which he justifies the Pottawatomie massacre as an act directed by God in retaliation for the Kickapoo Rangers' violence.

28. Frederick Douglass, the Women's Era Club of which Hopkins was a member, and black historian George Washington Williams all praised Brown as a martyr (Patterson 452).

29. For a description of Stowe's depiction of the idyllic Quaker settlement, see chapter 13, "The Quaker Settlement," in *Uncle Tom's Cabin.*

30. For a discussion of this poem and the reporting on Brown's execution, see Cecil D. Eby Jr., "Whittier's 'Brown of Ossawatomie.'"

31. For information on Louis Ransom's painting, *John Brown on His Way to Execution,* see Robert S. Fletcher, "Ransom's John Brown Painting." For more information on the pictorial portrayal of John Brown, see James C. Malin, "The John Brown Legend in Pictures."

32. Patterson assumes that Winona has been raped by Bill Thomson while enslaved in Missouri, referring to Thomson as "the man who had enslaved and raped her" (451), but, as I argue here, the novel never makes this clear.

33. Berlant's work on "diva citizenship" affords a compelling model for reading *Winona.* Using Jacobs's *Incidents in the Life of a Slave Girl,* Harper's *Iola Leroy,* and the Anita Hill testimony, Berlant identifies a form of political activism that deploys the "monarchial body" to "mime. . . the privileges of citizenship in the context of particular national emergencies" (227). Winona's queenly representation, followed by Aunt Vinnie's heralding of her promising future, intervenes in two national emergencies: the violent territorial dispute over slavery depicted in the novel, and the racial violence that marked the era from which Hopkins and Wells both wrote.

34. This statistic is available on the Timeline of African American History, 1901–1925, at www.memory.loc.gov/ammem/aap/timelin3.html.

4. FINDING MOTHER AFRICA

1. *Of One Blood* was the last novel Hopkins serialized in the *Colored American Magazine*; it ran from November 1902 to November 1903. She began another serialized novel, *Topsy Templeton,* in a new publication she undertook in 1916, the *New Era Magazine,* but she only published two installments before the magazine ceased publication. See Wallinger's chapter, "The 'New Era Magazine'" (270–76).

2. Full of mysteries, secrets, hidden cities, and ghosts, this novel invites a psychoanalytic reading, as the work of several scholars bears out. Essays by Cynthia D. Schrager, Thomas J. Otten, Valerie Rohy, and Dana Luciano all take psychoanalytic approaches to this novel. Although, as I have argued in the preceding chapters, all of Hopkins's novels can be usefully illuminated through psychoanalytic models, I agree with Schrager's contention that in *Of One Blood,* Hopkins appears intentionally to engage the "new psychology" emerging at the end of the nineteenth century "in order to represent the complexity of racial subjectivity in post-Reconstruction America" (Schrager 182, 184). Eric Sundquist discusses Hopkins's familiarity with the field of psychology. He points out that she drew the subtitle of the novel, "The Hidden Self," from William James's essay by that name. James's 1890, pre-Freudian essay contributed to the field of psychological research, speculating on the possibility of a subconscious self (Sundquist 571–72).

3. Hopkins had touched on the imperialist expeditions before in *Contending Forces.* John Langley, we recall, dies in the ice fields of the Klondike where he went with an expedition in search of gold.

4. Reuel's wish to watch the death of a person as means to insight about what lies beyond death recalls *Uncle Tom's Cabin,* offering a secular version of Tom's desire to watch Eva's death: "when that ar blessed child goes into the kingdom, they'll open the door so wide, we'll all get a look in at the glory" (319). For other references to *Uncle Tom's Cabin* in Hopkins's work, see Wallinger, 272–75.

5. Schrager convincingly argues that while Reuel's exploration of "psychology and mysticism initially appears to be disengaged from the sociological and political treatment of the race question that characterizes the majority of Hopkins's fictional and nonfictional work," the two are in fact closely linked. Reuel's "morbid psychological state" grows directly from his "social condition as a black man passing as white" (187).

6. Reuel has the mark of a lotus lily on his breast, which indicates that he is the awaited king of Meroe and savior of his people. Hopkins was not the first to use this trope. Nat Turner, the leader of the 1831 slave revolt in Southampton, Virginia, claimed that he knew he "surely would be a prophet" by "certain marks on my head and breast" (qtd. in Cole 267). And Sutton E. Griggs, in his 1902 novel, *Unfettered,* uses a birthmark to identify his character, Dorlan Warthell, as the descendent of African kings. (I am indebted to my LSU Press reader for drawing this to my attention.)

7. Hopkins's fascination with John Brown, pursued in *Winona,* appears again in *Of One Blood* through the character of Dianthe Lusk. John Brown's first wife was named Dianthe Lusk and according to Brown she, like Hopkins's Dianthe, had the gift of out-of-body communication. After her death, Brown wrote to his son that he believed he received messages from her (F. B. Sanborn 78n2). This letter was available to Hopkins through F. B. Sanborn's 1885 biography of Brown.

8. Rohy has offered an excellent reading of the return of the repressed in this novel, although she does not link it specifically to the mother.

9. See John Cullen Gruesser's *Black on Black* for an informative discussion of Ethiopianism as a crucial context for this novel. For a history of Ethiopianism, see Sundquist, 553–63; Moses 22–25.

10. Psalms 68:31.

11. The line comes from W. E. B. Du Bois's pageant, *The Star of Ethiopia,* first produced at the Emancipation Exposition in New York in 1913. The speaker of the program invites the audience to "learn the ancient Glory of Ethiopia, All-Mother of men" (Sundquist 578–79).

12. Rohy 220. Hopkins's portrayal of Telassar anticipates a comparison Freud would make between an ancient city layered with centuries of development and a human psyche "with a similarly long and copious past" (*Civilization and Its Discontents* 18). Several scholars have observed the psychoanalytic quality of this scene. See Schrager (197–98), Luciano (170), and Otten (229).

13. "The title 'Candace,' according to Pliny (*Naturalis historia* 6.35.186), was passed on through a succession of Meroitic queens for many years. . . . Though the exact significance of 'Candace' is not clear, the title seems to suggest its application to Queen Mothers, perhaps at times to the mother of a reigning king" (Snowden 297–98n14).

14. Tate notes that as part of their post-Reconstruction racial protest, African Americans sought to attain "middle-class social status," in terms of both values and economic stability. "Appropriation of gentility," Tate explains, "meant approximating racial equality" (*Domestic Allegories of Political Desire* 59). Hopkins's portrayal of wealth in this hidden community participates in that project.

15. Daphne A. Brooks notes that the song list for Hopkins's musical, *Peculiar Sam; or, The Underground Railroad, a Musical Drama in Four Acts,* shows the influence of the Jubilee Singers (295).

16. Hopkins Papers, box 1, folder 11.

17. Citing Booker T. Washington's famous description of his rise "up from slavery" and his efforts on behalf of the race, Scott DeVeaux argues for the practical possibilities of music in racial uplift: "had Washington been a more astute reader of trends, he would

have installed a conservatory at Tuskegee. . . music was a cornerstone of black cultural identity, so musicians could count on prestige, respect, and a degree of economic support from within their own communities even as they reached outside for a larger economic reward" (46–47).

18. Christopher A. Brooks discusses Du Bois's belief in the political importance of the sorrow songs in his essay, "The 'Musical' Souls of Black Folk" (274–75).

19. This dialectic resembles the structure of "Go Down Moses," which Dianthe sings at two points in the narrative. Daphne A. Brooks explains: "the structure of 'Go Down, Moses' charts a dialectic of communication and coalition building between the individual lead singer and her choral community" that functions as a "coded invitation to participate in this communal process" of racial uplift (308–309).

20. As Gruesser points out, here Hopkins anticipates later studies that established that "in their oral traditions African cultures for many centuries have had an accurate and extensive record of their pasts" (*Black on Black* 36).

21. Luke 12.2.

22. Although Aubrey does not know of his African heritage as Reuel does and Dianthe did before her accident, he too is a motherless child, without knowing the condition of his mother, Mira. Therefore, we might read his attraction to Dianthe as we read Reuel's: as an attempt to find his mother through his family. Through his own and his family's ignorance, however, Aubrey has been welcomed to identify with the father and his assessment of Dianthe as a sexual object follows that heritage.

23. Aubrey's tactics recall Langley's attempt to seduce Sappho with hidden information about her son in *Contending Forces.*

CODA

1. Paul Robeson, *Paul Robeson: The Complete EMI Sessions, 1928–1939,* EMI, 2008. CD; Louis Armstrong, *Louis and the Good Book,* Umvd Labels, 1949, LP, 2001, CD; Ike and Tina Turner, *Outta Season,* Blue Thumb Records, 1969, LP; Van Morrison, *Poetic Champions Compose,* Polydor/Umgd, 1987, CD; Hootie & the Blowfish, *Cracked Rear View,* Atlantic, 1994, CD.

2. Hopkins's addresses for these two events are included in Dworkin's collection of her nonfiction works.

BIBLIOGRAPHY

Ammons, Elizabeth. *Conflicting Stories: American Women Writers at the Turn of the Twentieth Century.* New York: Oxford UP, 1982.

———. "Stowe's Dream of the Mother Savior: *Uncle Tom's Cabin* and American Women Writers before the 1920s." *New Essays on Uncle Tom's Cabin.* Ed. Eric J. Sundquist. Cambridge: Cambridge UP, 1986. 155–95.

Anderson, Benedict. *Imagined Communities: Reflections on the Origin and Spread of Nationalism.* London: Verso, 1983.

Appiah, Kwame Anthony. "Race." *Critical Terms for Literary Study.* Eds. Frank Lentricchia and Thomas McLaughlin. Chicago: U Chicago P, 1990. 274–87.

Baym, Nina. *Woman's Fiction: A Guide to Novels by and about Women in America, 1820–1870.* Ithaca: Cornell UP, 1978.

Bederman, Gail. *Manliness and Civilization: A Cultural History of Gender and Race in the United States, 1880–1917.* Chicago: U Chicago P, 1996.

Beecher, Catherine E. *A Treatise on Domestic Economy, for the use of Young Ladies at Home and at School.* Boston: Thomas H. Webb and Co, 1843.

Bercovitch, Sacvan. *The American Jeremiad.* Madison: U Wisconsin P, 1978.

———. *The Puritan Origins of the American Self.* New Haven: Yale UP, 1975.

Berg, Allison. *Mothering the Race: Women's Narratives of Reproduction, 1890–1930.* Urbana: U Illinois P, 2002.

Bergman, Jill. "'A New Race of Colored Women': Pauline Hopkins at the *Colored American Magazine.*" *Feminist Forerunners: New Womanism and Feminism in the Early Twentieth Century.* Ed. Ann Heilmann. London: Pandora Press, 2003. 87–100.

———. "'Everything We Hoped She'd Be': Contending Forces in Hopkins Scholarship." *African American Review* 38 (Summer 2004): 181–99.

Berlant, Lauren. "The Queen of America Goes to Washington City: Notes on Diva Citizenship." *American Literature* 65 (September 1993): 549–74.

Blassingame, John W. *The Slave Community: Plantation Life in the Antebellum South.* New York: Oxford UP, 1979.

Bloch, Ruth. "American Feminine Ideals in Transition: The Rise of the Moral Mother, 1785–1815." *Feminist Studies* 4 (June 1978): 101–26.

Boris, Eileen. "The Power of Motherhood: Black and White Activist Women Redefine the Political." *Mothers of a New World: Maternalist Politics and the Origins of Welfare States.* Eds. Seth Koven and Sonya Michel. New York: Routledge, 1993. 213–45.

Bost, Suzanne. "Fluidity without Postmodernism: Michelle Cliff and the 'Tragic Mulatta' Tradition." *African American Review* 32 (Winter 1998): 673–89.

Brooks, Christopher A. "The 'Musical' Souls of Black Folk: Can a Double Consciousness Be Heard?" *The Souls of Black Folk One Hundred Years Later.* Ed. Dolan Hubbard. Columbia: U Missouri P, 2003. 269–83.

Brooks, Daphne A. *Bodies in Dissent: Spectacular Performances of Race and Freedom, 1850–1910.* Durham, NC: Duke UP, 2006.

Brown, Lois. "Out of the Mouths of Babes: The Abolitionist Campaign of Susan Paul and the Juvenile Choir of Boston." *New England Quarterly* 75 (March 2002): 52–79.

———. *Pauline Elizabeth Hopkins: Black Daughter of the Revolution.* Chapel Hill: U North Carolina P, 2008.

Brown, William Wells. *Clotel; or, The President's Daughter.* 1853. New York: Penguin Classics, 2003.

Campbell, Jane. *Mystic Black Fiction: The Transformation of History.* Knoxville: U Tennessee P, 1986.

Carby, Hazel V. *Reconstructing Womanhood: The Emergence of the Afro-American Woman Novelist.* New York: Oxford UP, 1987.

Cheng, Anne Anlin. *The Melancholy of Race: Psychoanalysis, Assimilation, and Hidden Grief.* Oxford: Oxford UP, 2001.

Chireau, Yvonne P. *Black Magic: Religion and the African American Conjuring Tradition.* Berkeley: U California P, 2003.

Christian, Barbara. *Black Feminist Criticism: Perspectives on Black Women Writers.* New York: Pergamon Press, 1985.

Clifford, Carrie W. "Votes for Children." *The Crisis* 10 (March 1922): 185.

Cole, Merrill. "Nat Turner's Thing." *The Psychoanalysis of Race.* Ed. Christopher Lane. New York: Columbia UP, 1998. 261–81.

Collins, Julia C. *The Curse of Caste; or, The Slave Bride.* 1853. Oxford: Oxford UP, 2006.

Collins, Patricia Hill. *Black Feminist Thought: Knowledge, Consciousness, and the Politics of Empowerment.* New York: Routledge, 1990.

Condict, Cornelia A. Letter. "Editorial and Publishers' Announcements." *Colored American Magazine* (March 1903): 398–99.

Cooper, Anna Julia. *A Voice from the South.* 1892. Ed. Henry Louis Gates Jr. New York: Oxford UP, 1988.

———. "Womanhood: A Vital Element in the Regeneration and Progress of a Race." *The Voice of Anna Julia Cooper.* Eds. Charles Lemert and Esme Bhan. New York: Rowman & Littlefield Publishers, Inc., 1998. 53–71.

Cullen, Countee. "Heritage." *Color.* New York: Harper & Brothers, 1925. 36–41.

Cummins, Maria Susanna. *The Lamplighter.* 1854. New Brunswick, NJ: Rutgers UP, 1988.

Davis, F. James. *Who Is Black? One Nation's Definition.* 1991. University Park: Pennsylvania State UP, 2001.

Denby, David J. *Sentimental Narrative and the Social Order in France, 1760–1820.* Cambridge: Cambridge UP, 1994.

Dever, Carolyn. *Death and the Mother from Dickens to Freud: Victorian Fiction and the Anxiety of Origins.* Cambridge: Cambridge UP, 1998.

DeVeaux, Scott. *The Birth of Bebop: A Social and Musical History.* Berkley: U California P, 1997.

Doreski, C. K. "Inherited Rhetoric and Authentic History: Pauline Hopkins at the *Colored American Magazine.*" *The Unruly Voice: Rediscovering Pauline Elizabeth Hopkins.* Ed. John Cullen Gruesser. Urbana: U Illinois P, 1986. 71–97.

Douglass, Frederick. *Narrative of the Life of Frederick Douglass.* 1845. *Classic American Autobiographies.* Ed. William L. Andrews. New York: Mentor, 1992. 229–327.

———. "Meaning of July Fourth for the Negro, Speech at Rochester, July 5, 1852." *The Life and Writings of Frederick Douglass, Vol. II, Pre-Civil War Decade, 1850–1860.* Ed. Philip S. Foner. New York: International Publishers, 1950. 181–204.

Du Bois, W. E. B. *The Souls of Black Folk.* 1903. New York: Penguin, 1996.

Dworkin, Ira, Ed. *Daughter of the Revolution: The Major Nonfiction Works of Pauline E. Hopkins.* New Brunswick, NJ: Rutgers UP, 2007.

Eagleton, Terry. *Literary Theory: An Introduction.* Minneapolis: U Minnesota P, 1983.

Eby, Cecil D., Jr. "Whittier's 'Brown of Ossawatomie.'" *New England Quarterly* 33 (December 1960): 452–61.

Ellison, Ralph. *Shadow and Act.* New York: Vintage, 1953.

Emerson, Ralph Waldo. "Self-Reliance." *Essays of Ralph Waldo Emerson.* New York: Book League of America, 1941. 15–31.

Eng, David L., and Shinhee Han. "A Dialogue on Racial Melancholia." *Loss: The Politics of Mourning.* Eds. David L. Eng and David Kazanjian. Berkeley: U California P, 2003. 343–71.

Equiano, Olaudah. *The Interesting Narrative of the Life of Olaudah Equiano, Written by Himself.* 1789. Ed. Robert J. Allison. Boston: Bedford Books of St. Martin's Press, 1995.

Etcheson, Nicole. *Bleeding Kansas: Contested Liberty in the Civil War Era.* Lawrence: UP Kansas, 2004.

Fanon, Frantz. *Black Skin, White Masks.* Trans. Charles Lam Markmann. New York: Grove Press, 1967.

———. *The Wretched of the Earth.* New York: Grove Press, 1963.

Fletcher, Robert S. "Ransom's John Brown Painting." *Kansas Collection: Kansas Historical Quarterlies* 9 (November 1940): 343–46.

Foner, Eric. *Reconstruction: America's Unfinished Revolution, 1863–1877.* New York: Harper & Row, 1988.

Foreman, P. Gabrielle. "Who's Your Mama? 'White' Mulatta Genealogies, Early Photography, and Anti-Passing Narratives of Slavery and Freedom." *American Literary History* 14 (2002): 505–39.

"The Freedman's Savings and Trust Company." www.archives.gov/research/african-americans/freedmans-bank.html.

Freud, Sigmund. *Civilization and Its Discontents.* 1930. Trans. James Strachey. New York: W. W. Norton and Co., 1961.

———. Introductory Lectures, footnote (1917). In *New Introductory Lectures on Psycho-Analysis. The Standard Edition of the Complete Psychological Works of Sigmund Freud,* vol. 22. London: Hogarth Press, 1964.

———. "Mourning and Melancholia." 1917. In *The Standard Edition of the Complete Psychological Works of Sigmund Freud,* vol. 14. London: Hogarth Press, 1957. 243–58.

———. "The Uncanny." 1919. In *The Standard Edition of the Complete Psychological Works of Sigmund Freud,* vol. 17. London: Hogarth Press, 1957. 217–56.

Gabler-Hover, Janet. *Dreaming Black/Writing White: The Hagar Myth in American Cultural History.* Lexington: UP Kentucky, 2000.

Gaines, Kevin. "Uplift Ideology as 'Civilizing Mission.'" *Cultures of United States Imperialism.* Eds. Amy Kaplan and Donald Pease. Durham, NC: Duke UP, 1993. 433–55.

Gardner, Eric. "Introduction." *Major Voices: The Drama of Slavery.* London: Toby Press, 2005. 589–92.

Gilbert, Sandra. "Rider Haggard's Heart of Darkness." *Coordinates: Placing Science Fiction and Fantasy.* Eds. George E. Slusser, Eric S. Rabkin, and Robert Scholes. Carbondale: Southern Illinois UP, 1983. 124–38, 188.

Gilman, Charlotte Perkins. *His Religion and Hers.* 1923.Westport, CT: Hyperion, 1976.

———. *Women and Economics: A Study of the Economic Relation between Men and Women as a Factor in Social Evolution.* 1898. Ed. Carl N. Degler. New York: Harper, 1966.

Gilroy, Paul. *The Black Atlantic: Modernity and Double Consciousness.* Cambridge: Harvard UP, 1993.

Greene, J. Lee. *Blacks in Eden: The African American Novel's First Century.* Charlottesville: U Virginia P, 1996.

Griggs, Sutton E. *Unfettered: A Novel.* 1902. Whitefish, MT: Kessinger Publishing, 2008.

Grimké, Sarah M. *Letters on the Equality of the Sexes and the Condition of Woman.* 1838. New York: Burt Franklin, 1970.

Gruesser, John Cullen. *Black on Black: Twentieth-Century African American Writing about Africa.* Lexington: UP Kentucky, 2000.

Gutman, Herbert G. *The Black Family in Slavery and Freedom, 1750–1925.* New York: Pantheon Books, 1976.

Hall, Charles Winslow. "Fascinating Bible Stories: IV Hagar and Ishmael." *Colored American Magazine* 2 (February 1901): 302–306.

Hall, Stuart. "Cultural Identity and Diaspora." *Identity: Community, Culture, Difference.* Ed. Jonathan Rutherford. London: Lawrence and Wishart, 1990. 222–37.

Harper, Frances Ellen Watkins. "Enlightened Motherhood." 1892. *A Brighter Coming Day: A Frances Ellen Watkins Harper Reader.* Ed. Frances Smith Foster. New York: The Feminist Press, 1990. 285–92.

———. *Iola Leroy.* 1892. Boston: Beacon Press, 1987.

———. "The Slave Mother: A Tale of the Ohio." *A Brighter Coming Day: A Frances Ellen Watkins Harper Reader.* Ed. Frances Smith Foster. New York: The Feminist Press, 1990. 84–86.

Hawthorne, Nathaniel. "Letter, Nathaniel Hawthorne to William D. Ticknor, January 19, 1855." In *The Letters, 1853–1856. The Centenary Edition of the Works of Nathaniel Hawthorne,* vol. 16. Eds. Thomas Woodson et al. Columbus: Ohio State UP, 1987. 304.

Hopkins, Pauline. "Address at the Citizens' William Lloyd Garrison Centenary Celebration," *Daughter of the Revolution: The Major Nonfiction Works of Pauline E. Hopkins.* Ed. Ira Dworkin. New Brunswick, NJ: Rutgers UP, 2007. 355–57.

———. "Black or White—Which Should Be the Young Afro-American's Choice in Marriage." *Daughter of the Revolution: The Major Nonfiction Works of Pauline E. Hopkins.* Ed. Ira Dworkin. New Brunswick, NJ: Rutgers UP, 2007. 208–14.

———. *Contending Forces: A Romance Illustrative of Negro Life North and South.* 1900. New York: Oxford UP, 1988.

———. "The Evils of Intemperance and Their Remedy." *Daughter of the Revolution: The Major Nonfiction Works of Pauline E. Hopkins.* Ed. Ira Dworkin. New Brunswick, NJ: Rutgers UP, 2007. 3–6.

———. "Famous Women of the Negro Race: Educators [Continued]." *Colored American Magazine* 5 (June 1902): 125–30.

———. *Hagar's Daughter.* 1901–1902. *The Magazine Novels of Pauline Hopkins.* New York: Oxford UP, 1988. 1–284.

———. "Letter from Cordelia A. Condict and Pauline Hopkins's Reply." *The Norton Anthology of African American Literature.* Ed. Henry Louis Gates Jr. New York: W.W. Norton & Company, 1997. 593–95.

———. *Of One Blood; or, The Hidden Self.* 1902–1903. *The Magazine Novels of Pauline Hopkins.* New York: Oxford UP, 1988. 439–621.

———. Papers. Fisk University Library Special Collections.

———. "Whittier, the Friend of the Negro." In *Daughter of the Revolution: The Major Nonfiction Works of Pauline E. Hopkins.* Ed. Ira Dworkin. New Brunswick, NJ: Rutgers UP, 2007. 251–58.

———. *Winona.* 1902. *The Magazine Novels of Pauline Hopkins.* New York: Oxford UP, 1988. 285–437.

Jacobs, Harriet. *Incidents in the Life of a Slave Girl.* 1861. New York: Norton, 2001.

James, William. "A Strong Note of Warning Regarding the Lynching Epidemic." 1903. *William James: Essays, Comments, and Reviews.* Eds. Frederick Burkhardt and Fredson Bowers. Cambridge: Harvard UP, 1987. 170–73.

Kansas State Historical Society, "Beecher Bibles: A Kansas Portrait." www.kshs.org/portraits/beecher_bibles.htm.

———. *Transactions of the Kansas State Historical Society, Vol. 10.* Charleston, SC: Nabu Press, 2008. ebrary, Inc. Web.

Kaplan, Amy. "Manifest Domesticity." *American Literature* (September 1998): 581–606.

Karcher, Carolyn L. "Rape, Murder, and Revenge in 'Slavery's Pleasant Homes': Lydia Maria Child's Antislavery Fiction and the Limits of Genre." *Culture of Sentiment: Race, Gender, and Sentimentality in Nineteenth-Century America.* Ed. Shirley Samuels. New York: Oxford UP, 1992. 58–72.

Kerber, Linda K. *Women of the Republic: Intellect and Ideology in Revolutionary America.* Chapel Hill: U North Carolina P, 1980.

Knight, Alisha R. "'All Things Work Together for Good': Pauline Hopkins's Race Woman and the Gospel of Success." *Loopholes and Retreats: African American Writers and the Nineteenth Century.* Eds. John Cullen Gruesser and Hanna Wallinger. Berlin: Lit Verlag, 2009. 125–40.

Koven, Seth, and Sonya Michel, eds. *Mothers of a New World: Maternalist Politics and the Origins of Welfare States.* New York: Routledge, 1993.

Kristeva, Julia. *The Revolution in Poetic Language.* New York: Columbia UP, 1984.

Lacan, Jacques. *The Seminar of Jacques Lacan, Book VII: The Ethics of Psychoanalysis, 1959–1960.* Ed. Jacques-Alain Miller. Trans. Dennis Porter. New York: Norton, 1992.

Ladd-Taylor, Molly. *Mother-Work: Women, Child Welfare, and the State, 1890–1930.* Urbana: U Illinois P, 1994.

Larsen, Nella. *Quicksand; and Passing.* Ed. Deborah E. McDowell. New Brunswick, NJ: Rutgers UP, 1986.

Limerick, Patricia. *The Legacy of Conquest: The Unbroken Past of the American West.* New York: W. W. Norton, 1987.

Litwack, Leon F. *Been in the Storm So Long: The Aftermath of Slavery.* New York: Knopf, 1979.

Logan, Rayford. *The Negro in American Life and Thought: The Nadir, 1877–1901.* New York: Dial Press, 1954.

Luciano, Dana. "Passing Shadows: Melancholic Nationality and Black Critical Publicity in Pauline E. Hopkins's *Of One Blood.*" In *Loss: The Politics of Mourning.* Eds. David L. Eng and David Kazanjian. Berkeley: U California P, 2003. 148–87.

Malin, James C. "The John Brown Story in Pictures: Kissing the Negro Baby." *Kansas Historical Quarterly* 9 (November 1940): 339–41.

Marsh, J. B. T. *The Story of the Jubilee Singers; With Their Songs.* 1881. New York: Negro University Press, 1969.

McCaskill, Barbara. "Anna Julia Cooper, Pauline Elizabeth Hopkins, and the African American Feminization of Du Bois's Discourse." In *"The Souls of Black Folk" One Hundred Years Later.* Ed. Dolan Hubbard. Columbia: U Missouri P, 2003. 70–84.

McClintock, Anne. *Imperial Leather: Race, Gender and Sexuality in the Colonial Contest.* New York: Routledge, 1995.

McCullough, Kate. "Slavery, Sexuality, and Genre: Pauline Hopkins and the Representation of Female Desire." *The Unruly Voice: Rediscovering Pauline Elizabeth Hopkins.* Ed. John Cullen Gruesser. Urbana: U Illinois P, 1996. 21–49.

McDowell, Deborah. *"The Changing Same": Black Women's Literature, Criticism, and Theory.* Bloomington: Indiana UP, 1995.

Milton, John. *Paradise Lost.* 1674. Cambridge: Chadwyck-Healey, 1992.

Mishra, Vijay, and Bob Hodge. "What is Post(-)colonialism?" *Colonial Discourse and Post-colonial Theory: A Reader.* Eds. Patrick Williams and Laura Chrisman. New York: Columbia UP, 1994. 276–90.

Moses, Wilson Jeremiah. *The Golden Age of Black Nationalism, 1850–1925.* New York: Oxford UP, 1978.

Mullen, Harryette. "Optic White: Blackness and the Production of Whiteness." *Diacritics* 24 (1994): 71–89.

Muñoz, José Esteban. *Disidentifications: Queers of Color and the Performance of Politics.* Minneapolis: University of Minnesota Press, 1999.

O'Brien, Colleen C. "'Blacks in all Quarters of the Globe': Anti-Imperialism, Insurgent Cosmopolitanism, and International Labor in Pauline Hopkins's Literary Journalism." *American Quarterly* (June 2009): 245–70.

———. "Race-ing toward Civilization: Sexual Slavery and Nativism in the Novels of Pauline Elizabeth Hopkins and Alice Wellington Rollins." *Legacy* 21 (2003): 118–33.

Otten, Thomas J. "Pauline Hopkins and the Hidden Self of Race." *ELH* 59 (Spring 1992): 227–56.

Painter, Nell Irvin. *Sojourner Truth: A Life, a Symbol.* New York: Norton, 1997.

Pamplin, Claire. "'Race' and Identity in Pauline Hopkins's *Hagar's Daughter.*" *Redefining the Political Novel: American Women Writers, 1797–1901.* Ed. Sharon Harris. Knoxville: U Tennessee P, 1995. 169–83.

Patterson, Martha H. "'Kin' o' rough jestice for a parson': Pauline Hopkins's *Winona* and the Politics of Reconstructing History." *African American Review* 32 (1998): 445–60.

Pedersen, Carl. "Sea Change: The Middle Passage and the Transatlantic Imagination." *Black Columbiad: Defining Moments in African American Literature and Culture.* Eds. Werner Sollors and Maria Diedric. Cambridge: Harvard UP, 1994. 42–51.

Peterson, Carla L. "Commemorative Ceremonies and Invented Traditions: History, Memory, and Modernity in the 'New Negro' Novel of the Nadir." *Post-Bellum, Pre-Harlem: African American Literature and Culture, 1877–1919.* Eds. Caroline Gebhard and Barbara McCaskill. New York: New York UP, 2006. 34–56.

Peterson, Bernard L. "Hopkins, Pauline Elizabeth." *Early Black American Playwrights and Dramatic Writers: A Biographical Directory and Catalog of Plays, Films, and Broadcasting Scripts.* Westport, CT: Greenwood Press, 1990.

Petry, Ann. *The Street.* Boston: Houghton Mifflin, 1946.

Phelps, Elizabeth Stuart. *The Story of Avis.* 1877. New Brunswick, NJ: Rutgers UP, 1985.

Porsild, Charlene. *Gamblers and Dreamers: Women, Men, and Community in the Klondike.* Vancouver: U British Colombia P, 1998.

Rafael, Vincente L. "Colonial Domesticity: White Women and United States Rule in the Philippines." *American Literature* 67 (December 1995): 639–66.

Randle, Gloria T. "Mates, Marriage, and Motherhood: Feminist Visions in Pauline Hopkins's *Contending Forces." Tulsa Studies in Women's Literature* 18 (1999): 193–214.

Rohy, Valerie. "Time Lines: Pauline Hopkins' Literary History." *American Literary Realism* 35 (Spring 2003): 212–32.

Romero, Lora. *Home Fronts: Domesticity and Its Critics in the Antebellum United States.* Durham, NC: Duke UP, 1997.

Ryan, Mary P. *Womanhood in America: From Colonial Times to the Present.* New York: New Viewpoints, 1975.

Sanborn, F. B., Ed. *The Life and Letters of John Brown, Liberator of Kansas, and Martyr of Virginia.* 1885. New York: Negro Universities Press, 1969.

Sanborn, Geoffrey. "Mother's Milk: Frances Harper and the Circulation of Blood." *ELH* 72 (Fall 2005): 691–715.

Schrager, Cynthia D. "Pauline Hopkins and William James: The New Psychology and the Politics of Race." *The Unruly Voice: Rediscovering Pauline Elizabeth Hopkins.* Ed. John Cullen Gruesser. Urbana: U Illinois P, 1986. 182–209.

Simpson, Lewis P. *The Dispossessed Garden: Pastoral and History in Southern Literature.* Baton Rouge: Louisiana State UP, 1975.

Sklar, Kathryn Kish. "Victorian Women and Domestic Life: Mary Lincoln Todd, Elizabeth Cady Stanton, and Harriet Beecher Stowe." *The Public and the Private Lincoln.* Ed. Cullom Davis et al. Carbondale: Southern Illinois UP, 1979. 20–37.

Slotkin, Richard. *Gunfighter Nation: The Myth of the Frontier in Twentieth-Century America.* New York: Atheneum, 1992.

———. *Regeneration through Violence: The Mythology of the American Frontier, 1600–1860.* Norman: U Oklahoma P, 1973.

Smith, Filipe. *American Body Politics: Race, Gender, and Black Literary Renaissance.* Athens: U Georgia P, 1998.

Smith, Rogers M. *Civic Ideals: Conflicting Visions of Citizenship in U.S. History.* New Haven, CT: Yale UP, 1997.

Snowden, Frank M. *Blacks in Antiquity: Ethiopians in the Greco-Roman Experience.* Cambridge: Belknap Press (Harvard UP) 1971.

Southworth, E. D. E. N. *The Hidden Hand; or, Capitola the Madcap.* New Brunswick: Rutgers UP, 1988.

Spillers, Hortense. "Mama's Baby, Papa's Maybe: An American Grammar Book." *Diacritics* 17 (1987): 65–81.

Sprengnether, Madelon. *The Spectral Mother: Freud, Feminism, and Psychoanalysis.* Ithaca, NY: Cornell UP, 1990.

Stowe, Harriet Beecher. *Uncle Tom's Cabin.* 1852. New York: Penguin, 1998.

Sundquist, Eric. *To Wake the Nations: Race in the Making of American Literature.* Cambridge: Belknap Press (Harvard UP), 1993.

Tate, Claudia. *Domestic Allegories of Political Desire: The Black Heroine's Text at the Turn of the Century.* New York: Oxford UP, 1992.

———. "Freud and his 'Negro': Psychoanalysis as Ally and Enemy of African Americans." *Journal for the Psychoanalysis of Culture and Society* 1 (Spring 1996): 53–61.

———. *Psychoanalysis and Black Novels: Desire and the Protocols of Race.* New York: Oxford UP, 1998.

Tompkins, Jane. *Sensational Designs: The Cultural Work of American Fiction, 1790–1860.* New York: Oxford UP, 1985.

Tracy, Steven C. "The Blues Novel." *The Cambridge Companion to the African American Novel.* Ed. Maryemma Graham. Cambridge: Cambridge UP, 2004. 122–38.

Turner, Frederick Jackson. "The Significance of the Frontier in American History." 1893. *Rereading Frederick Jackson Turner: "The Significance of the Frontier in American History" and Other Essays.* New Haven, CT: Yale UP, 1999. 31–60.

Varon, Elizabeth R. *Disunion! The Coming of the American Civil War, 1789–1859.* Chapel Hill: U North Carolina P, 2008.

Walker, Alice. *The Color Purple.* New York: Harcourt Brace Jovanovich, 1982.

Wallace, William Ross. "What Rules the World." Columbia Granger's World of Poetry Online. www.columbiagrangers.org.

Wallinger, Hanna. *Pauline E. Hopkins: A Literary Biography.* Athens: U Georgia P, 2005.

Ward, Andrew. *Dark Midnight When I Rise: The Story of the Jubilee Singers Who Introduced the World to the Music of Black America.* New York: Farrar, Straus and Giroux, 2000.

Ward, Carolyn, Transcriber. "Kickapoo Rangers." *Kansas: A cyclopedia of state history, embracing events, institutions, industries, counties, cities, towns, prominent persons, etc. with a supplementary volume devoted to selected personal history and reminiscence.* 3 vols. in 4. Ed. Frank W. Blackmar, Vols. I–II. Chicago: Standard Pub. Co., 1912, Volume II, 69–70. www.skyways.lib.ks.us/genweb/archives/1912/k/kickapoo_rangers.html.

Warner, Susan. *Wide, Wide World.* 1850. New York: Feminist Press, 1987.

Wegener, Frederick. "Charles W. Chesnutt and the Anti-Imperialist Matrix of African-American Writing, 1898–1905." *Criticism: A Quarterly for Literature and the Arts* 41 (Fall 1999): 465–93.

Welter, Barbara. *Dimity Convictions: The American Woman in the Nineteenth Century.* Athens: Ohio UP, 1985.

Wharton, Edith. *The House of Mirth.* 1905. New York: Penguin, 1985.
White, Deborah Gray. *Ar'n't I a Woman? Female Slaves in the Plantation South.* New York: Norton, 1999.
"The White House." www.whitehouse.gov/history/presidents/ug18.html.
Whittier, John Greenleaf. "Brown of Ossawatomie." *National Lyrics.* Boston: Ticknor and Fields, 1866. 89–90.
"Willard Hotel." www.nps.gov/history/nr/travel/wash/dc36.htm.
Williams, William Carlos. "Advent of the Slaves." *In the American Grain.* New York: New Directions, 1956. 208–11.
Wilson, Harriet E. *Our Nig; or, Sketches from the Life of a Free Black.* 1859. New York: Vintage Books, 1983.
Wollstonecraft, Mary. *A Vindication of the Rights of Woman.* 1792. New York: Penguin, 2004.
Wright, Richard. *White Man Listen!* 1957. New York: Anchor Books, 1964.
Yuval-Davis, Nira, and Floya Anthias, Eds. *Women-Nation-State.* London: Macmillan, 1989.

INDEX